HAYSEEDS,
MORALIZERS, AND
METHODISTS

HAYSEEDS, MORALIZERS, AND METHODISTS

The Twentieth-Century Image of Kansas

ROBERT SMITH BADER

University Press of Kansas

Published by the University Press of Kansas (Lawrence, Kansas
66045), which was organized by the Kansas Board of Regents and is
operated and funded by Emporia State University, Fort Hays State
University, Kansas State University, Pittsburg State University, the
University of Kansas, and Wichita State University

Library of Congress Cataloging-in-Publication Data

Bader, Robert Smith, 1925–
  Hayseeds, moralizers, and Methodists: the twentieth-century image
of Kansas/Robert Smith Bader.
     p. cm.
  Bibliography: p.
  Includes index.
  ISBN 0-7006-0360-3 (alk. paper). ISBN 0-7006-0361-1
(pbk.: alk. paper)
    1. Kansas—Civilization—20th century. 2. Kansas—
Civilization—20th century—Public opinion. 3. Public opinion—
United States—History—20th century. I. Title.
F686.B33 1988
978.1'03—dc19   88-97
                                                                    CIP

Printed in the United States of America
10 9 8 7 6 5 4 3

Where there is no vision, the people perish.
—*Proverbs 29:18*

CONTENTS

PREFACE

No STATE in the Union struggles more self-consciously with its image than Kansas. Perhaps in no state is the collective self-perception a more effective agent in stifling local creativity and in defeating community realization. Everyone agrees that, on balance, the image of Kansas is decidedly negative. Among young and old, natives and newcomers, Kansans and non-Kansans, the perception is universal that the state occupies an unenviable position in the national psyche as a drab and backward society. In recent years especially, this unhappy condition has attracted the attention of numerous academic, political, and business leaders anxious to further the economic development of the state.

In an earlier era the state occupied a very different niche on the nation's perceptual spectrum. Most Kansans are unaware that in this century and on these fifty million acres the commonwealth developed a robust reputation as a national leader in political and social affairs. Nor do they realize that in place of the modern inclination to diffidence and apology, the dominant attitude of the citizenry toward their state was once one of profound, often unbridled exuberance—a chauvinistic posture that nowadays we associate with the state of Texas.

The study of image is perhaps more an act of faith than is true of most historical work. When I earlier made studies of the state bond scandal and of prohibition, I found the topics reasonably circumscribed and the narrative lines clearly delineated. But in the disjunct world of image, anything and everything may be relevant, or only an idiosyncrasy. Since it is so amorphous, the topic goes unrecognized in the card files of the libraries and archives. To an extraordinary extent, then, the author must shape the subject and develop the narrative. The result may be only the diabolic product of his devilish mind. It is, as William Allen White said about his autobiography, "necessarily fiction."

In addition to exploring the more orthodox historical materials, my research made a nodding acquaintance with prose, poetry, painting, film, television, radio, and even science fiction, as they related to the state's image. The research ranged in scope from the collection and organization of primary materials in scrapbooks (chapters 6 and 7) to the tertiary-level review of secondary works (chapters 2–5). Because the study is primarily interpretive, the annotation is somewhat light. However, I have included an extensive bibliography of the most useful sources that were consulted.

The subject has been of intense interest to me for decades. I have long been dissatisfied with both the puffery of the professional touter and the derision emanating from national publications such as the *Wall Street Journal*. But my Kansas-conditioned character required that the topic be approached in a candid, unflinching fashion, even when I was confronted with unpleasant truths. The reader should be assured, however, that my motivation springs from a pure and profound affection for the Old Girl and an intense desire to see her restored to her rightful place among the community of nations.

The rise of the Kansas star in the national heavens and its subsequent eclipse form the central theme of the narrative. An unblinking review of the salient events may help convert an "unusable" past into a more serviceable history. Kansas provides a case study of the international march toward homogeneity and the loss of particularity. Once that truth is assimilated, who will care and how much? That question sets the primary cultural agenda for the state in the twenty-first century.

For material aid in various phases of the study I would like to express my appreciation to Nicolette Bromberg, Barbara Clark, Phyllis Couch, C. Robert Haywood, Norman E. Saul, and June Windscheffel. As before, I gratefully acknowledge the important contribution of editor Virginia Seaver to the readability of the manuscript. My special thanks go also to the staffs of the Kansas State Historical Society and of the Kansas Collection and the History Department of the University of Kansas. As always, my wife, Joan Larson Bader, has sustained and encouraged me in all ways, large and small.

1
PROLOGUE

IN 1857 my great-great-grandfather brought his family from Indiana to territorial Kansas to farm. The family has maintained a continuous presence in the fertile valley of the Neosho ever since. Just before the First World War, my father hired out on the Missouri Pacific Railroad as a locomotive fireman. The company sent him to Falls City, a small town whose principal asset, its geographical position—precisely equidistant between Kansas City and Omaha—had induced the railroad to locate there its divisional shops.

In due course I was born in Falls City. That prosaic fact takes on additional moment when we consult a regional map. There we find the blue-collar town sitting majestically on the left bank of the Nemaha, three miles *north* of the state line, just outside the state of Kansas. Though we may be innocent of little in this world, cold logic demands that the judgment scroll exclude the place of one's birth. Nevertheless, all my life I have considered it a black mark on my record, and by inference, my character. Some may worry about having been born out of wedlock; I fret about having been born out of Kansas.

During those Nebraska years we headed south at every conceivable opportunity. When our parents announced that we were going "home" for the weekend, my younger sister and I never had to ask the destination. Nor did it ever occur to us to protest that we were already "home." We knew better. "Camping out" would be an apt description of our years in exile, though that could reflect undeservedly on my mother. As might be expected of a home-economics graduate of Kansas State Agricultural College, she was a world-class homemaker.

Crossing the state line each time into Kansas was virtually a religious event, as the grateful family gave prayerful thanks for its deliverance, if only temporarily, from the wilderness. The enthusiasm of the parents at the crossing was rivaled only by their vocal pleasure on entering Coffey County. On each occasion the promised land had been found, and found to be good. And all the while the children were being indelibly imprinted with the saliency of place in the affairs of men, though at the time they were no more conscious of it than of cosmic radiation or the spinning of the earth.

Cultural geographers, who have studied the ontogeny of geographical awareness, report that typically the child holds in high esteem not only his immediate region but also distant centers of high population density and cultural visibility. It is perhaps not surprising, then, that in addition to the powerful bonding to Kansas, I developed, early on, a certain fondness for New York City. Such twists of the childish mind may be normal enough, especially if short-lived, as in my case. Nevertheless, to this day, I consider New York–worshipping to be an unnatural act, inexcusable even in the very young.

Kansas, then, became the be-all and end-all, the holy of holies. The impressionable young mind could scarcely frame a thought that might call its supreme status into question. A little later, in the growing restlessness of adolescence, the question was framed and even passed beyond the lips. "Have you ever thought about living someplace else?" I asked a favorite aunt. "Lord, child, why

2

would I want to live anyplace else?" she firmly responded. The look in her eye and the tone of her voice left no doubt that the conclusion was well considered and absolutely final. I never asked such a silly question again.

During the early 1930s, at precisely the time when I was learning that Kansas was the center of the universe, the universe was learning quite otherwise. Gradually but steadily the perception grew that Kansas wasn't widely held in such high esteem, that it was in fact regarded by the nation as a generic term for disaster. Of course, so long as you stayed close to the home hearth, it made little difference what the high and the mighty thought of you in such distant centers of power and influence as Boston, Philadelphia, and New York City.

My enlistment in the navy a few days after high-school graduation rudely shattered the innocence mothered by isolation. Now one could experience firsthand the superior smiles and pitiless taunts that had heretofore only been imagined. But after helping to make the world safe once again for democracy, the veteran returned to Kansas to count his medals and contemplate his future.

That future took him to Kansas State College, a bachelor's degree, and what had been regarded as an excellent undergraduate education. Recently that sanguine assessment had to be reevaluated after two eastern professors made the pronouncement that during those undergraduate years (the late 1940s) Kansas State was a mere "backwoods" institution. After reflection, however, the charge must be dismissed on its face. Anyone who is familiar with Manhattan knows that there are almost no woods in the area to be in back of.

After graduation, the deep-seated, geographically based feelings of inferiority came forcibly to the surface. I had decided to venture into deeper and hotter educational waters (a decision that my parents never understood; after all, I had a college degree). In Chicago I met the sons and daughters of the powerful and the influential from Boston, Philadelphia, and New York City. Many had never ventured west of Chicago; some, not beyond the Hudson River.

Although I was twenty-four years old, married, a navy veteran, and a college graduate, I was nearly paralyzed with fear. And that fear wore a palpable geographical face. Those easterners, of course, prime products of their scholarly and sophisticated colleges (no "backwoods" *there*), had forgotten more than I, a simple son of the prairie, would ever know. Like young Reinhold Niebuhr when he entered Yale Divinity School from a small town in Missouri, I felt "like a mongrel among thoroughbreds." The fact that most everyone from west of the Mississippi bore the same cross, in varying degrees, brought small consolation to the overanxious Kansan.

After those challenging, but exhilarating, Chicago years, I plied my trade in such exotic spots as Gainesville, Florida; Urbana, Illinois; and St. Louis, Missouri. Kansas, though, never left my heart or thoughts. Several years ago a latent interest in the state's social history began to manifest itself unmistakably. My voyage of self-discovery and search for identity was returning to its roots.

A few years ago, in the Watson Library at Kansas University, an undergraduate and I struck up a conversation about the social energy and cultural authority of the several states. He mentioned New York and California and then—with no felt need for further elaboration—added, "You know, the big boys." It was just an ordinary conversation between two Kansans, two generations apart in age. But in that phrase they could communicate volumes—without the loss of a nuance—about the historical distribution of power, prestige, and image within the United States of America.

IDENTIFYING THE MAJOR elements of the image of a socio-political unit and tracing them over time is a "soft" business certainly, not likely to challenge theoretical physics or molecular biology in its scientific beauty or its quantifiable exactitude. The cultural engine sputters, lurches, and veers, sometimes threatening to run entirely off the road and out of sight. Image is a function of reality, albeit a tardy function, but it never precisely reflects reality as commonly understood. In this work, where image diverges significantly from actuality, it is the perception, not the substance, that is followed.

In the ongoing tension between reality and image the outcome is often surprising. As a deeply entrenched set of expectations, image may stubbornly persist in the face of blatant evidence to the contrary. For example, novelist John Steinbeck long held a vivid, albeit highly romanticized, mental picture of Fargo, North Dakota, as being "blizzard-riven, heat-blasted, dust-raddled." When he finally visited the city, on a mild autumn day, he found only an unremarkable American urban center on the northern plains. He felt let down, almost depressed. But later he discovered "with joy" that "the fact of Fargo had in no way disturbed my mind's picture of it. . . . In the war between reality and romance, reality is not the stronger."

In the television era the tendency, followed here, has been to treat image as a near-synonym for reputation or publicly perceived character. A positive image evidently requires more than economic health. The public must perceive in the individual or in the group a valued condition or a contribution to contemporary society. Thus, in modern America the professional athlete, the multinational corporation, and the growth-hungry sovereign states all attend assiduously to their "image."

The chemistry of image may be amorphous, complex, and subjective, but its molecules do not move at random. A close inspection of the record reveals pronounced central tendencies, some variation around those modes or averages, and shifts in the modes at varying rates over time. Despite the mushiness, statements of some certitude may be made. The perceptual milieu in which Kansans lived, moved, and had their being differed unquestionably in, say, 1890, 1910, 1930, 1950, and 1970.

The image seems to operate with its own, often irrational, rules. It abhors the subordinate and the fragmented while embracing the dominant and the unitary. Thus the image of the Second World War, especially in the minds of the young, has distilled to the Holocaust in Europe, Hiroshima in Asia. All else has tended to become subordinated to those two mind-searing events. The image of Colorado is that of a mountainous state (a view encouraged by the icon on its license plates); the reality is that the eastern third of the state is as flat, arid, and arguably desolate as any region of Kansas. But the dominant view is all.

The image of a cultural unit tends to be democratic in at least two senses. Everyone in the society is subjected to the impact, though not necessarily to the same degree; and everyone, theoretically, is an image generator. Thus, in this study, as liberally as feasible, the voices of a range of individuals will be allowed to speak directly, both to capture the contemporaneous flavor and to document the necessarily subjective generalizations. But image also may be critically molded by a few—such as H. L. Mencken and Sinclair Lewis in the twenties—if their prestige and their platforms are sufficiently elevated. In the twentieth century the most important single image generator in and of Kansas was William Allen White. He spoke and wrote the majority view, at least as he perceived it. His voice dominated, in an exaggerated and perhaps unfair fashion, those of, say, Ed Howe, W. G. Clugston, and Emanuel Haldeman-Julius, who tended to champion causes that appealed only to a minority.

The interpretation of cultural image necessarily entails a consideration of the collective character and psyche. In the Age of Communication the population, just as the individual, receives the external view and subsequently internalizes it. The outsider's view has been critically important to Kansans' perceptions of themselves as a people. Only when this term is added to the cultural equation can we begin to understand the celebrated love/hate ambivalence that Kansans hold for their state.

Given the holistic nature of image, the centrifugal forces of race, ethnicity, and religion will not be considered. Nor will those ubiquitous intrastate clines such as rainfall, prairie-grass height, and violent crime rate, all of which diminish markedly as one moves from right to left on the Kansas map. The focus will be on the whole body of the Kansas anatomy—unity, not diversity; integration instead of dissection; majority history, rather than minority.

The coverage is primarily of the twentieth century, although reflections on seminal nineteenth-century events do occur at frequent intervals. Both professional historians and the general public have been somewhat reluctant to grant equal time to twentieth-century events. Until relatively recently, some have refused to acknowledge that much of significance has transpired since statehood. Writing in 1957, the historian William Frank Zornow complained that "trained scholars and dilettantes alike have labored under the notion that Kansas history ended [at] Fort Sumter." Additionally, concentration on the more recent past furnishes a sense of historic connectedness that contemporary Kansans are sadly lacking.

THE FIRST IMAGE of Kansas that was projected to the European world was favorable. In 1541, Francisco Vásquez de Coronado led a party of some thirty mounted men from the staked plains of Texas into central Kansas (Rice County). In their eyes the region compared well with their native Spain as a land of abundance. The soil was said to be "rich and black [and] well watered"; the fruits and nuts were "fine [and] sweet." Subsequent explorers, including Meriwether Lewis and William Clark, were generally impressed with the beauty and potential of the land. But in 1806, Zebulon Pike pronounced the country an uninhabitable desert, an arid zone that would inhibit further American expansion. After explorations in 1819/20, Major Stephen H. Long labeled as "The Great American Desert" the region that would subsequently become renowned as the nation's breadbasket. It was a reputation that would remain controlling for decades.

The Kansas-Nebraska Act of 1854 opened the territory to extensive American settlement for the first time. Under the principle of "popular sovereignty," the territorial residents would decide for themselves the vexed question of slavery. Thus, to the normal economic motives of settlement was added the moral issue of human bondage. The opening of a new territory for settlement, a common-enough event in the history of the United States, took on the coloration of a holy crusade. As a result of confrontations such as the Wakarusa War, the Pottawatomie Massacre, and the Sack of Lawrence, "Bleeding Kansas" gained a national reputation as the site of principled violence. And the violence was not contained within the new territory. A few days after delivering himself of an impassioned speech entitled "The Crime against Kansas" on the Senate floor, Charles Sumner of Massachusetts was clubbed into unconsciousness by an irate southern congressman.

At the conclusion of the Civil War, homesteaders by the hundreds of thousands poured into and across the new state. The dominant theme of the period from 1865 to 1890 is that of the imposition of the fruits of Western civilization on a region heretofore regarded as a wilderness, fit only for soldiers, missionaries, ignoble savages, and wild animals. The line of colonization moved irresistibly from the eastern to the central to the western section of the state. It was slowed only momentarily by recurrent drouths, by economic depressions such as that of 1873, and by the monumental invasions of grasshoppers, as in 1874. Although the desert image was vastly overdrawn, especially for the eastern section of the state, it contained a kernel of unerodable truth: the land and the climate could, in fact, be harsh and unforgiving. Its settling required a hardy, determined, and adaptable people.

One relatively minor facet of the westering movement has been remarkably fruitful as a generator of enduring images. As the railroads extended their steel ribbons to the west, a succession of Kansas towns served as railheads for cattle that were being herded up from Texas. From 1867 to 1885, Abilene, Hays, Newton, Ellsworth, Wichita, Caldwell, and Dodge City served the cow-town function in approximately that order. In these and similar towns the familiar stereotype of the wild and wicked West was spawned. Larger-than-life characters, such as Wyatt Earp, Wild Bill Hickok and Bat Masterson, live on in the fertile imaginations of the writers of songs, novels, and television and movie scripts. Among modern-day Kansans, the reputation of these cowboys greatly overshadows that of those who had an infinitely greater contemporary impact on society but lived more prosaic lives. The modern citizen has not made the acquaintance of such nineteenth-century giants as Charles Robinson, John J. Ingalls, and John P. St. John.

By about 1890 the last county had been formally organized and the frontier officially closed. The "moving in" phase of state development was ending, and Kansas was settling down to become whatever it was destined to become. But this final chapter of the nineteenth century was an unsettling one for the national reputation of the state. By the late 1880s the economic boom had collapsed, and in its wake, angry, debt-ridden farmers deserted the traditional political parties in droves to organize the People's party. Agrarian unrest spread throughout the nation, but Kansas remained a major center of the Populist movement. The state developed a national reputation as a land of "hell raisers," a commonwealth in which economic and moral wrongs were not suffered in silence. A good deal of that spirit, though in quite different guise, informed the Progressive movement that at the turn of the century supplanted the Populist revolt. In more recent decades the hell-raising proclivity of *Homo sapiens kansensis* has been known only to the historian and the archaeologist.

2
THE PROGRESSIVE ERA

TURN-OF-THE-CENTURY Kansans stood at the threshold of the most stimulating and auspicious period in the state's history. The two "golden decades" of the Progressive Era produced a level of cultural aggressiveness and societal confidence that is astonishing to the modern Kansan. Farmers and laborers joined businessmen, large and small, to create a purposeful society—indeed, a civilization—that significantly influenced national affairs and served as a model of the Jeffersonian agrarian ideal. The trying, often tumultuous era of experimentation and settlement had finally ended. After almost fifty years of development, Kansas as a society, a culture, and a philosophy was coming of age.

In contrast, the preceding decade had been a public-image nightmare. During the 1890s, bad weather and harsh economic conditions had conspired to make the very name of Kansas a generic term for disaster. A Chicago financial house had announced in 1896 that one might as well try "to sell stock in an irrigating scheme on the planet Mars as to dispose of securities bearing on their face the name of Kansas." Kansas had become an oath on the lips of thousands who had left the state in abject despair ("In God we trusted, in Kansas we busted"). The

11

defeated could be found in numbers from Florida to California, often living with "the wife's folks," bitterly contemplating in their newly found leisure the lessons learned in "the Kansas school of experience."

The political response of the population to these distressing times came in the form of populism. Their syllabus of grievances was urged by colorful advocates such as Mary "Yellin' " Lease and "Sockless" Jerry Simpson, who railed against the eastern "money power" in somewhat less than genteel terms. Their bombast, reinforced by that of Carry Nation, marked Kansas for ridicule as the natural habitat of the unstable zealot and the emotion-owned freak. The popular image of Kansans, William Allen White had written, included "green ears, striped backs, and iridescent tail-feathers." A national publication had declared that Kansas "cuts the worst figure of any State in the Union." The national lexicon had expanded to include the "Kansas cyclone," the "Kansas grasshopper," and the "Kansas crank." These conditions had wrought a profound change in the normally optimistic outlook of the ordinary citizen. The nineties often found him alternating in mood between sputtering anger and sullen defensiveness on every subject from economics to literature.

This unhappy state of affairs began to change in the late 1890s. The first faint, but distinct, glimmering of a major metamorphosis could be discerned as early as 1897. Those who persisted through the "bust" into the recovery were a chastened lot. They determined to build, or to rebuild, on a more substantial, less speculative foundation. Now ever so critical and cautious, they were down on growth schemes, developing an almost pathological hatred of debt. As they scrimped to pay off outstanding obligations, mortgages became fewer and smaller. The farmer and the businessman waxed, the plunger and the promoter waned. Land in additions surrounding boom towns now sold by the realistic acre, rather than by the speculative lot. The philosophy of fiat money reigned no more as the recovery unfolded in a "slow, easy, and unpretentious" manner.

The flowers of economic prosperity blossomed everywhere: in the public square, in the form of sidewalks, parks, electric lights, and street cars; in the private sector, as fresh paint, remodeled porches, flower gardens, and new automobiles. The citizens, both rural and urban, walked with a more sprightly gait and spoke with a more hopeful air. The defeatism and the inferiority complex that had been so characteristic of the nineties evaporated as the dew on a warm July morning.

The waves of prosperity splashed over into the social and political realms as well. Kansas became a foremost champion of Theodore Roosevelt and the Progressive Movement—a political philosophy that William Allen White characterized as "profoundly spiritual." "It would be hard to find a state with more progressive measures than Kansas," a social scientist noted in 1912. These legislative acts included woman suffrage, the direct primary, banking regulation, railroad-rate restructuring, public-health reform, and controls on drinking, smoking, and gambling, among dozens of others. Known as the "boss-busters" initially, the reformers, in theory at least, reduced the power of corporations, utilities, and political bosses while enhancing that of women, higher education, and the "little man"—all in the name of democracy, efficiency, and social justice.

The shift in the Kansas fortunes, as well as the attendant alteration of the Kansas psyche, attracted the attention of pundits both internal and external. In 1896, William Allen White had gained national notoriety for both his state and himself with the famous editorial "What's the Matter with Kansas?" Written in a fit of pique, the witty piece painted a vivid word picture of the backwardness of the state's economic policy and the bankruptcy of the Populists' economic philosophy.

Only a year later, however, White thought he had detected the growth of the "bacteria of confidence" in the body politic. "The Kansas man," he boasted, "lowers his flag to no other State. He accepts no imported traditions. In the bright lexicon of Kansas there is no good word but Kansas."[1] A few years into the century, in an article entitled "Lifting the Curse from Kansas," G. W. Ogden reported in a national magazine that the Kansas that had served as the marketplace of "freakish" ideas had ceased to be. "Its name is no longer a brand of misfortune; no curse of fleeing multitudes reverberates across its solitudes." Over the past few years, he said, Kansas had become "twice as rich, many times more respected and infinitely happier."[2]

Many of the ambitious young people who were moving into positions of responsibility in the civic, social, political, and business realms had been born, reared, educated, and married in Kansas. For them, Kansas was not an adopted state, as it had been for their parents; it was the site of their nativity and rearing, the only "sacred spot" they had ever known. No "movers" or "mere sojourners" could be found in their ranks, these proud descendants of the "stickers," the survivors. The state, they felt, had been purged of the weak and fainthearted through a process akin to Darwinian selection. "Kansas is consecrated ground to us who live here, labor here, and love here," a native enthusiast wrote in 1909; "Kansas is home at last."[3]

In 1902, Charles M. Harger, an Abilene newspaperman and a keen observer of the Kansas scene, wrote in a national publication that ever since the turbulent territorial period, commentary on Kansas and Kansans had tended to the extremes—"from extravagant eulogy to bitter abuse." But with the return of prosperity and self-confidence, the ordinary Kansan "exaggerates less and qualifys more. The sunflower state of to-day is being pictured to the world as it is." The watchwords of the dawning era were *thrift, savings,* and *stability.*[4] "Bleeding Kansas" was well on its way to becoming "Leading Kansas."

A poem entitled "Sneakin' Back to Kansas," published in 1901 by J. B. Adams, gives a sense of the early phase of the state renaissance as felt at the grass-roots level:

> They're sneakin' back to Kansas, Reps
>   and Dems, Prohibs and Pops
> They have heard the wondrous story of
>   the world-surprising crops,
> They have read it in the papers that
>   the old Jayhawker state
> Is a passin' the procession at a mighty
>   lively gate!
> In her days of woe they shook her, gave
>   it to her in the neck
> Just as rats out in the ocean'll desert
>   a sinkin' wreck,
> But she weathered every breaker an'
>   she's right in the advance,
> An' they're sneakin' back to Kansas as
>   repentant emigrants. . . .[5]

KANSAS HAD BEEN considered a puritan state, full to the brim with moral fervor, and had so considered itself since the days of "Bleeding Kansas" that had preceded statehood. Most citizens would have concurred with a YMCA director who in 1909 held that Kansas "stands preeminently for all that is uplifting and good [and] is the sworn enemy of that which degrades and dismantles manhood and boyhood." There were those, however, who claimed to find in the pious of Kansas a disturbing inclination to holier-than-thou-ness. The unctuous, their critics said, routinely began their day by thanking the Lord that He had not made them as other men—shiftless, profane, and beer drinking.

Everyone could agree that the state's moralistic ideal-

15

ism was not abstract but thoroughly pragmatic, "firmly fastened to a peg driven deep in the earth." The desire to manifest the ideal in the concrete could be found in many public enterprises. By 1915, social legislation to improve the lot of children, women, prisoners, the poor, the wayward, and the abandoned had placed the state "in the front ranks of the national welfare movement." Antitobacco and antigambling measures sailed through the legislature. But the most sparkling jewel in the reform crown was alcohol control—prohibition.

In 1880, Kansas had thrust itself dramatically onto the national temperance stage by endorsing a constitutional amendment prohibiting the manufacture and sale of intoxicating liquors, the first state in the Union to do so. Nineteenth-century enforcement had been difficult, especially in the cities and during periods of economic stress. But the Progressive movement—fired by equal parts of moral fervor and economic self-interest and not at all reluctant to expand the role of government—eagerly embraced the prohibition ideal. By 1910, law enforcement, broadly supported by an indignant public, had significantly reduced the level of alcohol consumption, even in the more reluctant urban centers. The era of greatest state pride coincided closely with the period of lowest liquor consumption.

During this interval, Kansas nudged aside Maine, the nineteenth-century model, as the premier prohibition commonwealth. As state after state voted on liquor-control issues, conditions in Kansas, real or imagined, often became the focal point of the campaigns. Both sides cried that Kansas prohibition was lied about enough "to make Ananias weep with envy." In 1914 the California prohibition referendum featured a forty-seven-page booklet entitled simply "Kansas." In Washington State, dry groups formed Sunflower Clubs, dedicated to tell "the truth" about Kansas prohibition. Their exaggerated claims about the salubrious effect that abstinence had on mental health led a Seattle newspaper to remark that apparently the question of liquor control in Washington was going to turn on how many crazy people there were in Kansas.

Warming to their task, state prohibition leaders proclaimed the good tidings to the region, the nation, and the world. *Our Messenger*, the newspaper of the Woman's Christian Temperance Union (WCTU), held up the state as "an object lesson for the world." The long-term (1909–38) president of the WCTU, Lillian Mitchner, said that Kansas had "helped to solve for the world the greatest civic problem of the age." The prominent congregational minister Charles M. Sheldon declared that prohibition had "done more than any other one thing to make Kansas the garden spot, morally, of the universe."

THE MARRIAGE of material prosperity and spiritual fervor produced a loud and sustained vocalization of state pride that is beyond the experience of the modern Kansan. Though the rhetoric often reached fanciful heights, it issued from the deep wells of self-confidence generated by genuine societal achievement. Kansas had become a national leader in the two most significant social and political movements of the day: progressivism and prohibition. The concrete accomplishments tasted all the sweeter when announced to a world that was still clinging to the outmoded images of the nineties. But the behavior of the populace broke no known laws of the natural or social sciences. Fervent and prosperous reformers are not inclined to keep their light hidden under the Biblical bushel.

One of the basic difficulties in telling the bald truth about Kansas, it was said, concerned believability. The truth was "so incredible," an enthusiast alleged, that some citizens felt constrained to alter the facts "lest they prejudice their case." Newspaperman and future governor Henry J. Allen embellished the theme. "The simplest statement of fact touching the modern conditions in Kansas," he said in 1909, "reads like the advertisement of a

17

real estate agent."[6] Initially the secretary of the Kansas State Historical Society, George W. Martin, held some reservations about what appeared to be "the constant extravagant bragging characteristics of Kansas." But additional contemplation prompted him to conclude in 1907: "The people of Kansas are the embodiment of modesty and self-abrogation. Kansas is a home-made state."[7]

Governor Edward W. Hoch (1905–9) fueled the upbeat mood in a 1905 speech to the state undertakers association. He surprised his audience by coming out flatly against the color black for funerals and the mourning period. As the emblem of darkness and despair, black was not a proper sign of sorrow for those who believed that there was "immortality beyond the grave." The mourning color of choice in a progressive Kansas, Hoch said, was white, a symbol of "sunshine, hope, justice, light and heaven."

The quintessential progressive governor, Walter R. Stubbs (1909–13), championed both the moral and the economic dimensions of the twentieth-century version of the "Kansas fever." In a private letter he let the hyperbole flow: "Of course Kansas is by far the most prosperous region on the face of the globe. Our schools, banks and bins are full to overflowing. Our farmers come to town in automobiles, their sons are in eastern schools and their daughters are touring Italy, Palistine and Egypt."[8]

Patriotic comments glorifying the state filled the publications of the period. Some addressed the economic conditions:

> Living conditions in Kansas may not be absolutely perfect, the milk may be too rich or the honey too sweet, but we don't like to have these flowing over our land anyway.

> The chief pursuit of the people of Kansas is making of crop records and their chief occupation is to keep from making all the money in the world.

Others remarked on the leadership exhibited by the state:

> Kansas is a synonym for advancement in moral, political, and material things. Kansas is an early state—Kansas never slumbers! The people of Kansas think and act!

> It is her unfailing ability to keep ahead of the band wagon . . . while she toots her own horn to let the world know something's coming . . . that challenges the admiration of even her enemies.

> [Kansas] is a state of ideas, . . . a gushing fountain of ideas, a swarming hive, an avalanche, a cyclone of ideas.

The classic statement of the period came from the pen of Carl L. Becker, then a historian at Kansas University. Becker had arrived from Dartmouth College in 1902 with the typical easterner's view of Kansas "as the land of grasshoppers, of arid drought, and barren social experimentation." His interest in local patriotic sentiments was kindled on the very day of his arrival when he overheard college girls exclaim "dear old Kansas!" as their train crossed over the state line.

Eight years later, Becker wrote his famous essay entitled simply "Kansas." The gestation period coincided precisely with the great swelling in state pride. Progressives of both political persuasions, proclaiming "a new heaven and a new earth," had placed Kansas squarely at the center of the universe. The eastern professor was impressed. He wrote that Kansas was "no mere geographical expression, but a 'state of mind,' a religion, and a philosophy in one."

Becker noticed especially the self-confidence of Kansans in their particular manners and mores. Their disregard for precedent was "almost an article of faith." Kansans "set their own standards." The state had become a veritable "experiment station in the field of social science." "In Kan-

19

sas, we don't care much what other states are doing," he was told by a legislator; "Kansas always leads, but never follows." The emotional attachment to the state, which Becker found to be nearly universal, was "devotion to an ideal, not to a territory." Having conquered the vicissitudes of their environment, both moral and physical, Kansans understandably displayed "the feeling of superiority naturally attaching to a chosen people."[9]

The horn tooting that was emanating from the state captured the attention of the national community. Kansas came to occupy the time-honored "Texas niche" of unreserved bravado and self-promotion. During the first decade of the renaissance, the national reaction ranged from surprise to supportive to "poking a little . . . fun at Kansas' advertising proclivities." The sharper barbs and rebukes would come later.

A national journalist thought Kansans had some cause for "thinking so well of themselves." Suggesting a reversal of the traditional flow of capital, the *New York Sun* in 1907 editorialized that the thriving banks of Kansas could help accommodate the financial needs of the New York business community. "Bleeding Kansas" was now bleeding money into its banks. In a long 1905 editorial on "Kansas and Kansans" the *New York Globe* said that "state booming" had become ingrained in its citizens. "A true Kansan, as soon as he discovers speech, begins audibly to congratulate himself on the place of his birth." It repeated, with a smile, the story of the Englishman who had asked a Kansan, in a London hotel, where he was from. On being told, the Englishman responded with, "Ah, yes, the largest state in the Union."

In 1909 the prominent Atchison journalist and novelist, Edgar W. Howe, asked a number of prominent easterners to respond to a simple question: "What comes to your mind when the word 'Kansas' is mentioned?" To no one's surprise, the encomiums flowed in from every quarter. From Samuel S. McClure of the New York publishing house (when "I have a sense of being out of touch with America, . . . more than once I have gone straight to Kansas to orient myself"); B. L. Winchell, president of the Rock Island Railroad ("Of late years, I confess that the word 'Kansas' is . . . associated in my mind with a rich state"); Leigh Mitchell Hodges of the *Philadelphia North American* ("Bleeding Kansas! And now it's leading Kansas, and feeding Kansas, and everything but needing Kansas. . . . I'm proud of Kansas because she grows more thinkers than any other state"); author Elbert G. Hubbard ("A land where there is so much that is noble and pure and true and beautiful and good"); and Arthur Brisbane, in an editorial in the *New York Journal* ("All over our country, and all over the world, the name of Kansas stands for fertility and prosperity, dignified success based upon honest work and honest intelligence. The state of Kansas is a great nation of itself within this nation").[10]

TURN-OF-THE-CENTURY Kansas was overwhelmingly a rural, agricultural state. When the farmers did well, everybody prospered; when the crops failed, everyone suffered. In 1900, 76 percent of the population lived in rural areas or in towns of fewer than two thousand souls. Through the painful process of trial and error the "survivors" had adapted—more or less—to the demanding prairie-plains environment. They had learned to diversify their crops and livestock: to raise kafir corn, sugar beets, barley, millet, and sorghum in addition to corn and wheat; sheep, hogs, horses, mules, and bees as well as cattle and chickens. An unflinching reality had forced them to relinquish their cherished theories—though often with much reluctance—that rainfall followed the plow or timber culture or human settlement or the frequency of dead snakes hung "belly-side up" along the fence row.

Kansas jumped to the front in wheat, alfalfa, and broom-corn production. It boasted the largest assessed

21

evaluation, bank deposits, and college population per capita of any state in the Union. The distribution of wealth was claimed to be "more equitable . . . than anywhere else in the civilized world." Whereas during the nineties the railroad platforms had been crowded with castoff clothing and donated seed from the benevolent East, they now groaned under huge sacks of grain ready for shipment to the East as a cash surplus.

A national agricultural expert, after a 1915 tour of agricultural colleges in seven midwestern states, was especially impressed with the independence displayed by the State Agricultural College at Manhattan. Echoing Carl Becker, he found an "overwhelming confidence in the efficiency of the Kansas viewpoint, no matter how materially it differed from traditions and standards that in other sections of the country were revered as infallible."

The man most responsible, by far, for bringing the golden gospel of Kansas agriculture and state prosperity to a skeptical world was Foster Dwight Coburn, secretary of the Board of Agriculture from 1894 to 1914. Heading up "the biggest press bureau on earth," Coburn was often called "the most useful" citizen of Kansas. Eulogized at the time of his death in 1925 in a lengthy *New York Times* editorial, Coburn had on occasion promptly received letters from Europe addressed only "To the Man Who Made Kansas Famous, Kansas, U.S.A."

Coburn's publications, sometimes in runs of one hundred thousand, included titles such as "The Hog and His Habitat," "The Helpful Hen," and "The Beef Steer and His Sister." The endless stream of solid information, interlaced at strategic points with unadulterated propaganda, often proved critical in attracting potential settlers from the states or from abroad. The Englishman who thought Kansas was the largest state in the Union had undoubtedly been influenced by Coburn.

Coburn's method was simple and direct, in the best

Kansas tradition. He established a grass-roots network of township officials and county clerks who faithfully reported every cackle, moo, and Hessian fly in the realm. The network was a model of Teutonic thoroughness, one perhaps envied by Kaiser Wilhelm himself. When the secretary's machine produced a favorable statistic, which was often, "we got up on the highest edifice on the highest ridge of ground in Kansas and shouted it out loud. We advertised Kansas, you bet."[11]

With the system in good working order, Coburn "fairly oozed facts from every pore." Kansas became known throughout the civilized world as "first in this and greatest in that and supreme in the other." Coburn proved so effective that Governor Arthur Capper (1915–19) was forced to make a public denial that Kansans were "much given to hot air and statistics." But Charles Harger said that Kansas "bows at the feet of the god of statistics. We have deemed it better to know the per capita of the currency than the story of the Iliad."[12]

During this period of high patriotic fever, Coburn and other prominent spokesmen adopted the practice, which has continued into the modern period, of personifying the state, often in the feminine form. William Allen White wrote frequently in this mode: "So there she stands— this Kansas of ours, a robust hard-working, wholesome old girl." "There is no love like that of a Kansas lover," Coburn wrote, "and no hatred like that of a suitor from whom . . . she has withheld her smiles."

Coburn's pronouncements covered a striking variety of topics: animal science ("The heaviest fleece ever produced was clipped from a Kansas sheep"); transportation ("Kansas is the champion motor-car commonwealth on the globe"); sex ("In Kansas women eat at the first table"); international relations ("The acres planted to wheat this year would cover Belgium or Holland with three million acres to spare"); economic development ("Why not advertise Kansas as a health resort?"); and pure bunkum ("The dollar will buy more latitude and longitude in Kansas than any other spot on the globe").

Some critics claimed that Coburn's success in advertising Kansas stemmed in large part from the convenient fact that he had dropped from his vocabulary such embarrassing terms as "drouth," "cyclone," "grasshopper," and "blizzard." Coburn himself denied the charge ("Tales of failure are told as faithfully . . . as are the statements of the State's unparalleled success"). But when the public read that Kansas produced "the richest alfalfa, the tallest corn, and the deepest floods of any commonwealth on the globe," it knew that the agriculture secretary had not been the author. Suspicious out-of-state newspapermen pored over the secretary's reports hoping to discover 'Kansas K-lamities." But alas, the news emanating from Topeka included only tales of plenty and progress.

THE VIRUS of optimism and confidence infected the cultural arena as well. The Kansas State Fair, the Kansas Authors Club, the Woman's Kansas Day Club, and the Native Sons and Daughters (whose sole organizational purpose was "the glorification of Kansas") were founded during this period. The *Kansas Magazine* appeared in its third incarnation, more feisty than ever. The Topeka painter George Melville Stone was hailed as "one of the greatest of our modern artists." In 1909 a musician soberly declared that "few states . . . have given music more prominence . . . for culture and refinement than has Kansas." The theater did not fare as well, however. Dramatic presentations tended to be "of the meagre sort." The nearest the state had come to grand opera, a critic sourly remarked, was a rear view of the star's special train as it "whirls past the squat-roofed prairie depot bearing a famous company from coast to coast." The sentiment anticipates the modern state slogan, "Midway, USA."

Kansas's reputation received a boost in 1914 from the author of one of the most widely read books in the travel-literature genre, *Abroad at Home*. The well-known New York journalist Julian Street wrote that "everything I had ever heard of Kansas, every one I had ever met from Kansas, everything I had ever imagined about Kansas, made me anxious to invade that State. With the exception of California, there was no State about which I felt such a consuming curiosity." Before he crossed the state line, what he heard in Kansas City from William Rockhill Nelson, publisher of the *Star*, did not diminish Street's anticipation. "Kansas is the greatest state in the Union," Nelson told him. "It thinks. It produces things. . . . All these new ideas they are getting everywhere else are old ideas in Kansas."

Street lamented the fact that there seemed to be little appreciation of art in Kansas (and in Missouri), and he grumbled that he had eaten the worst meal of his entire trip in Kansas. Several "religious manifestations," the ubiquitous "nasal voices," and the rustic mode of expression ("In Kansas we are hell on education") amused him. But he was impressed with the qualities that he perceived to be the core of the Kansas character: "directness, sincerity, strength, thoughtfulness and practicality." The University of Kansas ("anything but backward") and prohibition ("a prohibition State in which prohibition actually works") received high marks. He called Kansas "the most typical American agricultural state" and likened it to the "scriptural kingdom—a land of floods, droughts, cyclones, and enormous crops; of prophets and of plagues."

Western Kansas didn't fare quite as well. From his Pullman window, Street saw only a drab, treeless waste of brown and gray—"nothing, nothing, nothing." Images of incessant wind, violent cyclones, dust storms, tragic desolation. As the train approached the small town of Montony—which he felt was *most* appropriately named—near the Colorado border, he listened sympathetically to

25

the exclamations of a fellow passenger: "God! How can they stand living out here? I'd rather be dead!"[13]

At about the time of Street's journey, one of America's best-known young poets, Vachel Lindsay, began a cross-country walking tour from his home in Springfield, Illinois, to California. An idealist with socialistic and pacifistic leanings, Lindsay championed the "new localism"—a philosophical view that the most important things in life were those closest to hearth and neighborhood. A disciple of Walt Whitman's, Lindsay saw in the Midwest no "provincialism or cultural inferiority" but rather "the essence of America, the heartland," the national center of "visionary optimism." Progressive Kansas and Vachel Lindsay were made for each other.

In Lindsay's account of his lengthy journey, published in 1914 as *Adventures While Preaching the Gospel of Beauty*, he declared that "of all that I saw the State of Kansas impressed me most." He rhapsodized about the bees, the barns, the clouds, the orchards, the alfalfa fields, and the seas of wheat and grass. Lindsay entered Kansas, a biographer tells us, "with images of wild strawberries and white New England Churches" dancing in his head. In his diary he wrote: "I have crossed the mystic border. I have left Earth. I have entered Wonderland. . . . This morning I passed the stone mile-post that marks the beginning of Kansas."

Thomas Jefferson had called farmers "the chosen people of God," placing them at the vital center of the American republic. Lindsay, who has been accused by critics of "Sunday-school innocence," found the concrete realization of the Jeffersonian ideal in the rural communities of Kansas: "Kansas, the Ideal American Community! Kansas, nearer than any other to the kind of a land our fathers took for granted!" Relatively free of the evils associated with urbanization and industrialization, the state had developed "the type of agricultural civilization the constitution had in mind!" In Kansas could be found the epitome of "the church type of civilization! The newest New England! State of more promise of permanent spiritual glory than Massachusetts in her brilliant youth!"[14]

The heady environment had worked its magic on the local poets as well as on the sometime visitor. In 1911 a small group of visionaries at Kansas University published a modest collection of poems, *Songs from the Hill.* Full of youthful and progressive exuberance, they dreamt dreams that were not to be. Since "the centers of American literature" had been inexorably moving westward for a century, they reasoned, "the next logical camping place of the muses should be on the banks of the 'Kaw.' "

In 1914 a more ambitious collection was published under the title *Sunflowers: A Book of Kansas Poems,* edited by Willard A. Wattles. He selected the work of men and women who had recognized "the significance of our state" with poems that "smack unmistakably of our Kansas soil and are close to the grass roots." He conceded that Julian Street had been "more or less right" about the absence of Kansas art, but Wattles confidently predicted that the Sunflower State would soon eclipse the decadent and provincial East. The collection unabashedly celebrated the many and diverse dimensions of "Kansasness"—the land, the crops, the animals, the plants, the weather, and the people, both their eccentricities and their normalcies. Twenty-two of the eighty-four lyrical, often sentimental poems included the word Kansas in their titles.

The volume included contributions by Harry H. Kemp ("Let other countries glory in their Past, / But Kansas glories in her days to be"); J. B. Edson ("For the Lord's got back to Kansas and 'twill be a Kansas year"); and Wattles himself ("Kansas, Mother of us all, Bosomed-deep, imperial"). Wattles also included the best-known poem to survive the period—one that has been memorized by generations of Kansas school children—"The Call of Kansas," by Esther M. Clark, whose last stanza is:

CHAPTER TWO

> Kansas, beloved Mother, today in an
>   alien land,
> Yours is the name I have idly traced
>   with a bit of wood in the sand,
> The name that, flung from scornful
>   lip, will make the hot blood start;
> The name that is graven, hard and deep,
>   on the core of my loyal heart.
> O, higher, clearer and stronger yet, than
>   the boom of the savage sea,
> The voice of the prairie calling,
> > Calling me.[15]

A home-spun effort by "Doc" Divilbiss, published in 1909, identified many of the themes on the popular mind during the heyday of progressivism:

> Center of the greatest nation,
> With residents from all creation
> And every one writes his relation—
>   "Come to Kansas". . . .
> Once the "happy, happy home"
> Of Eastern men with coin to loan—
> Mighty few mortgages they own,
>   Now in Kansas.
> Cyclones, blizzards, dug-outs too—
> Seems as if all three have "flew."
> That's history now—they're all through
>   With Kansas. . . .
> You're a freak without a doubt,
> But you know what you're about
> And every child you've got will shout
>   "Here's to Kansas!"[16]

DURING THE PROGRESSIVE ERA, Kansans derived great satisfaction from both their bountiful condition and their future prospects. They also began to look back nostalgically on a "glorious past," in much the same manner that the Age of Reason had revered classical Greece and Rome. The nineteenth-century heritage comprised two overarching and transcending experiences: the Free State struggle of the territorial period and the peopling of the prairie and the plains. By the turn of the century the heroic phenomena had become thoroughly mythologized in the public and the creative mind. Henceforth, they would serve as twin cornerstones of something akin to a state "civil religion."

Kansans could legitimately claim that no other American state had experienced such a short, eventful, and morally significant gestation period, not even the original thirteen. For nearly seven years the newly organized territory had held center stage in the national theater, with the slavery question hanging in the balance. The "Kansas question" had become the overriding political and moral issue of the day. Intense disputation, sometimes violent, in the territory and in the halls of Congress, marked its course and ultimate resolution.

"All the world knows Kansas," a proud citizen wrote in 1905, "knows Kansas as the first battle ground in the war for freedom, knows Kansas as the very cradle of freedom." Union leaders such as Abraham Lincoln and Horace Greeley had made the Kansas cause their own because it was "the cause of mankind." "Perhaps no state . . . is so rich in historic interest as Kansas save Massachusetts alone," an officer in a state patriotic organization said. "What that state was to the Revolutionary fathers so Kansas was to the cause of freedom a century later." Kansas' most famous rhymester, Eugene F. Ware, reinforced the theme in his "Three States":

> Of all the states, but three will live in story;
> Old Massachusetts with her Plymouth Rock,
> And old Virginia with her noble stock,
> And Sunny Kansas with her woes and glory;
> These three will live in song and oratory,
> While all the others, with their idle claims,
> Will only be remembered as mere names.

Historians might quibble among themselves about the relative importance to the Free State cause of leaders such as Charles Robinson, John Brown, and James H. Lane. They could underline the bald fact that local and personal economic objectives had commonly overshadowed the national and moralistic antislavery crusade in governing the behavior of individual colonists. But the general populace did not overly concern itself with such refinements. It loved to tell and retell the heroics of the Free State champions, which had been memorialized in prose by Horace Greeley, in poems by John Greenleaf Whittier. In those "stirring times" the indolent, whiskey-drinking border ruffians had received their comeuppance from the thrifty, morally upright Yankees. The hand of God had manifestly been at work in this Holy Cause. The outcome itself was sufficient evidence of that.

The Founder Principle of geography, or the Doctrine of First Effective Settlement, holds that the cultural priorities of a region's colonizers will influence subsequent generations quite disproportionately to the absolute numbers of the colonizers' descendants. Citizens of a commonwealth "born of a moral idea" could be expected to remain especially responsive to moral crusades. The fight against chattel slavery could readily be transformed into righteous protests against other specific forms of "slavery"—for example, tobacco, alcohol, and gambling—or, indeed, against free-floating or "generic" sin. The so-called Puritan, or New England, conscience often came to find "a lodgment" in the laws of the prairie commonwealth. Thus Kansas came to be, or at least conceived itself to be, "the child of Plymouth Rock."

After the Civil War, thousands of Americans, including many veterans of the bloody conflict, augmented by restless Europeans, had sought their futures in Kansas. The young hopefuls had come to the nearly empty fifty million acres, as the ancient Hebrews to the promised land, "believing all things, hoping all things." They had emigrated to escape parents, spouses, poverty, a "crowded and decadent East," or, as one "mover" remembered, "because Daddy wanted to be his own boss." Or they came, as young people are want to do, simply for the high adventure, "for the pure hell of it."

From the mid sixties to the late eighties the huge rectangular land mass filled rapidly with towns, farmsteads, windmills, livestock, schools, churches, railroads, section roads, barbed wire, Osage-orange hedgerows, and buffalo bones. When the cyclic prosperity hit its "manic" phase in the mid eighties, people "went crazy" over land and railroad speculation, town-site development, "gold-bearing shales," and county-seat fights. Actually, two states had come into being: the realistic one you saw outside your dugout window and the paper one promised by the get-rich-quick schemes of the promoters. "Those were the days," an eyewitness recalled, "of railroads without trains . . . , irrigation ditches . . . without water, incorporated towns . . . without inhabitants, courthouses without courts, . . . and all kinds of public improvements without a use—all promoted in some semiwilderness region during the inflation of that . . . commercial gas bag commonly known as a 'boom.'"[17] In the late eighties the air went out of the "gas bag," and the "stickers" who remained in Kansas inherited huge public debts and an unsavory national reputation.

By the inception of the twentieth century, the surviving early settlers, now senior citizens, itched to tell about their pioneering experiences. Most concurred with an Oberlin man who wrote in 1905 that the pioneers had represented "the best class of brave, God-fearing people" from the East and the South. These "plain but sturdy" settlers had conquered the "barren and trackless plains" of Kansas in a region that had once been called the Great American Desert. "Through the hardships and sacrifices of those early pioneers whose patriotism and bravery and fidelity never ceased," he said, "the glorious future of Kansas was made possible."[18]

During the pioneering days, easterners often received letters from Kansas relatives and friends full of uncritical praise for the promised land. But twentieth-century reminiscences conveyed a more realistic picture than the contemporary "puff" pieces. The old settlers were not slow to criticize the state, establishing a tradition that their latter-day descendants have enthusiastically perpetuated, though for somewhat different reasons.

Some old-timers remembered frontier Kansas as "the graveyard of hopes," claiming that it could "promise more in June, and deliver less in August" than any state in the Union. Others, more forgivingly, spoke only about its "occasional cussedness." A Geary County woman recalled times in the early years when "I wouldn't have given the snap of my fingers for the whole of Kansas." Her husband had insisted that everyone should have a mission in life, but their purpose in coming to "this God-forsaken country" had left her mystified. Of course, she quickly added, "that was before the rains came."[19]

Some observers stressed the penchant for extremes in the Kansas personality. George P. Morehouse, president of the Kansas State Historical Society, said in 1918 that "we are a state of extremists and never take a conservative view of anything." Back in the seventies a Philadelphia newspaper had warned those who were headed west to give "a wide berth" to Kansas, whose climate was one of "extreme heat and cold." They would be well advised, it said, to choose a land "where New England hypocrites and humbugs do not rule one end of the state and highwaymen and horse thieves the other." In the nineties, Senator John J. Ingalls had declared that "the unprecedented environment has produced a temperament volatile and mercurial, marked by . . . insatiable hunger for innovation, out of which has grown a society that has been alternately the reproach and the marvel of mankind."[20]

The epic themes of the nineteenth century were, and continue to be, the inspiration for much of the fictional literature about Kansas. The preterritorial sagas—the tales of Coronado, Pike, the Indian Missions, the military forts, and the overland trails—have excited the literary imagination for over a century. So, too, have the border wars, John Brown, Quantrill's raid, and the image of the intrepid homesteaders struggling with the Indians, perverse nature, and one another. An especially appealing genre has been the rowdy cow town at the railhead with its colorful cowboy culture. Long-running television series, such as "Gunsmoke," have furnished millions of viewers the world over their only, but badly distorted, impression of the modern state of Kansas. The dominant themes of the nineteenth century have also attracted the talents of songwriters anxious to express their feelings about the state's history and culture. After a 1985 survey of the field, historians James H. Nottage and Floyd R. Thomas, Jr., concluded that the lyrics of patriotic songs typically celebrated Kansas as "a good land" which had been settled by "good people."[21]

During the Progressive Era, Kansans probably saw the core of their "goodness"—of their historically conditioned, collective character—somewhere near the intersect of genuineness, directness, industriousness, determination, individualism, piety, and democracy—the nuclei of what would later become known as "traditional" and "puritanical" values. They prided themselves on the uniqueness of the society they had built on "the trackless prairies" in five short decades. Carl Becker put it succinctly: "Kansas is a community with a peculiar and distinctive experience. . . . [It] is a state with a past."

DURING THE PROGRESSIVE period the state "with a past" enjoyed a dynamic present that included a good deal of attention from the national press. A variety of political and social issues and a number of attractive personalities elicited the publicity, some of it favorable, some of it not. But whatever the content of a given message, the state was noticed, respected, and attended to. Though removed from the eastern centers of power, the prairie civilization informed and influenced national public policy to a significant extent. Win, lose, or draw, Kansas was in the social, political, and cultural ball game.

Some of those in the surrounding states became irritated at the volume and the intensity with which Kansas events were being reported in the media. In 1918 a touring reporter for a national magazine told a veteran resident of western Missouri that his next stop was Kansas, which he considered "a steaming hotbed of news." At that, the old Missourian lost his composure. He said he was tired of hearing about Kansas wheat, Kansas inventiveness, the "Kansas push." Yes, he was sick to death of reading about "Kansas, Kansas, Kansas—nothing but Kansas!"

Kansas events were more likely to receive favorable notice in the eastern press if they fit the "progressive" mold. The *New York Times's* salute to the state in 1911 on the fiftieth anniversary of statehood is a typical example. The Civil War fight for liberty, it said, had ignited in Kansas, making the state both "morally and materially the battleground of the struggle." But in these more serene days, it had become the field of battle only for "industry, enterprise, and intelligence, contending solely with the problems of an orderly and progressive community."

Even in these halcyon days, Kansas sometimes became "the butt of jokes and criticism." Before the turn of the century the story had circulated about the Kansas man abroad who, when asked his home state, responded with "Well, if you must know. I'm from Kansas. Now laugh, dern you." In some of the more-refined social circles, the fashion remained "to speak jestingly of Kansas." Echoing the popular image of the calamitous nineties, even progressive Kansas, for some sophisticated easterners, remained only "a hot, dry place, way out on the edge of things."

A state of proclaimed "puritan" virtues—one that struggled against long odds to control, indeed eliminate, alcohol, tobacco, and gambling—became an easy target for the fabled hard-drinking, cigar-chomping journalists. For these cynical brethren, Kansas was "the hypocrite headquarters of the world and Topeka was its capital." In this vein the saloon-smashing activities of Mrs. Nation received far more attention than did any other single phenomenon. In an 1901 editorial entitled "Civilization in Kansas," the *New York Times* considered her a bad joke and worse. To have her running amok was "incompatible with . . . even a tolerable state of civilization." The paper recommended "some exemplary punishment" to salvage "the reputation of the State of Kansas as a civilized commonwealth."

The well-known radical Emma Goldman paid a visit to the state in 1911. After a brief survey of the scene of "dreary calm," she said that Kansas, like Massachusetts, lived on "past glory." No longer could Kansas claim to be the "stronghold of free thought," as in the days of John Brown. Liberalism now lay gasping under the dead weight of prohibition and the church. "Lack of interest in ideas, smugness, and self-complacency" characterized most Kansans, she sniffed. A decade or so later, many Americans would come to agree.

In a 1916 editorial the *New York Times* lampooned the rural-dominated state culture. The paper had finagled a copy of a book report on the noted novelist Joseph Conrad by a member of the Monday Study Club of Sabetha (Nemaha County). The book report referred to Conrad as a "highbrow" whose message couldn't be understood by normal human beings, at least none in Sabetha. He expressed himself in a mode entirely foreign to "the Kansas language." The *Times* noted that although Conrad's work had been acclaimed by the literati of the entire world, heretofore "all judging Kansas, the Brains Belt, had not spoken." As to the literary choice of a Sabethan between Conrad and "such local masterpieces as Capper's Weekly," there could, of course, be no doubt.

Two months later, the *Times* quoted approvingly a Montgomery, Alabama, paper which had said that "we do not like Kansas . . . because it is always flaunting its virtue in the face of other States." "In a mad world," the *Times* sarcastically noted, "Kansas is the one sane asylum." Perhaps the empty Kansas jails could be converted to "Shelters for the Unuplifted from Other States." "Kansas is one grand sweet song of prosperous goodness," the paper said. It is "the purest, the most peaceable, the soberest, the most enthusiastic, the most uniform, and the best advertised Commonwealth in the whole forty-eight."[22]

During the teens the nation edged ever closer to adoption of the "Kansas idea," that is, constitutional prohibition. The tone of national comment shifted from the lighthearted and jocular to the humorless and harsh. The most bitter attack came from Albert Jay Nock, writing in the prestigious *North American Review*. In the 1916 article entitled "Prohibition and Civilization," Nock conceded that prohibition in Kansas had prohibited "within limits." But he insisted that it was far more important to know "what life is like under a general social theory of negation and repression: for such is what life in Kansas comes to."

The ultimate test of any civilization, Nock argued, was "its power of attracting and permanently interesting the human spirit." If the psychologist William James, a distinguished "lover of the humane life," were to make a "candid examination of the civilization of Kansas . . . one knows at once what the verdict would be." If we observed "the type of people" produced by such a civilization, it was easy to conclude that "no amount of social benefit would be worth having if we had to become like them in order to get it." The "tyrannical imposition" of the Puritan "Kultur" had produced in Kansas only a "flat hideousness" and an "arid provincialism," a society that was totally devoid of "charm."

A lengthy and cogent defense emanated from a powerful and surprising quarter. The *New York Times* acknowledged that puritanism might be considered "a system of busybody interference." But William James, it felt, would have been at home either in Kansas or in the Athens of Socrates. James would have concluded that even prohibition Kansas was "not naked of civilization and charm." Throughout its history, Kansas had produced "picturesque characters" who had "a flavor and savor strictly Kansan. Either in their temperament or their air is some exuberance, sparkle, and 'kick' that makes alcohol superfluous." The *Times* agreed that it was better to have "too much" of the Puritan spirit than not enough of it. "With its enthusiasms, its curiosity, its interest in everything, . . . its love of discussion and novelty, in its aberrations and sporadic 'crazies,' . . . Kansas civilization must be potent in charm."[23]

THE PROGRESSIVE ERA closed on an unexpected public-image note. From the territorial period forward, Kansans had been widely advertised as fighters. The grit and determination needed to tame the wilderness is, after all, not far removed from combativeness. The frontier community had become notorious the world over for its armed violence; even the "Pioneer Woman" on the Statehouse grounds resolutely holds a rifle on her lap. In the days of Bleeding Kansas, Sharp's rifles, known euphemistically as Beecher Bibles, had signified the "Old John Brown militancy." Chock full of eager young men, Civil War Kansas had had the most enlistees and the most casualties per capita of any state in the Union. In the Spanish-American War, the Philippine heroics of the famous Twentieth Kansas Regiment and its daring leader, Frederick Funston, had evoked the admiration of a grateful nation. ("There goes Kansas," General Arthur MacArthur had said, "and all Hell can't stop her.")

But after the outbreak of European hostilities in 1914, a

number of Kansas men and women, along with some of their midwestern neighbors, adopted firm antiwar positions. Inspired by Quaker pacifism and progressive idealism, augmented modestly by German sympathizers, they urged nonresistance and opposed war preparedness. By early 1916, teacher, farmer, and labor organizations with combined memberships of 150,000 had taken antiwar stands. In addition, 40 women's clubs, 100 churches, and over 150 fraternal groups had joined the chorus.

On January 30, 1916, peace delegates from across the state, attending the annual meeting of the umbrella organization, the Kansas Peace and Equity League, filled to overflowing a Baptist church in Topeka. Governor Arthur Capper himself headed up the organization. Charles M. Sheldon, the well-known Congregationalist minister; Frank Strong, chancellor of the University of Kansas; Tom McNeal, a prominent journalist; and other noted Kansans joined the governor on the platform. They declared that hostilities could best be prevented by "educating and Christianizing ourselves and the world," instead of by armed preparedness. And they sharply criticized President Woodrow Wilson for his planned military build-up.

Three days later, President Wilson made a previously scheduled stop in Topeka to deliver himself of a strong argument for preparedness. He had been shocked at the reports that many Kansans opposed military preparedness ("If Kansas will not fight, who will?"). In an outspoken speech to a large but reserved crowd, he appealed to the fighting Kansas tradition: "If I were to pick out one place which was likely to . . . get hot first about invasion of the essential principles of American liberty, I certainly would look to Kansas among the first places in the country."[24]

The national press, led by the *New York Times*, responded quickly to what it termed "the beautiful blindness of certain high, transcendental, impracticable Kansas theorists." In a series of biting editorials spread over 1916 and early 1917, the *Times* reminded Kansans of their fight-

ing heritage ("the old Kansas stock and spirit") and accused Governor Capper of "a spineless pacifism." It
counted twenty-one Kansas counties named in honor of
military men, deeming this an "evil omen" for the "peace-
at-any-price flock." Some Kansans joined the *Times* attack,
declaring in angry tones that the pacifists, far from representing "the true Kansas spirit," had brought "shame and
humiliation upon every son of the State." Others noted
sadly that it was but another example of the historic tendency to extremism.

Undaunted, the antiwar advocates responded that the
informed Kansan rejected the "go-it-blind sort of jingoism"
common in the East. The Allies should take seriously the
possibility that Germany really wanted peace. The war
scare had been generated by the propaganda of those who
stood to profit from war. If munitions absolutely had to
be made, the government should take over the industry
so as to eliminate the profit motive. The true "Kansas spirit" still existed, one independent-minded partisan said,
and "still dares to have an opinion at variance . . . with
opinions held elsewhere."

A proclamation by Governor Capper declared January
28, 1917, as Peace Sunday and January 29 as Peace Day,
in addition to the traditional Kansas Day. Answering the
charge that as provincial rubes, Kansans viewed the world
through an isolationist prism, Capper said that they had
"a world-grasp" and would "not be content to stand before
the world as onlookers through any fancied geographical
isolation." He called for the "calm and deliberate discussion of this tremendous question" and urged stepped-up
efforts to increase state membership in organizations dedicated to peace. And so, thousands of Kansans, through
their churches, lodges, clubs, farm organizations, and labor
unions—and four hundred thousand school children—
observed the Peace Days in study and contemplation.

However, in early February, after diplomatic ties had
been severed with Germany, the legislature pledged its

support of the president "to the fullest extent." Governor
Capper declared April 6 as Loyalty Day (by coincidence,
the day on which war was to be declared). But in a late
March editorial entitled "Capper and His Kind," the *New
York Times* labeled as irresponsible the appeals from Kansas
for "pacifism and disarmament" while the "peril grows
daily." The pacifists, it said, were scattered but influential.
"They constitute in the present hour a much more dangerous element than the Copperheads of the North in the
war between the States."

But in the end, Kansas completely redeemed her
hard-earned reputation for bellicosity. The state, of course,
participated fully and enthusiastically in every phase of
the war effort. Religious groups, such as the Mennonites,
who were reluctant to buy war bonds and who balked
at military service, received mob justice from their "patriotic" neighbors for their temerity in standing by their
principles. At a 1918 Liberty Loan rally in Topeka, a dough-
boy described the most advanced methods of modern
warfare. Employing "graphic language," he demonstrated
the delicate technique of sticking the "cold steel bayonet"
into the "arrogant Huns," twisting the point to cut the hole
larger "in order to pull the blade out and be ready to . . .
stick another." The large audience of men, women, and
children "went wild with fervor, and entering into the
spirit of his bloody talk, cheered him to the echo."[25] In
1919 the state legislature condemned the secretary of war
for releasing over one hundred conscientious objectors
from Fort Leavenworth. Demanding a full congressional
investigation, the righteous resolution charged that such
action placed a premium on "slackerism, cowardice and
mawkish sentimentality." So much for Kansas pacifism.

3

THE TWENTIES

THE PERIOD between the First World War and the Great Depression, variously known as the Jazz Age, the Age of Flaming Youth, the Roaring Twenties, and the Age of Mencken, was a critical one for the Kansas image. The era that allegedly "discovered" sex featured bobbed-haired, flat-chested flappers, the Scopes trial, the Lindbergh flight, and national prohibition. Evangelists Billy Sunday and Aimee Semple McPherson trod the sawdust trail, while the novels of F. Scott Fitzgerald, Ernest Hemingway, and Sinclair Lewis captured the imagination of the Lost Generation. Societal critics concerned themselves with the Teapot Dome scandal, the execution of the anarchists Sacco and Vanzetti, and the revival of the Ku Klux Klan. The more devout found cause for alarm in the closed automobile, the rising hemlines of women's dresses, and scholarly skepticism about the traditional claims of inerrancy of the Bible.

A robust postwar prosperity served as the economic backdrop for a major cultural confrontation that grew more intense as the decade unfolded. The nation had essentially become divided into "two Americas," as remarked by numerous observers, including the novelist John Dos Passos and the journalist Walter Lippmann. Making up the "backbone" of the country was a pietistical, conforming middle class, sympathetic to business and the values it exalted. Liberals, intellectuals, artists, and writers constituted a disaffected but noisy minority whose influence grew steadily as the decade advanced. They worshipped more permissive gods, or none at all, and viewed the benighted mainstream—especially that current flowing in the rural areas of middle America—as impossibly dull and repressive, even antediluvian.

The Kulturkampf resolved itself into several distinct, but correlated, spheres. In alcohol control, the drys clashed with the wets; in sexual affairs, the strait-laced with the liberated; in religion, the fundamentalists with the modernists; in politics, the traditionalists with the progressives; and in their overarching philosophies, the ruralists with the urbanists. At or near the center of this struggle stood the dry, strait-laced, fundamentalist, traditional, and rural state of Kansas. Symbolizing for better or worse the puritanical philosophy and life style, Kansas gained an inordinate amount of national notoriety during the decade. From a secure, even triumphant, position as an examplar for the nation in 1920, the state was driven into a fully defensive posture, characterized by a siege mentality, ten years later. The ultimate resolution of the conflict would have consequences for the state image for the remainder of the century.

The bullish climate of the Progressive Era extended into the early years of the Roaring Twenties. When its "agricultural empire" produced total farm products that grossed over $1,000 million in 1919, Kansas began to advertise itself as the Billion Dollar State. In 1922 a New Jersey editor observed that Kansas had become "the pyrotechnic display among States. Where other commonwealths are satisfied to let off a few sparks, Kansas desires to light the heavens." Patriotic exuberance moved a former state supreme court justice (1899–1905), William R. Smith, to demand in 1921 a drastic overhaul of the "archaic" state seal.

Calling for a special session of the legislature, Smith declared that the seal was "a primitive, inartistic picture of a semi-civilized region," depicting nothing in which "we now take pride." Reflecting the "glorious spirit of the present day," the revised seal should show women with the ballot, a broken demijohn symbolizing prohibition, and an icon of the Court of Industrial Relations ("our most modern institution").

Proposed in 1920 by the progressive governor Henry J. Allen (1919–23), the controversial Industrial Court stimulated a great deal of national comment and enhanced the Kansas reputation as a prolific creator of novel approaches to deep-seated societal problems. In theory the Industrial Court placed the public interest above that of both business and labor by requiring arbitration in "essential" industries ("to compose industrial differences as the best sense of the community wants them composed"). Though denounced by labor leaders and contested by captains of industry, the court became a model for a number of similar proposals across the nation. The plan had been proposed as "progressive" legislation, but in later years it has come to be viewed as a conservative measure designed primarily to bust unions. The liberal William Allen White won a Pulitzer Prize for a polemic opposing the court. However, many contemporary liberals hailed the measure as a significant step in the modern movement to subordinate individual rights of property to the interests of the "integrated community." The Industrial Court, the liberal journal *Survey* said approvingly in 1925, derived from the same inspirational source as the one that had produced socialism in England and communism in Russia.

But the prosperity of the twenties brought a conservative turn in the political road for both Kansas and the nation. The *New York Times* noted that even the violent winds, which had elevated the cellar to prominence as "one of the most important fixtures in Kansas architecture," seemed to have subsided, leaving the state "a tame place to live in." In mid decade, Henry J. Allen, publisher of the *Wichita Beacon*, rued the conservative rut into which a fabled Kansas journalism seemed to have fallen. He yearned to read the "fearless, slashing words" of yore, which had caused men "to sit straight and pound tables." Too much prosperity had produced a fat and complacent press that no longer boldly sought public dragons to slay. The *New York Times* noted presciently that a new generation had grown up in Kansas "not so sharply differentiated as its predecessors from all the known varieties of mankind. The young people believe in neither the dragons nor the dragon-slayers."

But Kansas became known as a bellwether among the states for more than its recent turn to conservatism. During the progressive period, both Kansans and non-Kansans had labeled the state the most typical or the most American in the Union. Carl Becker put it poetically: "The Kansas spirit is the American spirit double distilled. . . . Kansas is America in microcosm." During the irenic days of Warren G. Harding and Calvin Coolidge the identification became even more firmly established. Kansas was portrayed as the quintessence of the American democratic ideal. The Kansas journalist William G. Clugston developed the theme in a national magazine. In no place, he said, did the "average, ordinary individuals generally referred to as the common people" dominate more completely. In no state had the democratic ideal been "cherished more fondly or exalted more highly." No people could be found striving "more energetically, or with more confidence in themselves and their ideals. He concluded that the verdict of history could very well be "As Kansas went, so went Democracy."[1]

Indeed, during the early twenties, Kansas reached the height of its influence. In the 1921 editorial "The Dream State," commemorating the sixtieth anniversary of Kansas statehood, the *New York Times* recognized the state's role in national affairs: "Nothing too good can be said of Kansas and her dreams." Kansas had become the national piper, while the rest of the country "dances to her piping." "In the heart of Kansas," it quoted William Allen White, "is a spiritual tuning fork."

A year later, flush with the state's heady successes, White wrote his famous "prophecy" piece:

> Kansas is the Mother Shipton, the Madame Thebes, the Witch of Endor, and the low barometer of the nation. When anything is going to happen in this country, it happens first in Kansas. Abolition, Prohibition, Populism, the Bull Moose, the exit of the roller towel, the appearance of the bank guarantee, the blue sky law . . . these things came popping out of Kansas like bats out of hell. Sooner or later other states take up these things, and then Kansas goes on breeding other troubles. . . . There is just one way to stop progress in America; and that is to hire some hungry earthquake to come along and gobble up Kansas. . . . Kansas is hardly a state. It is a kind of prophecy![2]

By FAR THE GREATER number of observations on the Kansas character centered on her puritanism. A liberalizing, irreverent era that esteemed the fox trot, the black bottom, the hip-pocket flask, and the heroines of F. Scott Fitzgerald had no use for the self-appointed guardian of public morality. Nor did those who characterized the Eighteenth Amendment—the "Kansas Idea" which went into effect in 1920—as the most reactionary piece of legislation since the halcyon days of Louis XIV.

By the mid twenties, much of the national press was exuding anti-Kansasisms from every pore. Even the French social scientist André Siegfried, in an influential book on the United States, labeled Kansas "the heart of western Puritanism." Sometimes the focus was on the influences that had an impact on the political scene. The "political vagaries" of the state, the *New York Times* waggishly suggested, could be explained by the simple mete-orological fact that "the wind get on their nerves. Then they get on the nerves of the rest of the country." Kansas farmers, it said, loved to cheer for the public man "who is good to his old mother and does not forget the little ones." "The situation has become such," a critic noted in a national magazine, "that a man must be either a hypo-crite or a fanatic if he hopes for any sort of political prefer-ment." The ultimate political purpose of the common-wealth was "to regulate the personal conduct of the indi-vidual—the policy of trying to legislate morality into morons."

Comments on "moral conditions" in Kansas were ubiquitous. Easterners chided Kansans for pressing for prohibition enforcement elsewhere while the state's anti-cigarette law went unenforced. Kansans were accused of establishing a national division of labor whereby they sup-plied the nation with "great political ideas" which were then funded by federal taxes extracted largely from the populous East. The newly established *New Yorker* maga-zine snickered that the state legislature had been known to go for weeks at a time "without seriously interfering with the people's habits." Kansas was the Commonwealth of Good, a detractor noted sarcastically; if evil ever ap-peared there, it was immediately declared "an alien impor-tation, usually from New York."

The commentary even touched that holy of holies—religion. The *New York Times* learned that the *Topeka Capi-tal*—a favorite target since publisher Arthur Capper had led the prewar pacifistic movement—had been inviting readers to comment on their favorite books. For one cor-respondent, the *Times* reported with glee, the favorite reading material had turned out to be the *Wesleyan Method-ist Magazine* of 1825. The *Times* was also fascinated by the fact that another Kansas newspaper had serialized the Bible in a regular column that proved to be its most popu-lar feature. How "curious" that Kansans would employ a secular vehicle to encourage the reading of the Good Book. Only "heathens" would consider anything in the Bible as news. Once again, it said, Kansans had proven that they were "hard to understand."

In 1924 the noted humorist Irvin S. Cobb produced one of the most witty and widely read impressions of Kansas in the twenties: *Kansas: Shall We Civilize Her or Let Her Civilize Us?* Cobb managed to convey the urbane easterner's view of a rustic, puritanical culture, though he coated it with a liberal patina of good-natured humor. On his tour of the state he had had the misfortune to stay in a "deplorably bad" hotel where a "fat lumpy" little girl practiced—no, "preyed"—on the piano outside his room. Inside the room "the aroma of rotted oilcloth contended with the perfume of a leaky gas fixture." Frustrated by the insufferable conditions, he lay down on the lumpy mattress and "called the State of Kansas hard and unforgivable names."

Cobb was no more impressed by the physiography of the surrounding landscape, with its "unromantic horizontalitudenessities." He fervently hoped that someday a sensitive poet or architect might make the towns more attractive, but in the meantime they could only be described as "homely when they're not actually grotesque." The locals deluged him with Coburn-type statistics about everything from the size of the average bank deposit in the state to the number of party telephone lines in the county. "But still," he mused, "there can't be as many trains leaving here for outside points as they let on, or practically everybody would have got away before now."

However, not all was bleakness and rusticity in the wilds of Kansas. She might be "a trifle shy on natural beauties," Cobb said, but she had "plenty of mental Alps and moral Himalayas to compensate." Unfortunately, for some time, Kansans had "resolutely . . . undertaken to attend to the other fellow's business." "Am I my brother's keeper?" they had asked him rhetorically, and had responded with a resounding "You bet your sweet life I am!" Still, Kansas had "shaped her people into as orderly, as godly, as uniformly prosperous, as well-content,. . . as generally educated a mass of citizenry as is to be found [in] the Union."[3]

THE ONGOING cultural struggle between the city and the countryside framed the several views of Kansas. For decades the American population had been forsaking a rural environment for an urban one. The demographic shift implied a major reorientation of values. The greater degree of urban tolerance and anonymity encouraged the city dweller to loosen the moral restraints associated with the small-town milieu. In the urban environment, individualism and social isolation tended to increase, family-and-community-oriented behavior to decline. Self-discipline, piety, and the homely virtues came to be seen as old-fashioned, as superfluous baggage that one left, or should have left, back on the farm.

In the twenties the trend received a major boost from the inexorable forces of modernity: the radio, the movies, the toaster, and the vacuum cleaner—the rich cornucopia of modern gadgets and widgets made possible by the genie of electricity. These technological innovations, the rapidly increasing power of advertising to influence behavior and the antiestablishment works of authors such as Fitzgerald, Hemingway, and Lewis—all conspired to portray an exotic, fast-paced urban life, which was especially attractive to the young. By contrast, the traditional society seemed boring, sleepy, and outmoded—a way of life for dullards and the old folks, but hardly an inviting future for the aspiring and the go-getter.

The portrayal of Kansas as a national symbol of a waning rural culture began early in the decade. In a 1922 critique of American civilization, a social psychologist found life to be dominated by the bucolic philosophy of politicians such as William Jennings Bryan and "the beatitudes of a State like Kansas." The *New York Times* chortled over the Kansas predilection to exalt hicks who were "still eating [their] pie with a knife, drinking [their] coffee from a saucer and picking [their] teeth in public with a pocket knife."

In 1922 the *Times* turned on its head the most obvious implications of a Census Bureau report that Kansans enjoyed the greatest longevity in the nation. Their enhanced life expectancy, it said, derived principally from the fact that they were "powerful sleepers, thanks not only to their climate and quiet nights, but to self-complacence. In such a commonwealth there is nothing to worry about." The life expectancy of New Yorkers was several years shorter, the paper acknowledged, but its "stimulating" environment made Kansans "envious." "All Kansans want to go to New York, but few New Yorkers yearn to see Kansas. It is not the land of their desire."

In 1923 the *Chicago Tribune* drew a more explicit comparison between urban culture and rural culture. In a lead editorial it reminded its readers that during the Populist period, White had reported that the greatest aspiration of Kansas was "to bake in the sun" and that little had changed in the interim. In contrast, in urban America, "men push cathedrals of steel high into the air. . . . Life is bold and full of accomplishment. . . . Here music gets its subsidies, art its home, science its laboratories. . . . Here is where a million fires make the steam of a nation. Here are its dynamos, its achievements and its records." If "the Kansas will" were to be fully imposed on the nation, the paper warned, "the greatest architectural monument of the land will be a silo, the greatest work of art a crazy quilt and the greatest thrill in life a snooze in stocking feet by the base burner."

Although they had much more limited resources to catch the national eye and ear in this cultural war, Kansans did on occasion go on the offensive. The Kansan with the most opportunities to speak out to the wider audience—

and to be heard and appreciated when he did—was, of course, William Allen White. He had come to be recognized as the national spokesman for the small town and its conventional middle-class values, now under the siege guns of the alienated in the urban East.

In the Progressive Era, White had frequently touted Kansas as a middle-class utopia dominated by farmers and small businessmen. He once made a detailed comparison between Emporia and New York City. In Emporia, he had said, "we see some things more sanely and more humanly than they do in New York." Emporians were more friendly, closer to nature, and had produced a more democratic society. There the little man "counts for more." In the class-conscious metropolis the social lines were drawn, producing a servile class that "fawns for a quarter." Rigid class distinctions represented the saddest spectacle in the city for one who was familiar with "the frank, wholesome, clean, happy faces of the country."

Among White's several defenses of the values of small-town America, an article in 1922 stands out for its caustic, even bitter, tone. White had joined the national chorus of those who were calling for a more restrictive immigration policy. For over a century, he said, Americans had pinned their hopes for a decent democratic society on education and a growing economy. But the plan had gone awry. The cities were being overrun with immigrants from "the world's sunny climes" who fostered graft, corruption, and boodling. And these "darker-skinned [Mediterranean] neighbors breed faster than we." The total cultural and political dominance of the cities was just a matter of time. "We have written our Constitution, created our laws, established our government for one kind of people—and the ships from across the sea have brought us another kind of people."[4] White's indictment drew a heated response from the liberal New York journalist Heywood Broun. White's theoretical premises were askew, Broun said, and in any event, White shouldn't have used "moron" as a synonym for "immigrant."

Within a year, White was generating a great deal of publicity for himself and his state in a very different—and partially contradictory—cause. He had become disturbed at the rapid growth of the Ku Klux Klan in Kansas and the rural Midwest: "To make a case against a birthplace, a religion, or a race is wicked, un-American and cowardly." He attempted to laugh the Klan out of Kansas with colorful characterizations of the "Kleagles, Cyclops and . . . Whangdoodles" parading in bed sheets in the state's cowpastures. In 1924 he drew 150,000 votes as an independent, anti-Klan candidate for governor. The campaign publicity and the rapid demise of the Klan after the election helped to nip Kansas' budding reputation for bigotry.

THE OVERSHADOWING figure in the urban/rural confrontation was the Baltimore journalist and social and literary critic Henry Louis Mencken (1880–1956). The outspoken Mencken came to symbolize opposition to the domination of American culture by the small-town puritanical mentality. His admirers have proclaimed him a giant in American cultural history, "a shaper of the national taste and temper." Most historians have concurred. They agree with Walter Lippmann's contemporary assessment that Mencken represented "the most powerful personal influence on this whole generation of educated people." Sentimental intellectuals continue to keep the lamp burning brightly at the Mencken shrine for his intemperate attacks on conventional mores. This despite the multiple embarrassments of his pro-German sympathies before both world wars, his unshakable opposition to the ideal of democratic government, and his congenital inability to consider women any higher on the evolutionary scale than Persian cats.

The *American Mercury*, founded in 1924 for "the urbane and the washed," was the principal vehicle for Mencken's satirical views of mainstream society. Under his editorship the iconoclastic magazine quickly became "a national institution." Carrying a bright green copy of the *Mercury*, as a kind of "mental hipflask," marked the man of "liberated intelligence." By the late twenties the journal was handily winning "favorite magazine" polls on college campuses across the land, including, *inter alia*, the University of Kansas. This generation of college students, said the Socialist Norman Thomas, has shed all illusions but one: "that they can live like Babbitt and think like Mencken."

Although it has been alleged that the "Bad Boy from Baltimore" hated everything, the record hardly supports this assertion. It is true that a wide variety of individuals and enterprises felt the sting of his acerbic wit and the sledge-hammer blows of his dogmatic vituperation. But he persistently focused his attention on those elements of the sociocultural milieu closely associated with small-town manners and mores: on the rubes, Rotarians, Babbitts, uplifters, pecksniffs, sentimentalists, and fundamentalists—all captured smartly by the anthropological taxon he made famous, "Boobus americanus."

Mencken's territorial interests centered on what he called the "far places," that is, on the "Methodist prairies of the Middle West [and] the Baptist backwaters of the South." A lifetime spent in Kansas or Arkansas, he said, was less attractive to the enlightened man than only a few years lived in "a genuinely civilized and happy country." Within this geographical range he concentrated on a few favorite targets. They included hicks ("the farmer is . . . predominantly a fraud and an ignoramus, [who] richly deserves nine-tenths of what he suffers from our economic system"); politicians ("Tammany [Hall] . . . is not perfect, but compared to the gang of thieves . . . in any American country-town it almost seems like a mob of saints"); Methodism ("a theology degraded almost to the level of voodooism"); puritanism ("the haunting fear that someone, somewhere, may be happy"); and prohibition ("It was set going by fanatics, it was spread by fools, and it is being kept up by scoundrels").

Mencken's simplistic opinions on prohibition were particularly vitriolic. A German of the old school, he fantasized that beer was "completely harmless" and that alcohol consumption under prohibition had "at least doubled." The underlying cause of these "crazy enactments" was "the yokel's congenital and incurable hatred of the city man—his simian rage against everyone who . . . is having a better time than he is." For Mencken, the alcohol issue needed no public forum to air its complexities. He rejected out of hand a piece with a differing point of view submitted by the well-known novelist Upton Sinclair. The *Mercury,* its editor said, was committed to the policy of the return of the American saloon. So far as he was concerned, alcohol control was a question "which did not permit of discussion."

The frequency, intensity, and variety of the Baltimorean's dicta elicited a rather emphatic response among those who had been called before the judgmental bar and found wanting. In their more ardent expressions of affection for the editor, one can often spot zoological metaphors such as "weasel," "buzzard," "maggot," "howling hyena," and "little skunk." One admirer called Mencken "an 18-karat, 23-jewel, 33rd degree, bred-in-the-bone and dyed-in-the-wool moron." The more restrained *Wichita Beacon* could only suggest that Mencken was full of "hokum, pose and flapdoodle." Some accused him of trying to establish a new religion, Mercurianity. But a pious Illinois woman declared that "the more we read of Mr. Mencken the more we love the Methodist church."

"H. L. Mencken is rude and insulting," a reader of the *Kansas City Star* said. "He might speak of our mental deficiencies with a more restrained tone." The journalist Frederick Lewis Allen said that reading a bombastic

Mencken article was a lot like "hearing a whole piano piece played fortissimo." But it remained for White—who could be vicious when the occasion demanded—to administer the *coup de grâce* in distinctly Kansas language: "With a pig's eyes that never look up, with a pig's snout that loves muck, with a pig's brain that knows only the sty, . . . he sometimes opens his pig's mouth, tusked and ugly, and lets out the voice of God, railing at the whitewash that covers the manure about his habitat."[5]

Given Mencken's "prejudices," it is not surprising that he and his minions frequently brought a harsh public light to bear on the state of Kansas. As the quintessential "cow state," chock full of hayseeds, moralizers, and Methodists, Kansas symbolized everything that H.L. deplored. During the twenties the *Mercury* carried more negative articles on Kansas than on any other individual state.

Mencken delighted in the hypocritical image of "howling boozers" cavorting merrily in the country clubs of "fanatically dry" Kansas. To charge a Harvard professor with agnosticism would be banal, he said; but a Kansas teacher, faced with the same circumstances, "would go damp upon the forehead." "The Wesleyan code of rural Kansas," he forecast in 1924, "will be forced upon all of us by the full military and naval power of the United States." In comparisons with prominent easterners, Kansans tended to come off second best—to say the most. "A Jerry Simpson [the rough-hewn Kansas Populist] and a Charles Evans Hughes [the sophisticated secretary of state] seem to belong to different genera, even to different solar systems."

Mencken took a dark view of the Kansas literary scene. "To be a Kansan and a *littérateur* is in itself a feat of respectable intricacy and derring-do," he said; "the man who harnessed a sheep and a hyena scarcely performed a more amazing. Literature regards Kansas as a desert swarming with Knights of Pythias, and Kansas regards literature as peopled with men too lazy to do honest work."[6]

In 1909 Mencken had brought his finely honed critical powers to bear on William Allen White's just-published novel *A Certain Rich Man*. Set in "sun-baked, unwashed" Kansas, the novel demonstrated a style that was "a miraculously exact imitation of Thackeray at his worst." White's work conveyed an "essentially feminine" viewpoint since it esteemed "sentiment above reality, piety above progress." The mawkish novel, the review concluded, should have great appeal for "every high school girl" in the country.[7]

Surprisingly, one prominent Kansas writer drew nothing but effusive praise from the Great One. Mencken set Ed Howe, the Atchison newspaperman and novelist, apart from all other Kansas mortals. Indeed, he felt that Howe should be designated as a "super-Kansan." He deserved that singularity because he was "an absolutely honest man—perhaps the only one in Kansas." The plain-spoken "Howe de Kansas" had earned those plaudits from the master because he was fond of railing against the cant and sham of the Kansas reformers and of evangelical religion, favorite Mencken targets. Mencken wrote an introduction to one of Howe's books, and at Howe's death in 1937, Mencken stated, with pardonable exaggeration, that the Atchisonian had been "the most adept master of language ever heard in America."

Because Mencken's knowledge of the Kansas scene was understandably circumscribed, he sought someone of similar philosophy who could furnish details. He found his man in Charles B. Driscoll, a former Kansan who had edited the *Wichita Eagle* for five years. Driscoll not only shared the Baltimorean's world view, but along with a number of his contemporaries, he attempted to fashion his public statements in the inimitable Mencken style. Driscoll made three contributions to the *Mercury* on exclusively Kansas topics in the twenties. "Urbane and washed" Kansans who read the hyperbolic pieces would hardly have recognized the place.

In the first effort, provocatively entitled "Why Men

Leave Kansas," he dwelt on the "Kansas Complex," which turned out to be a medical condition—namely, "a pathological desire to do good." An endless stream of tiresome cranks, crackpots, uplifters, and spiritualists had pressed their precious causes on him as editor of the *Eagle*. The Kansas ethos required that they be given a respectful hearing, though in any really civilized locale they would have been summarily booted out. Driscoll reminded his readers that Kansas had been settled by "John Brown types." "Anybody who will drive a covered wagon from Boston to Topeka for the sole purpose of finding a fight has a lot of energy and determination."[8]

A 1926 piece by Driscoll, entitled "Major Prophets of Holy Kansas, " remains a classic among the many contemporary efforts to fix an image of religious fanaticism on the state. In this view, Kansas was not just unobtrusively devout, in an All-American, garden-variety sort of way; it was the very buckle of the fundamentalist and fanatical Bible Belt. Among the "primitive religionists of the plains," Driscoll said, one found many "shining and tiresome souls" who waited impatiently for the imminent return of Billy Sunday, Aimee Semple McPherson, and/or the Lord. One of the most "picturesque prophets" in the entire West had been committed to a hospital for the mentally impaired in Chicago. But back in Kansas, he had not only been considered sane but had even been accorded "the highest honors as a front-rank pillar of the church and of civilization." A golden belt of saved souls ran from the Canadian border to the Gulf of Mexico. And embedded at the center of this national girdle, Driscoll said, was "a resplendent jewel which sends out rays . . . that reach from pole to pole. . . . This jewel is Holy Kansas."[9]

THE CHAMPIONS of modernity received a welcome assist in 1927 with the publication of one of the era's most consequential literary works by one of America's premier writers. Widely read and even more widely discussed, the novel fairly brimmed with anticlerical—and anti-Kansas—propaganda. Perhaps more than any other single volume of the period it both epitomized the cultural struggle and molded the public perception of Kansas. And it did so at a critical hour—at a time when the war was heating up, especially on the prohibition front. The novel was *Elmer Gantry*; the novelist, Sinclair Lewis.

It has been said that Lewis's novels "sketched the decade." "To be a fan of Sinclair Lewis," critic Alfred Kazin wrote recently, "was to proclaim oneself an independent thinker." Lewis had burst into the national consciousness with his scornful views of middle-class conformity in *Main Street* (1920) and *Babbitt* (1922). Americans had added the word "babbittry" to their vocabulary as a synonym for the spiritually numbing materialism allegedly associated with conventional respectability—to be found most typically in the rural precincts of middle America. After another major success (*Arrowsmith*), Lewis began work on his "preacher novel."

That Lewis would turn to a religious theme at this time is not surprising. The rapidly increasing prestige of the natural sciences and the relaxed morality of the Jazz Age had produced an unprecedented tension between the "fundamentalists" and the "modernists." The position of a communicant along this axis revealed a good deal more about his social and theological attitudes than about his denominational affinity. Fundamentalists believed in the infallibility of the Bible, the virgin birth, and the literal Second Coming. Public religious expression, they felt, should be restricted to the otherworldly directed activity of soul saving. The modernists, or social gospelers, concerned themselves less with doctrine than with secular activism. They wanted to change social conditions—on this earth and now. If they mentioned sin at all, it was likely to be in the context of social reform rather than individual transgression.

The religious dichotomy carried a geographical correlate: fundamentalists were concentrated in the rural areas of the South and the West; modernists, in the larger cities of the Northeast and the Middle West. In 1925, at the famous Scopes, or "monkey," trial in Tennessee, the irreconcilable nature of the two positions became painfully apparent. Two giants of the age, William Jennings Bryan and Clarence Darrow, furnished the most dramatic moments in what was basically a clash of cultures. A native son of Kansas, Dr. Vernon L. Kellogg, director of the prestigious National Research Council, testified for the defense that the teaching of evolution was a proper and necessary part of the high-school curriculum. Otherwise, Kansas, along with the rest of the nation, remained on the sidelines as an engrossed observer of the trial.

While in utero, Lewis's book received much more than the usual prepublication attention. In the spring of 1926 he moved to Kansas City, Missouri, ostensibly to do research in the religious community. There, amid much fanfare, he rejected the Pulitzer Prize for *Arrowsmith*. He again attracted widespread attention when, from the pulpit of the Linwood Boulevard Christian Church, he challenged God to strike him dead within fifteen minutes—if He really existed. And he organized a "Sunday School Class" of fifteen or so ministers from across the city's theological spectrum. In well-publicized weekly sessions in his hotel suite, Lewis badgered the masochistic clerics on everything from obscure theological doctrine to their own personal lives and beliefs.

The preacher novel was an immediate sensation when it was published in March 1927. The publishers had ordered 140,000 copies printed, said to have been "the largest first printing of any book in history." Selection by the Book-of-the-Month Club and scattered reports of banning helped to boost sales. Over 200,000 copies were sold during the first ten weeks. No novel had ever sold "in such quantities" in Kansas.

Rarely if ever had an American novel generated more widespread or more heated discussion. Lewis had indeed "stirred up the animals." The churchgoing public heard the book condemned "in measured and unmeasured terms from a thousand pulpits." The most pious decried it as "venomous," "sordid and cowardly," and "slime, pure slime." Some called for the cessation of publication; others wanted the author jailed. Billy Sunday cried that the Lord should have "socked Mr. Lewis so hard that there would have been nothing left for the devil to levy on." Despite the outcry, in time the public added Lewis's image of the evangelist to its permanent inventory of cultural types.

The novel, of course, was not without its contemporary supporters. The unflappable *Topeka Capital* thought that the book would "give people a chance to talk about something else than the neighbors." A "modernist" member of Lewis's "Sunday School Class" in Kansas City declared that the author had "stamped his personality on the country." H. L. Mencken, to whom the work had been dedicated "with profound admiration," was knocked "clear over the fence" by it. "A civilized man," he said, "viewing a Kansas Baptist or Methodist, is urged to laugh by a process almost as irresistible as that which prompts a galled jade to wince. . . . The Heaven they yearn for, though it may be only a sublimated Kansas, is as grand and glorious in their sight as the fields of asphodel that enchanted the Greeks."[10]

Students of the Lewis canon have not ranked *Elmer Gantry* artistically with his best work. Literary critics have largely ignored the novel because it manifests so little creative tension or character development. Although Elmer is a religious professional, he is essentially a stranger to the moral dilemma or the spiritual impulse: he is more the amoral yokel than an immoral monster. Given the cultural context of the day, the novel succeeded far more as propaganda than as art. In a widely quoted front-page review in the *Kansas City Times,* William Allen White implied that God had struck the novelist in the Kansas City church, after all. "Sinclair Lewis, the artist," White solemnly intoned, "is dead."

The central theme of the satire is religious hypocrisy—the gulf between the public utterances of men of the cloth and their private beliefs and behaviors. Lewis serves up a cornucopia of deceit and duplicity masquerading under the cloak of piety and righteousness. A couple of belts of moonshine whiskey in "dry" Kansas enormously facilitates Gantry's "spontaneous" call to preach. When he becomes "tortured by boredom" at the seminary (which was often), his morale is materially improved by visits to the wicked city, where he is "in closer relation to fancy ladies and to bartenders than one would have desired in a holy clerk." From the first page, where Elmer is "eloquently . . . lovingly and pugnaciously drunk," to the last page, where he lusts for the new girl "with charming ankles" in the choir, Lewis brilliantly portrays a life of unrelieved moral corruption.

And the corruption has a particular geographical fount. The novel's persistent subtheme is defective character formation arising from a stultifying hinterland culture. Elmer was no fortuitous sport or mutant springing *de novo* from the fertile prairie soil. Lewis's message was unmistakable: Elmer was an amoral, duplicitous boob, and Elmer was the natural product of his Kansas environment. The projected images faithfully mirrored the stereotypical view of Kansas as the quintessential realm of rubes, puritanical fanatics, and a repressive, suffocating dullness. When the novel's story line moves beyond Kansas, the locale becomes symbolically irrelevant and, therefore, fictitious.

Lewis's geographical preparation had been much less thorough than his religious research. Consequently, his descriptions of the Kansas social and physical environment tended to be crude, often humorous extravagances. Elmer's hometown of Paris, Kansas, and his widowed mother formed the "foundation of his existence." Villages such as Paris ("a settlement of nine hundred evangelical Germans and Vermonters") consisted largely of "plodding yokels" noted chiefly for their "dead eyes and sagging jaws and sudden guffawing." At social gatherings the yokels "milled like cattle, in dust up to their shoelaces, and dust veiled them, in the still heat, under the dusty branches of the cottonwoods."

Before he left for college, Elmer's understanding of most everything in the universe had been gained from the local Baptist church—everything, that is, except "any longing whatever for decency and kindness and reason." From his conception, his devout mother (who was "owned by the church") had wanted him to become a man of God. But by his adolescence she thought it more likely that he would go to Congress and "reform the whole nation into a pleasing likeness of Kansas."

Gantry's school, Terwillinger College, a small Baptist institution, was in Gritzmacher Springs, Kansas. Foreshadowing the mass migration of the thirties, Lewis reports that "the springs have dried up and the Gritzmachers have gone to Los Angeles." The town "huddles" on the lonely prairie, which is "storm-racked in winter, frying and dusty in summer." The school couldn't possibly be mistaken for an Old Folks Home because it contained "a large rock painted with class numerals." Along with nine other denominational colleges, Terwillinger belonged to the "East-Middle Kansas Conference"—"all of them with buildings and presidents and chapel services and yells and colors and a standard of scholarship equal to the best high-schools."

Early in his religious career, Gantry pursues Sister Sharon Falconer, a charismatic and physically attractive evangelist, probably modeled after Aimee Semple McPherson. He competes for her favor with her English-bred manager, a refined, erudite, and snobbish Oxonian. Sharon enjoys the immense difference in the cultural backgrounds of her two suitors. She teasingly asks Elmer if he had gone to Oxford, too. "I did not, by golly!" he says. "I went to a hick college in Kansas! And I was born in a hick town in Kansas!" Apparently one of Elmer's few redeeming qualities is his candid and guileless manner—a Ronald Finney in clerical garb.

Lewis reinforced and embroidered the images of Kansas as the land of rubes, dullards, and hypocrites for a large and impressionable public. He also introduced a new dimension to the composite portrait, one that would remain dormant for years before blossoming forth: Kansas as an irrelevancy, as the "eclipsed" state.

Sister Sharon had invited the amorous Elmer to her family's plantation in Virginia. The beautiful Shenandoah valley, the Blue Ridge Mountains, and the Old Mansion, with its white pillars, formal gardens, and uniformed black servants—all duly impressed the Kansan. But the hoary tradition associated with one of the First Families of Virginia, replete with "high-nosed aunts and cousins," petrified him, a mere piece of Kansas "provinciality." Before this "older world," Elmer stood diminished, like "a little beaten boy." "I came from Paris, Kansas," he cried, "and I'm not even up to that hick burg." "You're going to stop being poor Elmer Gantry of Paris, Kansas," she reassured. "Oh, I'm glad you don't come from anywhere in particular!"[11]

By THE LATE TWENTIES the national propaganda had begun to work its inevitable way. The Kansas star remained among the brighter in the national firmament, but the dominant mood on the home front had shifted from bullish exuberance to a tightly reined optimism. The aggressiveness and celebration that had characterized the beginning of the decade yielded to nervous explanation and calls for restoration.

Patriots suggested that Kansas Day should be made

a state holiday and that state history should be urged more forcefully in the public schools. In 1929 the editor of the *Jayhawk* magazine observed that if young Kansans would take a greater interest in politics—with the turbulent but heroic "Kansas tradition" to spur them on—the state would "again" occupy a place second to "no such modest commonwealths as California, New York and Florida." In religion and morals Kansas "probably" was as "progressive as any state . . . all wails and sneers . . . notwithstanding." An older expatriate, who had returned after an absence of several years, noted among the signs of "progress" a diminished sense of physical isolation. "Airplanes put us within thirty-six hours of Los Angeles or New York City," he said. "One wonders sometimes where one will go soon to find a nice quiet place to rest."

Local champions of the puritan life style began to acknowledge its deficiencies publicly. No one had stressed the puritan influence more often or more persuasively than William Allen White. But he came to admit that this heritage had been purchased at a high price. Pragmatic Kansans seemed to lack "a sense of beauty and the love of it." The epic struggle of the human spirit with "ruthless fate" in Kansas had been recorded by no great poet, painter, philosopher, or musician. "Surely all joy, all happiness, all permanent delight that restores the soul of man," he said, "does not come from the wine, women and song, which Kansas frowns upon."[12]

While no one could argue with White's basic premise, the arts were far from dead in Kansas. Poetry flourished in the twenties, under the leadership of the Kansas Authors Club. A frustrated, disowning tone had begun to appear, although it did not dominate until the next decade. Most of the decade's published poems sounded a cheerful, upbeat note. The major collection, edited by Helen Rhoda Hoopes in 1927, included chiefly "happy lyrics," which sang "the beauty of the prairies and the plains." The urban/rural confrontation provided inspiration for several contributors. Helen Griffith McCarroll made an unfavorable comparison between "the beautiful sleek houses purr[ing] on velvet grasses" in Kansas City and the state of Kansas, "mothering all the world at her great bosom. . . . Here she is unadorned—God, what a Beauty!" One of the period's leading poets, May Williams Ward, developed the same theme:

> I pity the dwellers in cities
> Who see but a scrap of the sky
> And a scrap of the earth. . . . O wonderful plain,
> Where the world and the worlds go by![13]

The advocates of modernity preached a dogma that asserted the cultural sterility of the hinterland. A major challenge for artists who produced work in a local, especially midwestern context, therefore, was the avoidance of the curse of "provincialism." The most important Kansas-bred painter of the twentieth century felt this tension as few others did. And whatever the tortures of his personal ambivalence, his first significant work became a major propaganda statement for the urbanists.

In 1928 John Steuart Curry (1897–1946) burst onto the national art scene with his *Baptism in Kansas*. It established him as a major artist, and in the early thirties he joined Grant Wood of Iowa and Thomas Hart Benton of Missouri as the "Midwestern Triumvirate of American Regionalism." Subsequently, Curry became the foremost, if controversial, artistic interpreter of rural Kansas for the state and the nation.

Baptism was painted from Curry's memory of a childhood event. It portrays a group of Campbellites (Disciples of Christ) conducting a barnyard baptism in a cattle-watering tank. The simplistic rustic scene looks innocent enough to modern eyes. A recent reviewer in a Wichita newspaper found it "incredible" that both contemporary eastern critics and well-educated Kansans could have regarded the "straightforward and objective" painting of pietistical farmers as devastating social satire.

But in the boiling cultural caldron of the late twenties, with its emotion-laden dichotomy, it could not have been otherwise. Kansans understandably looked askance at a picture that could well have served as an illustration for *Elmer Gantry* or a Charles Driscoll satire. In this and subsequent Curry depictions of tornadoes, religious fanatics, and lynch mobs, they resented his apparent attempts to rekindle the stereotypes that they had been trying so hard to live down.

Although eastern critics viewed the work from an entirely different perspective, they concurred with the local interpretation. The *New York Times*'s art critic, Edward Alden Jewell, characterized *Baptism* as "a gorgeous piece of satire. . . . Religious fanaticism of the hinterland saturates the scene. . . . On all sides spread the flat Kansas prairies, stretching to a horizon that fences from the outer world this shut-in frenzy of the human soul."[14] The painting so touched the soul of the New York art patron Gertrude Vanderbilt Whitney that she purchased it and agreed to subsidize Curry's work for the next two years. At the opening of the Whitney Museum of American Art in 1931, the founder posed regally for photographers beside her prize purchase.

What message did Curry intend to convey with the painting that became the linchpin of his career as the major artistic interpreter of Kansas? A native of Jefferson County, he had left his farm home as a teenager ("as quickly as he could," his wife said later) for art training in Kansas City, Chicago, and eventually Paris. By the early twenties his career as a magazine illustrator had enabled him to forsake a modest Greenwich Village loft for a more genial abode in the fashionable art colony at Westport, Connecticut. But by 1928, his commercial career was foundering, and as he recalled years later, "I was in a state of desperation trying to get along at illustration, or anything I could do."

During this era the young artists and writers who poured into New York City from the hinterland invariably brought "one great Hate," writer Waldo D. Frank has said—namely, "the Hate of Puritan ideals." By the late twenties, Curry had become a fully integrated member of one of the major artistic communities of the country. In affluent Westport, art historian M. Sue Kendall tells us, he served as an auctioneer at lively "bohemian" parties, where "paintings and sculpture in parodies of local styles were held up to ridicule."[15]

Curry had to be keenly aware of the standard view of Kansas held by eastern intellectuals, which included most of his friends and neighbors. In 1927, the year of *Elmer Gantry*, a fellow Kansan and Westport neighbor, Mateel Howe Farnham, Ed Howe's daughter, published a major novel, *Rebellion*. The protagonist, a Kansas girl, learns while attending a selective eastern college that "the very word Kansas, for some unaccountable reason, seemed to be cause for laughter." Another close friend and neighbor, the literary critic Van Wyck Brooks, had led the twentieth-century attack of the intellectuals on the corroding influence of puritanism on American culture. Scattered across the rural landscape, he had written, one could find thousands of small towns "frostbitten, palsied, full of a morbid, bloodless, death-in-life."

Although *Baptism* portrayed pious folk, we can be certain that piety was not the message. As a freethinker, Curry was said to be "opposed to organized religion." Furthermore, he did not paint a familiar scene from his own religious tradition; instead, he reached for an exotic one that eastern art patrons would almost certainly find more arresting and suggestive. His puzzled mother once asked him why he didn't paint the somber practices of his own Presbyterian heritage instead of the alien raptures of the Holy Rollers. Whatever his motivation in subsequent work, including the Kansas Statehouse murals, there can be little doubt that in the seminal *Baptism*, Curry con-

sciously capitalized on the contemporary eastern stereotype of his native state.

AS THE DECADE drew to a close, the "two Americas" marched
toward Armageddon on the liquor issue, with Kansas at
the epicenter of the bitter conflict. Reliable data on the
per capita consumption of alcohol in the state and nation—the core of the efficacy quarrel—was necessarily un-
available. The most scientific study of national consumption wasn't published until 1932 and was widely ignored
after it was.

Under the circumstances, every man could and did
become his own expert on the success of the "noble experiment." One saw what one wanted to see, believed what
one wanted to believe, unembarrassed by data on the collective behavior. With the facts blowing in the wind, the
image and the media became all. Both sides unblushingly
mangled the truth, ushering in what author Herbert Asbury has called the era of the "Big Lie." "The drys lied
to make prohibition look good," he said; "the wets lied
to make it look bad; the government officials lied to make
themselves look good . . . ; and the politicians lied through
force of habit."[16]

The presidential contest of 1928 exacerbated the social,
religious, and geographical tensions within the nation.
The dry Iowan Herbert Hoover defeated the consummate
New York wet Al Smith, 58 to 42 percent. Kansans chose
Hoover over the "city feller" by 70 to 30 percent, one of
the top pro-Hoover votes in the nation. But that was the
last major victory the predominantly rural drys were to
enjoy. The crude public-opinion polls confirmed what
even the staunchest of the drys had to admit, at least to
himself: prohibition as public policy was in deep trouble.

The dry leaders of Kansas fought determinedly against
the rising tide of adverse national opinion. For them, prohibition was as momentous and valued a life style and

67

philosophy as abolition had been for their grandfathers. The history of the prohibition movement, Kansas Supreme Court Justice Richard J. Hopkins (1923–29) said, was "the history of the most relentless fight ever made by the sons and daughters of men against a great evil." "The prohibition philosophy," said William Allen White, "is not that it will make others good, but that it will make life in a complex civilization safer and simpler and more profitable."

The legendary basketball coach at Kansas University, Forrest C. ("Phog") Allen, thought that prohibition had produced "the best crop of girls and boys this old world ever saw." "Kansas is so much drier than most of the other states," Attorney General William A. Smith (1927–30) said, "that it is foolish to talk about it being wet at all." Republican Governor Clyde M. Reed (1929–31) was "certain" that prohibition had been an "economic success." His Democratic successor, Harry H. Woodring (1931–33), declared grandly that "triumph over the forces of lawlessness, so far as prohibition is concerned, will come eventually in the nation as it came to Kansas."

But in this war of words the urban wets held the higher ground. In 1927 the journalist Frederick Lewis Allen noted that over the previous five years the word "reformer" had deteriorated to a term of "contempt" among the nation's urban and intellectual leaders. An *American Mercury* article entitled "Government by Yokel" complained about the rural domination of the national life. People in the cities were forced to "submit to the constant . . . restriction of their liberties by hinds who seldom think of them save to wish them evil."

Buoyed by the encouraging shift in public opinion, the wets intensified their campaign for repeal in 1929/30, often targeting Kansas as the premier prohibition state. The titles of articles appearing in national magazines told much of the story: "Cocktails in Kansas," "Kansas, the Beer State," "The Truth about Kansas," "Holy Hypocritical

Kansas." "Bleeding Kansas" had become "Boozing Kansas," one article began. "It's only the jackass politicians running for office before a yokelry very nearly as ignorant as themselves," wrote Frank Doster, a former chief justice of the Kansas Supreme Court, "who any longer affect regards for the old-time Puritan as a model of civic and religious virtue."

In his popular column in the *Nation*, Heywood Broun noted that "somebody in Kansas said that a man who took a high-ball was as much a public enemy as one who threw a bomb." The nation might be more efficient and prosperous under prohibition, he conceded, but "you cannot have dry poets, painters and dreamers." Drinking had always been a form of protest, a sign of rebellion. It was impossible, Broun insisted, to be "politically dry and at the same time progressive."[17]

Charles B. Driscoll continued to titillate his *Mercury* audience with an exaggerated portrayal of Kansas as a hotbed of pietistical fanaticism. When Billy Sunday had visited Wichita, Driscoll wrote in 1929, Henry J. Allen had "grasped the great evangelist's hand, weeping, while the inspired community arose as one man and shouted, 'Glory to God!' " During the pre-Volstead years, Kansans popped up "everywhere, tirelessly . . . preaching Prohibition. They went into the far fields . . . for silly-looking Prohibition party candidates . . . , taking defeat with the same angelic smile with which an idiot takes castor oil."[18]

In 1929 the noted author Herbert Asbury made a major contribution to the debate with the first, and arguably the best, biography of Carry Nation. In the very first sentence he describes her as an "industrious meddler and busy-body" who was a product of her hinterland environment—that "hotbed of the bizarre and the fanatical." She had followed the "well-beaten trail of . . . extravagant religious zeal . . . urged onward . . . by a deep rooted persecution mania and a highly developed scapegoat complex."[19] The book was well received, especially in urban America.

The most powerful and persistent voices for the wet cause were the big-city dailies. Although it had virtually no circulation in Kansas, the *Chicago Tribune* ran a series of feature articles devoted exclusively to social and political conditions in the state. It was one thing to declare prohibition a failure in Chicago or New York, but it was much more devastating to the dry cause to find it wanting in Kansas. After a whirlwind tour, Inspector X reported in the *Tribune* that the state provided "a study in applied hypocrisy. . . . Sanctified statesmen never weary of painting [it] as the Holy Land of America." But in truth, Kansas was the "birthplace of the dual personality politician who votes dry and campaigns in the churches with dry speeches, but keeps a private bottle in his locker." He found Topeka the "dryest of its size in the country," but in Wichita he claimed he saw more drunks in two nights than "in a four months tour of Europe or in a trip . . . through 36 states."[20]

For more than two decades the *New York Times* had kept a keen editorial eye trained on Kansas. While it often disagreed with the political and social philosophies emanating therefrom, its tone had typically been mild and respectful, often droll and whimsical. But in the late twenties the mood became more strident and more voluble. Kansas made the editorial page so frequently that one reader admonished the newspaper that it was "in danger of playing favorites." A 1929 editorial entitled "Backward Kansas" is characteristic of the period. It also furnishes a concluding—and ominous—note for the decade.

"In few States, if any," the *Times* said, "has there been so much pretense and proclamation of 'progressivism' as in Kansas." Office seekers, "wearing the white robe of progressivism," seize upon a "phobia," while failing to keep the state "abreast of the times." The "phobia of phobias" was, of course, prohibition. "The chief trouble with Kansas is that her wheels are continually revolving without going forward the ghost of an inch." Perhaps "the snorer" would eventually wake up; "the backward child" would ultimately learn. The editor fervently hoped that it would not be necessary to send a "Progressive Colonization Society" from the East to come to the aid of "receding Kansas."[21]

Those who set the intellectual tone for the nation—Cobb, Mencken, Driscoll, Lewis, Asbury, Curry, and Whitney, among the many others—all spoke a single language with only slightly different accents. They influenced especially the upper middle classes, who, in turn, served as models for those lower on the socioeconomic scale. The seeds sown during the decade would soon bear a richer harvest than even the most optimistic modernist could have imagined. Although Kansas was not without influence and respect at the close of the decade, the world was slipping away from her, and at an accelerating rate. If hard times should come, the result could be catastrophic.

4

THE THIRTIES

THE THIRTIES brought to Kansas the most calamitous conditions since statehood. The crash of 1929 ushered in a new day and, in solution, a new political philosophy. The Great Depression meant low crop prices, farm mortgages, tax sales, governmental relief, and dispirited emigration to more hospitable climes such as California. The hard times affected the entire nation; indeed, the whole planet. But the impact in Kansas was especially severe. Per capita personal income in the state, as a percentage of the national average, dropped from a near-normal 96 percent after the First World War to 67 percent in 1933, at the nadir of the economic disaster. The population loss during the decade (80,000) was greater than that for any other state.

The economic calamity was accompanied by a meteorological catastrophe. Cruel heat, blinding dust storms, voracious grasshoppers, and a prolonged drouth, punctuated by destructive floods, matched the trauma of the 1890s and more. The dust-bowl conditions came in the wake of the repeal of national prohibition, a social theory that had become intimately associated in the national consciousness with Kansas. What had been bold, imaginative, and "progressive" legislation in the teens became, almost overnight, repressive and reactionary, an ongoing source of ridicule and embarrassment. In the New Deal the troubled nation (and to a surprising extent, the state) embraced a novel collectivist philosophy that implicitly rejected the rugged individualism for which the agricultural commonwealth had for so long been noted. The greatest public scandal in the state's history severely tarnished the "clean" political image that had been earned over the years. And the rise of the goat-gland charlatan Dr. John R. Brinkley and the fascist preacher the Reverend Gerald B. Winrod polished anew the perception of Kansas as the home of political freaks.

Given these circumstances, the state's reputation necessarily plunged precipitously in the estimation of both the nation and Kansans themselves. Within a few short years the self-confident, harmonious, and influential commonwealth turned diffident, divided, and inconsequential. Its sense of itself—its role, purpose, and mission in the Grand Design—had been severely shaken. What vanguard thinkers such as H. L. Mencken and Sinclair Lewis had been preaching in the twenties emerged as the conventional wisdom of the Dirty Thirties and beyond.

The outlines of the shift in perception may be traced by reference to a few particularly revealing commentaries scattered across the decade. In 1931 a politically radical young woman named Meridel LeSueur won a *Scribner's Magazine* contest designed to "encourage the spirit of seeking what is true and valid in our own culture." In "Corn Village," LeSueur bitterly recalls her Kansas experience in Fort Scott (Bourbon County), where her parents had helped establish the People's College, a Socialist institution, just before the First World War. Although she had spent a scant three years in the state during her adolescence, she wrote that "like many Americans, I will never recover from my sparse childhood in Kansas." "Kansas," she said, "I have seen your beauty and your terror and your evil." She complained about her fundamentalist, revival-loving grandmother who had shown her no real affection. She remembered the "dreary villages, the frail wooden houses, the prairie ravished, everything imper- manent as if it were not meant to last the span of one man's life." Their house was "shambling," she said, "and the barns were better than the house and the stock better than the people."[1] Elmer Gantry would have felt right at home.

Her condemnation produced a conciliatory defense from a Greeley County woman, Maureen McKernan, which Scribner's agreed to publish. McKernan admitted that LeSueur's charges contained more than a modicum of truth. A Kansas City friend had often referred to Kansas as the "land of sunshine, sunflowers and sons of bitches." "We've made ourselves a national joke [by] fanatical loyalty to a few acres of buffalo grass and sandy river bottoms." But, she added, "we know that to deny that heritage . . . is to deny some tenet of faith that is as strong in our blood as religion—perhaps stronger." She then evoked the dual images of the "glorious past" of the nineteenth century. Territorial Kansas had been settled "for an idea" by "fanati- cal missionaries." A "hard working, hopeful people" had wrested the land from a recalcitrant nature, as "weaklings" by the droves had fled to less demanding environments. "The Middle West is a hard country," she said; "Kansas, the heart of it, is hardest. . . . But Kansas and the people who live there should not be altogether damned as dull and sordid and unhappy."[2]

The changing temper and tone had not been lost on that veteran recorder of the state fortunes William Allen White. In 1934 he published a short, but revealing, piece entitled "Just Wondering." It issued from a far different psyche than the boastful, chauvinistic statements he had authored repeatedly in the past. He wondered if the popu- lace and the politicians were not becoming "dull." Had increasing cosmopolitanism reduced the sense of Kansas as "a local habitation and a name?" "Where has the old delight in Kansas gone," he asked, "the old state pride that loved the story of John Brown, that kept hero tales going about the pioneers of each section? . . . Why is this Kansas begot from the loins of the old Kansas, such a different Kansas? Times change and men change with them, but where in our hearts is the blood that begot us?"[3]

National Geographic stories on individual states tend to be uncritical and flattering, gentle pieces that bring broad smiles to the faces of Chamber of Commerce members. In this context the 1937 treatment of Kansas by the magazine must be considered as outspokenly critical. Although food production was stressed ("a big shelf in the national pantry"), a major theme was the new status of the state as the national joke. Exaggerations of cyclones (the "Kansas twister"), droughts, dust storms, grasshoppers, and "odd human behavior" had all contributed to the merriment of the nation. So, too, had "odd laws that forbade men to eat snakes or that regulated the lengths of shirttails." For some unexplained reason the Kansas people had begun to develop the habit of "poking fun" at their own state. But beneath the "surface levity" one could still discover "that same grim self-reliance that sustained the pioneers, . . . undismayed even by dust, drought, or hard times."[4]

In 1939, one of the world's leading psychiatrists, Dr. Karl A. Menninger, psychoanalyzed the Kansas population en masse. A cofounder of the famed Menninger Clinic in Topeka and a born-and-bred Kansan, "Dr. Karl" reflected on the condition of the Kansas psyche at the close of the decade in an insightful article entitled "Bleeding Kansans." Ten years earlier he had spoken of Kansas, "her glories, her virtues, her progressive steps." But the crash had wrought unwanted psychological as well as economic consequences.

Menninger concluded that the now-familiar attitude of Kansans toward their state—the defensiveness, the apologetic manner, the "bantering ridicule"—reflected "a far deeper psychological origin" than the normal envy of greener pastures. The root cause was a profound and pervasive "feeling of inferiority." This state of mind did not derive from an "innate modesty" or a "feeling of revulsion" against the loud self-promotion of states such as California and Texas. Rather, Menninger said, "Kansas does not refrain from announcing that it has the best of this or the best of that because of our essential good taste; Kansas does not announce it because Kansas does not believe it." Obviously the world had changed since the Coburn era, with its robust, statistically bolstered patriotism.

The major political movements in the state—abolition, prohibition, populism, Brinkleyism, etc.—had earned for Kansans a reputation, Menninger said, as a "humorless, puritanical people, incapable of joy and grudging in their attitude toward those happier than themselves." Although this was "not a pretty reputation," Kansans accepted it "almost unanimously and meekly endure[d] the opprobrium and ridicule of other states. This I believe to be due to a humility and self-distrust so great as to be crippling to our energies."[5]

KANSANS DID NOT develop their diffident, self-deprecating attitudes in a social vacuum. The self-image of a circumscribed, inland locale must necessarily be decisively shaped by the larger, all-encompassing society. Eastern advocates of modernity had resented the perceived role of Kansas in national affairs as the smug, self-complacent censor. Many felt that they had a score to settle with the commonwealth that had been widely advertised as "his brother's keeper." The national press could barely suppress its glee at the embarrassing circumstances in which the erstwhile "moral leader" found itself. It became "open season" on Kansas, and everyone, it seemed, took to the field.

The greatest public scandal in Kansas history, the Finney bond scandal, came to light, most inconveniently, at the nadir of the Great Depression. The sensational events not only threatened the fiscal stability of the state but also cast a dark shadow over its reputation as a bastion of virtue in governmental affairs. The reaction of the *Chicago Tribune* to the affair in 1933 was characteristic of the national press. The paper confessed to "a mite of satisfaction" at the public embarrassment of "this highly self-esteemed state." "Probably if Kansas had been less militantly and assertively virtuous, less the national censor and less the common scold, less the state self-appointed to set the moral standard for the whole country . . . , there would be more generosity in the feeling for it when a first rate scandal rocks the dome of government."[6]

Political extremism, sired by the economic conditions, became a favorite topic of the national media. The recurrence of hard times, *Newsweek* said in 1938, had intensified the historical affinity of Kansans for crackpots and political "isms." Lumping political categories indiscriminately, it claimed that the "lunatic fringe," which had effected populism in the nineties and Klanism in the twenties, had now produced "goat glandism" (Dr. John R. Brinkley) and "fascism" (the Reverend Gerald B. Winrod).[7]

Along with its sister states on the Great Plains, Kansas became a metaphor for agricultural disaster. Verbal and photographic images of an uninhabitable, dust-choked wasteland filled the national consciousness. "Mounds of dust," the *New Republic* reported in the mid thirties, "may still be seen banked around the fence posts, reminders of the drought, and where whole counties have given up the fight, almost to the last man."[8]

Painful comments by outsiders about the plains environment cut all the more deeply because Kansans themselves were increasingly harboring doubts about the economic viability of the region. Several times over the previous one hundred years, scientists had revised their judgments of the inherent hospitality of the Great Plains to the development of human culture. Till about 1905, the romantic notion of a Great American Desert, which had been subsequently tamed by man, predominated. In this view the early settlers had literally "converted a desert into a garden." But during the Progressive period the desert notion had lost currency. The harsher characteristics of the environment were played down; the bountiful plains were seen as a rich, subhumid extension of the eastern corn belt. With the return of drouth and dust in the thirties, the desert concept firmly reestablished itself. Environmental students raised serious doubts about the long-term future of a region in which "catastrophe was endemic."[9]

The Kansas landscape had rarely received rave reviews from the transcontinental traveler; in the thirties it became especially vulnerable. In 1931, Heywood Broun, the "highbrow magazine writer" from New York, made the long coast-to-coast trip by train. From the vantage point of his Pullman window, in a widely publicized statement, he solemnly pronounced the state of Kansas "a place devoid of beauty, where existence is an endless and deadly monotony." On a similar journey a few years earlier, his wife, author Ruth Hale, had expressed her feelings poetically. Published in the *Literary Digest* as a "personal" to Murdock Pemberton, a Kansas native who had become a literary figure in New York, the poem did not share the enthusiasm of Vachel Lindsay, who had contemplated the same scene several years before:

> Dear Murdock, how could a poet
> Come out of Kansas?
> All day I've watched this flat ignoble country
> Meaching and creeping outside my window
> And there's not a foot of it anywhere
> That you could tell from any other foot
> Except that a few poor shacks
> Have humped themselves together into
> What the maps call towns. . . .[10]

The editorial pages of the *New York Times* reveal much about the "fall" of Kansas during the 1930s. Through mid decade the paper continued to pay an inordinate amount of attention to the Sunflower State. The general thrust of opinion may be inferred from the titles of some of the editorials: "Stationary Kansas," "Sorrows of Kansas," "Kansas Perplexed by Much Confusion," "Wherefore Art Thou Kansas!"

The New York paper pounced on adverse stories in Kansas newspapers that spoke about the "apparent lack of enterprise" among Kansans or reported the deep trouble of the "holier-than-thou" forces. After the gubernatorial election of 1930 the *Times* noted that "almost 200,000 of the sternest Puritans of ever-bleeding Kansas" had voted for Dr. Brinkley and his goats. Kansas "sings [woe] louder than all the other choristers of calamity." Carl Becker's definition of Kansas as "a state of mind," it said, could appropriately be changed to the "state of talk."

The *Times* kept alive the image of Kansas as the symbol of a sleepy rural culture that modern progressive man had rejected. "Folks don't stay up very late [,] Way out West in Kansas," the paper chanted; "They take the sidewalks in at eight [,] Way out West in Kansas." More unkindly, it alleged that the state harbored a "hatred of the East" and a "contempt for 'foreigners' and Negroes." An editorial by a worried William Allen White in the *Emporia Gazette* about the steady emigration of young people from Kansas drew a studied response. A few Kansans such as White ("the head philosopher of the Bucolic School"), the *Times* said, "expose themselves to the wickedness of Manhattan to make their pleasure in Kansas greater by the contrast of Babylon with Paradise." Perhaps the young who were deserting the state in such numbers had grown "tired of homogeneity, found Kansas too uniform, fervid and 'respectable,' sighed for life on a lower plane but richer in change and fun."[11]

The most unkind cut of all, of course, is to be ignored.

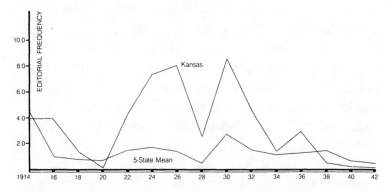

Figure 1. The frequency of editorials in the *New York Times* devoted to Kansas and to five neighboring states (Nebraska, Oklahoma, Missouri, Iowa and Colorado), expressed as a mean value, over the period 1913 to 1942. Each value is a two-year average.

From the Progressive Era through the mid thirties Kansas received far more than its proportionate share of attention from the *Times* editors. But from the late thirties the state essentially disappeared from the editorial page. A contemporary Kansas farmer noted: "When Kansas breaks into the New York headlines, it usually means one of two things. Either we have suffered an act of God or else we have made fools of ourselves."

As plotted in figure 1, from 1913 through 1932, an average of 4.50 *Times* editorials per year focused primarily on Kansas, in comparison to a mean of 1.69 for five neighboring states (Nebraska, Iowa, Missouri, Oklahoma, Colorado). The difference is highly significant statistically ($t = 2.94$; $P<.01$). Over the 1933 through 1942 interval the Kansas average dropped to 1.00, and the five-state mean dropped to 1.24, a statistically insignificant difference ($t = 0.38$; $P>.05$). Over the full thirty-year interval the Kansas average (3.33) is over twice that of the five-state mean (1.54), a statistically significant difference ($t = 2.07$; $P<.05$). For the entire interval, the total number of editorials about Kansas is 100; for the neighboring states the totals range from 43 (Colorado) to 49 (Iowa).

THE EVENTS of the decade had a devastating impact on the morale of the citizens. The high-spirited pride of the early decades melted away, leaving a bitter residue of lowered self-esteem, shattered confidence, and a curious tendency to combine senseless defensiveness with a confused self-criticism. When they were abroad, Kansans no longer crowed loudly about the land of their fathers. Rather, as an observant easterner noted, former Kansans living in metropolitan centers were not likely to reveal their geographical origin "unless you asked them."

In no arena of public life was the change more abrupt, profound, or complete than in that of liquor control. No state had been associated more intimately with one section of the federal constitution than Kansas had been with the Eighteenth Amendment. Incorporation of the "Kansas idea" into the organic law of the republic in 1920 had largely allayed any lingering local concerns about the difficulties of enforcement or the wisdom of the principle. Most Kansans rejoiced at the prospect of the entire nation's realizing the "material, moral and spiritual blessings" of an alcohol-free society. Never did a people look forward with more confidence to the political realization of their social ideals than did Kansans at the dawn of the era of national prohibition.

The repeal of the Eighteenth Amendment in 1933 meant the loss of the principle of prohibition as a national ideal. The Kansas idea had auditioned on the national stage and had failed—or more precisely—had been rejected. "When the 18th Amendment was adopted, everybody thought we had reached the promised land," said the president of the state WCTU, Lillian Mitchner; "but like the Children of Israel, we seem now to face a journey through the 'wilderness,' where there are yet 'idols' and 'golden calves' to be destroyed." When Kansas voters reaffirmed their state's fifty-four-year-old prohibition policy in 1934, they became even more vulnerable to national charges of being "backward," "unprogressive," "unsophisticated," even "antediluvian."

Not all criticism of the puritan ethic emanated from the unsympathetic East. The "Brother's Keeper" philosophy, said the Lyons, Kansas, publisher Paul Jones, had made "a comic strip of this verdant parallelogram." Kansans were forever striving, and forever failing, to build "a prairie Utopia." While other states were busying themselves producing educators, artists, scientists, and other useful citizens, Kansas was occupying itself with "advising, correcting and punishing" the wayward and the wicked.

Although he had grave misgivings about the puritan ethic, Jones became the Kansas "bulldog" of the thirties. He conceded that outsiders such as Heywood Broun thought that the natives stayed on only through "ignorance or lack of initiative." And that a favorite theme of big-city editors had become "our drabness and dullness, both physical and mental." In response he turned to a largely irrelevant ancient history in defense of the contemporary Kansas culture:

> The tourist from the Atlantic seaboard . . . expresses . . . a feeling of pity for those who . . . reside in a state where vistas are unbroken by forests, mountains or dashing waves; a section without history and traditions. . . . He is surprised when told that [Coronado] traveled through Kansas, remarking the fertility of her soil, the beauty of her skies and the majesty of her plains, 79 years before the Pilgrims set foot upon Plymouth Rock, 66 years before Captain John Smith . . . and 235 years before the Declaration of Independence.[12]

In this anxious hour, other social commentators evoked the reassuring images of the puritanical and traditional past, reminding Kansans of their "stirring" heritage. The home of John Brown and Carry Nation still "stood for the freedom of man." Kansas had a "glorious history," a commercial puff piece declared in 1932, and "the restless blood of the pioneers still surges in her veins." Here also, it said, in a failed attempt at flattery, was "a foundation too deep for disturbance." In William Allen White's 1938 presidential address before the Kansas State Historical Society—a rather philosophical overview of state history—his remarks dwelt almost exclusively on the heroic events of the nineteenth century. It was as if the twentieth century had not arrived.

Beleaguered Kansans, however, were in no mood for a root-and-branch philosophical introspection. Many became supersensitized to the outpouring of invective from home and abroad. The tradition of self-ridicule had yet to become so firmly established that it could be accepted with equanimity by all. The Reverend Charles M. Sheldon fretted about the misguided souls who "do not like Kansas." He sent to an enquiring New York acquaintance a lengthy list of reasons "why I prefer to live in Kansas." A citizen complained that in New York you were "applauded" if you criticized Kansas, but back home, if you were public-spirited enough to point out a few faults to the neighbors, you were both "hated and disliked." Locals said that they wanted to hear "less outside satire, caustic sarcasm and national snubbing." They "flared with indignation" at articles authored by "ungrateful" expatriate writers. Irate subscribers pressured the editor of the Kansas Magazine to suppress adverse stories about Kansas. "Much of the criticism of Kansas has been inspired by our own habit of declining to admit our faults," the editor coolly responded; "those who are so uncertain as to the desirability of their place or mode of living as to want nothing but praise can scarcely blame others for declining to supply it."[13]

In 1938, Raymond Clapper, a Kansan who had achieved national recognition as a political reporter, related national political events to Kansas traditions and the "Kansas spirit." In this "frightened" age, he wrote, "I find myself going back for inspiration and reassurance to Kansas." The comforting image that he recalled was of "the progressive Kan-

sas" shortly after the turn of the century. A strong supporter of the national administration, he discovered in
President Franklin Roosevelt "a good deal of the Kansas
spirit" and, in the New Deal, the spiritual "cousin" of the
Kansas Populist and Progressive movements. They all
shared a common search for "political and economic
equality and justice."[14]

The Kansas politician of the decade was the 1936 Republican presidential candidate, Alfred M. Landon. His
identification with an egalitarian, agrarian society (just "a
typical prairie state," his opponents said) attracted many
voters to his banner, though clearly not enough. His plain-
spoken manner, no-nonsense attitude, and advocacy of
traditional virtues, such as fiscal conservatism and responsible individualism, placed both his public policies
and his private behavior firmly in the Kansas tradition.
So, too, did his eye-catching sunflower campaign buttons,
his expedient support of state prohibition, and his refusal
to talk politics on Sunday.

However his roots may have influenced the outcome,
Landon's big chance surely enhanced the self-esteem of
the home state. But in itself it could hardly reverse the
tidal wave of adverse publicity that was washing over the
citizenry. Interestingly, the collapse of the image occurred
during precisely the period in which the state was enjoying
an unprecedented presence in the national capital. During
the decade, in addition to the presidential candidacy, Kansas could boast of a vice-president (Charles Curtis), three
prominent senators (Arthur Capper, Henry J. Allen, Clyde
Reed), two nationally significant congressmen (Frank Carl-
son, Clifford Hope), a secretary of war (Harry H. Woodring), an internal-revenue commissioner (Guy T. Helver-
ing), and leaders of the national Republican (John D. M.
Hamilton) and Democratic (Jouett Shouse) parties. The
coincidence of events strongly suggests that the reading
of a political subunit on the national barometer is not sig-

nificantly influenced by the quantity or the quality of its federal representation.

THE GREAT DEPRESSION induced a substantial change in the salient values of the American literary establishment. During the affluent and self-confident twenties, many of the most popular authors thrived by heaping scorn and ridicule on the conventional values of family, church, and marketplace. But in the stressful and self-doubting thirties the search for a "usable past" headed the literary agenda. Leading writers resurrected heroes and traditions from a proud past that would provide guidance and reassurance for the daunting present. In the cultural awakening of the depression years the public rekindled an interest in Americana—the history, literature, paintings, folklore, and legends of the American people. The humble homespun man of the soil—Mark Twain, Walt Whitman, Andrew Jackson, Abraham Lincoln—emerged as the ideal American type.[15]

Under the circumstances, homespun Kansas should have fared better on the national platform than she did, which only added to the mounting local frustration and penchant for self-deprecating criticism. The absence of major artistic interpreters of the state's culture proved a continuing and embarrassing problem, especially to those who had the sensitivities of William Allen White. He became a bit prickly about the constant stress during the depression on "material things," such as roads, airfields, and factories. What the state needed most, he said in 1932, was an organization to promote "ideas and ideals," a Kansas Chamber of Truth and Beauty. "A first rate poet in Ford County," he said, "would do more to bring Western Kansas into the approval of mankind than a packing house." With just one generation of "noble thinking and deep wise feeling," Kansas could "contribute more to the world than all the Chambers of Commerce . . . can contribute in all the rest of this century."[16]

Nelson Antrim Crawford, a former Kansan who had become editor of *Household Magazine,* fired some hard shots in the *Kansas Magazine* at the literary pretensions of the state. Virtually an entire meeting of the Poetry Society of Kansas, he claimed, had been devoted to the question of whether "the word *Kansas* could ever be used as an adjective." He ranked a widely used Kansas grammar as "possibly the worst work ever written" in the field. He recalled with dismay a conversation he had held with a farmer, when he still was serving on the faculty of the Kansas State Agricultural College. "That sure is a great school, Perfesser," the enlightened farmer had exclaimed. "It's practical. They don't teach no goddam grammer there."

Crawford had researched the question of the nature and distinctiveness of the "Kansas language." It implied, he suggested, "directness, bluntness, simplicity of speech, with an admixture of homely and often exceedingly effective humor." He considered White's "What's the Matter with Kansas?" the type specimen. But when a pussyfooting contemporary politician claimed that he spoke the "Kansas language," it meant only that he believed "in God, the Constitution, the sacredness of . . . womanhood, the beauty of the Kansas sunset, the peerless quality of Kansas hard winter wheat . . . and the abolition of graft in all places where it is likely to be discovered by the opposing political party." As a professional observer of national trends, Crawford also noted a recent inclination toward cultural convergence. Significant differences among the states had grown "steadily less," as transportation and communication systems had increased in power. Kansas had become "a conservative state," he said, and most of its citizens "consciously seek to become like the people of other conservative states."[17]

The quantity and the quality of Kansas literature were affected by the vicissitudes of the period. "Great creative art," critic W. G. Clugston said in a scolding 1938 review, had fallen victim to the "Kansas craze for action." The "distressing situation" in prose writing, he said, could be laid squarely at the feet of "our holier-than-thou political leaders" who had "kept us so occupied with [the] material and spiritual" that the creative and reflective had suffered. Kansans needed to appreciate that "soul-satisfying accomplishments" could come from activities other than "political power-seeking and commercial money-grabbing." Clugston also railed against the State Text Book Commission for having adopted a text on Kansas history that left the state's children in "ignorance" of many "stirring events." (The book declared that the "spirit of the pioneers is the true Kansas Spirit.") It was a "disgrace," he said, that the book ignored the contributions of such "strong personalities" as Mary Elizabeth Lease, Dr. Brinkley, Charles Sheldon, and Arthur Capper.[18]

The situation in poetry, if anything, was worse. "The Kansas poetry harvest," said Kenneth Porter, the leading poet of the period, "which 20 years ago was of a stalk-bending heaviness, is now . . . apparently both sparse on the ground and scant in the ear." Did Kansas poetry, he asked, like Kansas agriculture, suffer "merely from an unusually protracted drought, or have seed and soil definitely declined in fertility?" Echoing the sentiments of New Yorker Ruth Hale, the local bards had shown some concern for the status of the cultural arts in efforts such as "Poetless Kansas" and "Kansas Has No Poet." But Porter marked an "astonishing fact" of Kansas poetic life: the modern "sons and daughters of Abolitionist, Populist, Prohibitionist Kansas" manifested in their poetry no interest at all in either the historic or the contemporary "social struggle."[19]

But the thirties poets did expend gallons of printer's ink on lamentations about the cruel climatic conditions to be found on the prairie and the plains. Many of these efforts fully confirmed the time-honored outsider's view

of the region as a desolate wasteland. The melancholy of-
ferings bore titles such as "Black Blizzard," "Dust Cloud
over Kansas," and "In Time of Drought." They spoke de-
jectedly of "a dirty-faced world," "the long and listless
plains," and the "grey, discouraged endlessness" of the
landscape. "Apart from the bone-bare field and the chok-
ing herd," wrote May Williams Ward, "there is drought
of heart." A 1940 poem by Clare Harner, "Cry from the
Dust Bowl," seemed to say it all: "This heat! . . . This
wind! . . . This dust! . . . This Hell! Why can't there be
rain?"[20]

DURING THE THIRTIES the career of painter John Steuart
Curry came to be more intimately associated with the Kansas image than that of any other artist. From the moment
that *Baptism in Kansas* propelled him into national recognition, the relationship of the talented Kansan and his native
state had been difficult. Throughout the decade their
paths intersected intensely and frequently. In the early
forties the often-stormy association ended abruptly and
unhappily for both parties.

Curry followed *Baptism* with paintings that reinforced
the stereotype of Kansas as a "primitive" land of unrelieved monotony, hardness, and fanaticism. *Tornado over
Kansas, Kansas Posse, Holy Rollers,* and *The Gospel Train,*
among others, received wide and critical acclaim. By 1931,
six Currys were hanging in the Whitney Museum of
American Art, and the *New York Times* had hailed him as
the "Homer of Kansas." In paintings such as *Kansas Wheat
Ranch,* it said, Curry had been able to convey realistically
both "the seemingly unending spaces" of the prairie and
"the aching monotony of life" on the plains.

As Curry's reputation as *the* interpreter of life in the
state grew, his New York agent recognized the critical importance of the acceptance of the painter by Kansans. "It
would [have been] immensely helpful," art historian M. Sue

Kendall writes, "if the folks back home could [have been] induced to cooperate." But a 1931 exhibit that toured several Kansas towns was a resounding "flop." Not a single painting was sold, and even worse, the public resented the "crude angle towards Kansas." In a review of the exhibition, the Lawrence poet Florence Snow hoped that henceforth Curry would give "his Eastern patrons a much better and more beautiful idea of Kansas customs and character." Art patron Mrs. Henry J. Allen labeled Curry's choice of "freakish subjects," which professed to portray the spirit of Kansas, "entirely wrong." She charitably hoped that this was just "a phase" through which the young man was passing and that he would soon come to depict "the glories" of the Kansas people and their landscape.

By mid decade, both Curry's painterly reputation and his transcendent mission had become inseparably fused with that of Grant Wood of Iowa and Thomas Hart Benton of Missouri. As the earthy Regionalists, the triumvirate celebrated the homespun virtues of the Middle West while disdaining the "colonial" preoccupation of the eastern art establishment with the European fashion. Each man became indelibly associated not only with the region but also with a particular place and subculture within the region. With Wood and Benton happily settled in their respective states after extended residences in the "too effete" East, the pressure on Kansas to receive her own mounted. But after repeated attempts to locate him in a Kansas college had failed, the disillusioned Curry accepted in 1936 an appointment in the Agricultural College of the University of Wisconsin as the nation's first artist in residence. Mr. White decried the fact that Kansas could find "no room at the inn" for her distinguished son. *Life* magazine plunged the dagger deeper by loudly declaring that it had apparently been Wisconsin's purpose "to steal" Curry from his native state, which had "notably failed to buy his pictures."

A quiet, self-effacing young man, Curry was constitutionally incapable of loudly tooting his own horn. But just as Charles Darwin had his "bulldog" in Thomas Huxley, Curry found his in fellow Kansan Thomas Craven. A Salina native, graduate of Kansas Wesleyan, and major New York art critic, Craven noisily took up the Curry cause in state and national publications. Once called the "Henry Mencken of the world of art" for his outspokenness, he was able simultaneously to defend his misunderstood friend and to unburden himself of some pent-up hostility that he apparently had been harboring toward his native state.

Craven wrote about the love that Curry carried in his heart for the ungrateful homeland. Wisconsin had profited from the "negative, apathetic, don't-give-a-damn-for-art attitude of Kansas," a backward state that didn't "deserve to have a great artist." Could it possibly be, he asked, that Kansas had "no need for cultural improvement?" Flying directly in the teeth of the facts, Craven asserted that Curry's choice of subject matter had been strongly influenced by a "devotional upbringing [that] rendered him susceptible to the frenzied [religious] behavior of his people." Kansans had long complained that Curry painted only "obsolete conditions, the storm-stricken, plague-infested Kansas that was." But this objection had been answered of late—with "burning irony"—by the return of "the old Kansas," chock full of "plagues and droughts." The harsh reality of Kansas, he said, made Curry's representations seem "idyllic" in comparison.

The clamorings of Craven and those of like mind encouraged a group of prominent Kansas newspapermen to gain a commission for Curry to paint an extensive series of murals for the Statehouse. In 1937 the artist began to give concrete form to his overarching theme: man's epic struggle with the forces of Nature, as it had unfolded on the Kansas prairies. He said that he wanted to paint in "the Kansas language," depicting "the iron" in the Kansas people. "I want Kansas to like this," he said.

But from the initial planning stage to the final bitter brush strokes five years later, the project evoked a continuous stream of outspoken, often superficial, criticism from the public. This vocal outpouring reinforced the national image of Kansas as the natural habitat of hicks, prudes, and fanatics. It also reveals something of the collective mind set of a community that for nearly a decade had been undergoing a cultural crisis and struggling self-consciously to reaffirm its identity.

Although the funds derived largely from private donations (including about $8,000 in coins from schoolchildren), self-appointed art critics did not hesitate to give Curry the benefit of their advice. The reactions ranged from the "highly commendatory" to "violent denunciations," with the modal expression being much closer to the latter than to the former. Many feared that the Curry themes emphasized "the ugly and repulsive" in state history, reinforcing the "freak" reputation of Kansas' people, politicians, and weather.

Some claimed that the wild-eyed figure of John Brown actually frightened them. Other complaints issued directly from the concerns of a conservative agrarian people: the bull in the pastoral scene had the wrong stance and the wrong color and looked as if he had contracted "lumpy jaw"; Coronado's palomino horse seemed "weather-beaten," a mere "scrub" of an animal; the pigs looked as if they were walking "on stilts," and their tails curled in the wrong direction; the tornado resembled an elephant's trunk; the pioneer woman's skirt stopped much too soon.

The core of mural support was located among the journalists who had initiated the project. The veteran newspaperman A. L. ("Dutch") Shultz said that Curry's critics wouldn't know whether he mixed his paints "with beeswax or oil of cloves." Men whose art experience had been limited "to the time when they dabbed paint on grandpa's door," he said, qualified as art critics "in the same measure that the relief clients who loaf on the First

National Bank steps become authorities on world finance." In general, the more artistically aware minority seemed pleased. "He has not prettied us up," said William Allen White approvingly; "he has painted us, warts and all."

But majority displeasure found an outlet when Curry asked state officials to remove slabs of imported marble in the capitol rotunda to allow him to complete the last phase of the work. The public suddenly felt a great attachment to Italian marble. In a formal statement the Kansas Council of Women objected to the removal because the completed murals did "not portray the true Kansas." Bowing to the public pressure, the Executive Council refused Curry's request.

The legislature debated and almost unanimously approved a resolution commending the Executive Council for its enlightened stand. One legislator called the murals "grotesque"; another said he would approve an appropriation for "white paint to cover them up." Ironically, the only black member of the body demanded that the figure of John Brown be "erased" from the scene. "John Brown," said another legislative critic, "was a lazy old coot, rascal, thief [and] murderer . . . whose memory should not be perpetuated . . . in these hideous things called murals." The unsettled culture had turned on a major hero of its "freedom" epic.

The frustrated and bitter artist refused to sign the unfinished work because it did not represent his "true idea." But he believed that in "the fragments," especially in the figure of John Brown, he had accomplished "the greatest paintings I have yet done." The art world has since concurred. When he did the final touching up, Curry decided to add a family of skunks because "no Kansas scene would be complete without a skunk." Four years after he stopped work on the murals, John Curry died at the age of forty-eight. The attending physician called it a coronary failure; his more insightful wife said that he had died of "a broken heart."[21]

5

THE MODERN ERA

THE INTERVAL since the thirties may be called the modern era. During the wartime forties and subsequent decades both the economy and the climate made conspicuous improvements. Per capita income in the state, as a percentage of the national average, rose from 72 percent in 1940 to 95 percent in 1945. In 1970 it stood at 97 percent and in 1980 at 105 percent. But the image of the state did not follow the economic and meteorological improvements. With minor fluctuations it remained at the same level to which it had tumbled in the Dirty Thirties.

A "modern," permissive, urbanizing, and industrialized nation marched off to its own drummer, leaving the traditional, puritanical, rural, and agricultural province in its wake. In essence the story of the modern era is that of a persisting and futile struggle to improve the negative image—to catch up with the ever-accelerating national parade. The struggle has been accompanied by an increasing sensitivity to the outsider's view, for economic as well as cultural reasons, and by a concurrent reduction in state salience and purpose as a sociocultural entity.

The first two decades of the modern period—which may be called the early modern—had a flavor and a temper somewhat distinct from the years that followed. Frustrated and angered at the dramatic fall in prestige and respect for the state, interpreters of the Kansas scene railed at the political conformity and the puritanical backwardness that they perceived in their surroundings. Nevertheless, during those early postwar years one could detect a sense of fluidity, a pervasive and not illogical expectation that the state could, and probably soon would, return to the national niche it had so grandly occupied earlier in the century.

As Kansas became more prosperous, not surprisingly it became more conservative. The public idealism associated so intimately with the prosperity of the Progressive Era did not return. The conservative turn drew hot fire from commentators, especially those of a more liberal persuasion. Elicitations of a "glorious past" that had been irretrievably lost filled the prairie air. The disappointed sounded a theme commonly found in Faulknerian novels: the elegiac contrast between the virtue of the ancestor and the degeneracy of the descendant.

In a 1951 piece in *Holiday* magazine, Debs Myers reported that Kansas had recently become "staid and prosperous—a symbol of orthodoxy and starched respectability." The state, she said, was seen "almost as an island unto itself, strong in quiet, neighborly virtue, but increasingly barren of the ferment that produces challenge and conflict of ideas." In view of their "colorful past and sizable achievements," Kansans wondered why so many Americans had come to regard them in so "unflattering a light." Journalist Clyde M. Reed, Jr., shared his thoughts in a 1951 article in the *Kansas Teacher*, which was provocatively entitled "Once Kansas Was—Young, Daring, Venturesome!" As a "testing ground" for experimental legislation, he said, the state had given to the United States "progressive legislation and ideas by the carload." But in recent years, "awed by the dollar sign," Kansans had mounted a "blind, unrelenting opposition" to economic and social reforms.[1]

In 1950, Nelson Antrim Crawford fondly recalled the

good old days when the state of Kansas was "crazy half the time." Now, busily trying to live down that "eccentric" image, it only wanted "to conform." Newspapers had abandoned their "hell-raising" tradition, and the legislature had adopted a "don't rock the boat" philosophy. From infancy, pliant Kansans were taught that God was "a Republican and a Methodist." The "forthright, unequivocal" Kansas language, he said, was now in the employ of those who "excoriated" the imagined enemies of home and motherhood, farmers and veterans.[2]

A noted journalist from Kansas, Doris Fleeson, wrote in 1955 that her former teacher at Kansas University, the outspoken liberal economist John Ise, had spent much of his life "trying to drag his native Kansas into the twentieth century [and] nobody can say Kansas hasn't put up a fight." Ise had experienced firsthand the burden of the Kansas cultural cross. A reviewer of his well-received textbook on economics had written that "oddly enough, it comes from Kansas."[3]

In 1950, Milton S. Eisenhower, then president of Kansas State College, issued a major statement on the Kansas condition and its prospects. The youngest brother of Dwight Eisenhower, he had been an eager protégé of Charles M. Harger, "Abilene's one intellectual." As president, his eastern biographers tell us, Eisenhower had "stirred up a sleepy campus and put a backwoods college in the forefront of educational initiative in the United States." His general-education reforms, especially, had made the school's supporters proud of "their little school on the prairie." From the time of his arrival in the midwar year of 1943, the president had unerringly "guided Kansas State into the twentieth century." With that awesome task largely accomplished, he proposed a similar transformation for the state of Kansas.

Eisenhower characterized the first eighty years of state history as "five decades of epic poetry . . . followed by three decades of pedestrian prose." In the nineteenth century the creative tension between New England Yankees ("men of conscience") and southerners ("rugged individualists") had produced a bold and progressive culture. Strong personalities such as John Brown, Jim Lane, Carry Nation, Ed Howe, and William Allen White had led the charge. "They stood for something, these people," he said. But Kansas had lost its "sense of direction." "Our once-glorious and creative state pride," he wrote, has "degenerated into a half-ashamed provincialism."[4]

The most eloquent and influential statements came from Kenneth S. Davis, a Kansas-bred free-lance writer. In "That Strange State of Mind Called Kansas" (1949) and "What's the Matter with Kansas?" (1954), both published in the *New York Times Magazine*, he functionally replaced William Allen White as the foremost interpreter of Kansas for the national audience. Occupying a position to the left of Eisenhower on the political spectrum, Davis spoke in a more candid and aggrieved tone about the state. He scolded his fellow Kansans for their "timid conformism," their "smug conservatism," even their "middle-of-the-road" tendencies. The Kansas voice, he said, had "ceased to command a national respect." State leadership had passed to those who "apparently kept all their values in cash registers." The "gaudy old girl" courted by William Allen White had become merely "sad and drab." An "almost impenetrable crust of mediocrity," Davis cried, had been allowed to form over the formerly vital commonwealth.[5]

In those early postwar years the puritan moorings of the state took a frightful beating from both local and national critics. Among its sister states, Kansas had developed a reputation for social repression, of suffering from a "Puritan hangover." As the number of states clinging to some form of prohibition dwindled to a precious few and as the "noble experiment" became permanently fixed in the national psyche as the grotesque product of the hypocritical mind, the image of Kansas as a puritanical backwater matured. Curiously, in their elegiac enthusiasms, critics usually slighted the Progressive Era in favor of nineteenth-century accomplishments, evidently feeling uneasy with a movement that had so warmly embraced the strict control of alcohol.

When the state repealed its constitutional prohibition in 1948, reporter Clarence Woodbury registered the shock of the nation in *American Magazine.* When prohibition ended in its "most famous and most traditional stronghold," he wrote, Americans could not have been more surprised "if all the leopards in the nation's zoos had changed their spots overnight." Settled by zealots of the "John Brown ilk," Kansas had admittedly always "set high ideals for itself." But unfortunately the Prohibition State had come to be caricatured, he said, as a "strait-laced spinster with a glass of ice water in one hand and a militant umbrella in the other."[6]

Debs Myers noted that the popular stereotype portrayed Kansans as "uniformly austere and melancholy, tortured by heat, dust, cold, tornadoes and their own consciences." The state's "remarkable energies," Milton Eisenhower said, had too often been dissipated upon social issues which were "no longer of central importance in a world struggling to organize itself for the atomic age." A widely read 1952 survey of the states, *U.S.A. Confidential,* put the matter in a more distorted and sarcastic form. Drinking, gambling, illicit sex, and homosexuality, it claimed, ran rampant in the puritan stronghold, now a "dependency of the [Kansas City] Pendergast mobs." But there was no cause for national alarm, because "when Kansas does anything, it means the rest of the country did it years ago."[7]

When doing research for his influential *Inside U.S.A.* in the mid 1940s, John Gunther discovered in the state that had produced Carry Nation—"that . . . holy crone on broomstick"—sufficient evidence of puritanism to label it "the most intense in America." Among the major sources of power within the state he identified the Methodist Church and "the do-gooders . . . a fine collection of wonderful old ladies, who will chew your eyes out." He also offered a theological explanation for the "remarkable fact" that the "underpossessed," such as Kansas, tended to be "stubbornly conservative." The answer was puritanism: "The poor man goes to heaven easier than the rich."[8]

At the territorial centennial in 1954 the distinguished American historian Allan Nevins found puritanism a major and persisting element in the Kansas character. "That Kansas has had a special character and peculiar destiny," he said, "most of her citizens have always believed." A core element of that special character had been contributed by the "New England mind," making Kansas "the unique Western child of Puritanism." The puritanical tendency, along with those toward bellicosity and extremism, Nevins argued, were the persisting products of the Free State struggle.[9]

The most strident voice denouncing puritanism-run-amok was Kenneth Davis. The robust idealism of the Founding Fathers had been replaced by mere "Puritan pieties," the champions of "bold social experimentation" by the "earnest advocates of petty prohibitions." Prohibition had long been a "phony" issue, "designed to distract" the unsuspecting public from such political questions as roads, schools, and tax reform. Misguided moral fervor had also been responsible for the puzzling penchant of Kansans to contribute actively to their own negative stereotype. "Puritan masochism" manifested itself in self-deprecatory advertising of the state's misfortunes. Kansans themselves, Davis said, had encouraged the national view of the state as a place "of monotony so boring and dull as to be in itself a sufficient cause of religious and moral excesses."

Although the state's image had been badly bruised, the concept of Kansas as the quintessential "average" or "typical" American community managed to survive the

thirties, though barely. "No state is more accurately representative of America as a whole than Kansas," said Milton
Eisenhower. John Gunther said that Kansas was an "extraordinarily well-integrated state," with only a few minorities
"of any consequence." This somehow qualified the Kansan
as the "most average of all Americans, a kind of common
denominator for the entire continent." In a piece memor-
ializing William Allen White after his death in 1944, *Life*
magazine sketched an image of traditional Kansas that
would have warmed the heart of the Emporia editor. Prosperous, outdoor-loving Kansans, it said, raised "fine families" to a "wholesome manhood." As typical of the nation
as apple pie, "Bill White's state" was an "open window
through which one can look and really see America."[10]

Years before, one "typical American" had left the
home of his God-fearing parents on the Kansas prairie
to head up ultimately the largest concentration of military
power in the annals of the human race. Neither Dwight
David Eisenhower nor the nation ever forgot his humble
origins. In June 1945 a grateful people welcomed back the
conquering hero in the "greatest" procession ever in the
history of New York City. The first sentence in the lead
story in the *New York Times* proclaimed the momentous
happening to the world: "A homespun American from
the plains of Kansas came back from the wars yesterday
to a triumph such as Rome never gave a conquering
Caesar." On an inside page of that same edition of the
Times, a professor from Kansas University conveyed a very
different, more representative, message. In Kansas, he told
a meeting of professionals, "you can look farther and see
less than anyplace in the world except Texas. . . . [A Kan-
san] is just an average man with a sense of humor. He
must have a sense of humor or he wouldn't have stayed
in Kansas."[11]

In the early modern period, evaluators of the state
often concluded their critical comments on a hopeful note.
They conveyed a genuine conviction that an economically

sound Kansas would soon reassume its position near the head of the progressive parade. John Gunther, who had traveled to all forty-eight states for his survey, wrote that "no state is prouder of itself" than Kansas. One of these days the agitation would start again, said Debs Meyers, and then things would pop "hotter than hog grease on a griddle." The nation had felt "disappointed," even cheated, said Allan Nevins, that Kansas had "relapsed" into conservative ways. "Let us hope that after the soft prairie zephyr has blown mildly awhile," he said, "the rousing Kansas cyclone will return."

Kenneth Davis saw no "iron necessity" that the state had to remain "second-rate" forever. "Surely it is time for us to rise again," he said, and "restore our vital connection with a great creative tradition." The "old crusading spirit" had gone into hibernation, admitted Nelson Antrim Crawford, but it might break loose at any time. A member of the legislature had recently assured him that "we got money here in Kansas. . . . Let's make every institution in Kansas the best damn thing of its kind in the world."

The most grandiose vision of the future was put forward by Milton Eisenhower. Perhaps Kansas had taken "a well-earned rest," but she was now coming alive. The most compelling evidence of the "awakening" was the warm response of Kansans to UNESCO, an astonishing fact that a special State Department bulletin had lauded. Eisenhower even found a useful purpose for the recent Kansas predilection for the moderate in political and social life. "Kansas," he confidently declared, "is now ready to serve as the sane moderator of ideological extremes, the firm core of the American culture and the vital center of creative compromise."

In the period from 1960 to the present the state's image, on balance, has remained decidedly and stubbornly negative. During this interval the decline of the small town has emerged as a major theme in the characterizations of Kansas. Many counties have been losing population since the 1920s or even earlier. In the fifties, 70 of the 105 counties decreased in population, with the outmigration especially pronounced in the most rural areas and among young people. Population loss from the agricultural areas has continued, even accelerated, since that time. Rural farm residents in Kansas have decreased from 23 percent of the total population in 1960 to 7 percent in 1980.

Most Americans have romanticized the small town on the prairie as the "repository of thrift, hard work and the other Puritan virtues," the traditional qualities that made America great. Critics, however, have applauded the scornful view of Sinclair Lewis that the small town was "dullness made God." But increasingly all those "nice little places in Kansas" are being threatened with morbidity, if not with outright extinction. The implacable urban gods may yet effect the "final solution" to Lewis's problem.

Most studies of the dwindling rural culture are statistical and therefore impersonal. The more poignant, and image-generating, focus on a single community. For example, a 1972 case study of Russell (Russell County), reported in *Reader's Digest*, described the farm-and-oil town as "withering." Kansas, it noted, "exported" even more people than did the other troubled Great Plains states. In the mid seventies the prominent southern novelist Erskine Caldwell visited a number of midwestern towns and then wrote a book about his impressions. He described Iola (Allen County) as "plainly dormant. . . . Its era of glory has passed into history."

In a 1968 survey of the plains states published by Time-Life Books, the editors selected La Harpe (Allen County) as a representative of the troubled rural culture. Both materially and spiritually, La Harpe was "slowly crumbling to dust." The "depressed nature of life . . . is shockingly evident at the quickest glance. . . . Bereft of all economic purpose, La Harpe nevertheless does struggle on, touchingly attempting to deny its irrelevance." In 1986 the *Wichita Eagle-Beacon* published an extensive series of features on the Flint Hills town of Hamilton (Greenwood County). The town was chosen as representative of the nearly three hundred towns in the state that had populations of less than five hundred. The well-researched articles portrayed an unrelieved scene of futility, depression, and hopelessness in the "dying" town. The Hamiltons of Kansas were "peopled by the old, the independent and the poor, . . . tiny remnants of the old ideals. Without stopping, the economy has passed them by."[12]

On occasion a minority report has been filed. The internationally known travel writer Berton Roueche devoted a chapter of his 1987 book *Sea to Shining Sea* to Pratt (Pratt County). He found the county seat (population 6,900) in "conspicuously robust health." "These people here have money," he was assured by the Cadillac dealer. The world traveler was impressed by the "rich" library and the half-dozen "satisfactory" places to eat. He found that the reduced pace of life in the small community promoted longevity ("we don't have all that stress") and a low crime rate ("we're . . . blessed with the kind of people who try not to intentionally break the law").[13]

But the dominating image of the region was quite otherwise. In a widely read 1973 overview of the plains states—which was extended in 1983 to cover all fifty states—the journalist Neal R. Peirce pronounced the entire state of Kansas, not just the La Harpes and the Hamiltons, "irrelevant." During the postwar decades, he wrote, the plains region had become "an economic and political backwater. . . . [But] these states are in a way a comforting presence—a reminder of a simpler America that not only was, but lives on."

Among these living fossils, Peirce singled out the "eclipsed state" of Kansas for special commendation: "Nowhere on the American continent can the eclipse of a region or a state as a vital force—a focal point of creative change or exemplar of national life—be felt so strongly or poignantly as in Kansas. . . . [This] slide into obscurity is all the more tragic for Kansas, simply because she stood for so much and gave so much to the nation in her earlier years."

Peirce recalled the glorious past with its "great personalities." William Allen White almost singlehandedly had been able to keep the name of Kansas "alive," but since his death, "the Sunflower State seems to have slipped into the shadows." Recently tourism had been bringing in more revenue, he said, though "the 'sights' are relatively few." The Menninger Clinic had achieved an international reputation despite its "unlikely" Kansas location. The once-vital commonwealth had become virtually invisible, without meaning or usefulness for the ongoing American experience. Occasionally a noteworthy politician or the continuing liquor saga might raise a national eyebrow or two, but in the main, "people or events in Kansas are rarely of enough importance to be reported outside the state's borders. Kansas seems to have become an extraordinarily ordinary place, unnoticed by most Americans."[14]

IN THE FACE of such devastating criticism from abroad, those local prophets who had been peering into the Kansas soul scrambled to make sense of the state's progress among the civilized nations, or the lack thereof. With diffidence now well established in the state's character, many Kansans tended to agree, albeit grudgingly, with harsh assessments such as Peirce's. The keen expectation of an imminent cultural "awakening," so characteristic of the immediate postwar years, had evaporated completely. The "Second Coming" would have to be postponed into an indeterminate and increasingly ambiguous future. During the sixties and the seventies, both the economy and the weather continued to behave themselves in a generally acceptable manner. In fact, the resultant prosperity itself was often blamed. Perhaps it had produced such a "well-heeled stability" and "pleasantly stagnant" society that the state had lost its "fighting spirit."

Progress in historical work consists largely in the imposition of new interpretations on old realities. The revisionism associated with the Civil War and the Reconstruction Era is a classic example. Throughout most of Kansas history, students of the state have remarked on the homogeneity and the distinctiveness that characterized its people and culture. William Allen White, Charles Harger, W. G. Clugston, and Charles Driscoll, among many others, commonly spoke of the state in unitary terms. In 1894, J. Willis Gleed wrote that in contrast to the "heterogeneous" New Yorkers, "the people of Kansas are homogeneous; they are of one race. They have inherited common impulses, common customs, common religion, and common ideals." In 1910, Carl Becker wrote: "What strikes one particularly is that, on the whole, native Kansans are all so much alike. It is a community of great solidarity . . . an identity of race, custom, habits, needs; a consensus of opinion in . . . morals and politics." As late as 1947, John Gunther remarked on both the uniformity and the "extreme particularity" of Kansas. Throughout his 1950 book *Wheat Country,* William B. Bracke argued that Kansans were "unlike any others in the nation in their particular frame of mind." In 1952, in *This Place Called Kansas,* Charles C. Howes wrote about the "distinctive character" of Kansas and about the "peculiar essence of an entirely unique state."

But more recent interpreters have viewed the state's development and historical character through glasses of a different hue. They may perceive Kansas as a "special place" with a "special character." But the nature of that uniqueness has become much more illusive as the state's singularity, measured against national norms, diminishes appreciably. "Endurance," "suffering," and "surviving" remain in vogue as salient features of the historic character, but they appear anachronistic in affluent, urbanizing Kansas. Unitary elements and holistic explanations of the past have faded away. In their stead has come an emphasis on variety and contrast and a long-overdue recognition of the role of minority groups. Intrastate variation appears to have waxed as interstate differences have waned.

College president Emory Lindquist sounded the keynote for the new outlook in 1961. After presenting a detailed review of the state's history at the centennial, he grappled with the problem of unifying themes. Kansas, he said, couldn't be as neatly encapsulated as states like New York, Virginia, and Massachusetts. Instead, Kansas was like a man who has returned from a long trip. "He is glad he made the journey, but he isn't sure what it really meant, nor does he know how to profit fully from it."

Most modern historians and journalists have been inclined to agree. In the last general history of the state that has been published (1974), Robert W. Richmond titled his text, *Kansas: The Land of Contrasts*. In his 1974 presidential address before the Kansas State Historical Society, Dudley T. Cornish questioned whether Carl Becker had fully appreciated the "infinite varieties" of the Kansas experience, the "contrasts" stressed by Richmond. Historians George L. Anderson and Terry H. Harmon wrote in 1974 that it was difficult to define "the meaning of Kansas . . . because the word has been invested with diverse meanings." Many cultures and societies have contributed to the Kansas past, historian Rita Napier wrote in 1985; "complexity and diversity were its hallmarks." A 1986 article reviewing the state's image, written by historian Burton J. Williams, is entitled "Kansas: A Conglomerate of Contradictory Conceptions." In a 1980 article in the *Wichitan* magazine, editor L. David Harris longed nostalgically for the "old Kansas," with its sense of "morality and integrity." Nowadays, he lamented, "it's difficult to tell the states apart. . . . There's a certain sameness everywhere."

In a 1985 article in the *National Geographic,* native Kansan Cliff Tarpy concluded that the "unpredictable" state was so varied that it seemed impossible to "lump the coal mines, hickory groves, and the Ozark Plateau of the far southeast with the sagebrush and sunflowers around the Cimarron River." Political scientist Francis H. Heller wrote in 1972 that Kansas could be viewed as "a stage for unending conflict. Prohibition, yes—but also open saloons; the piety of the Brethren—but also the violence of the cattle trails; the imaginative creation of a legislative research agency—but also an almost totally atomistic approach to party organization." Recently, historian C. Robert Haywood has noted the frequency in interpretive texts of words such as *dichotomy, ambivalence,* and *divergent.* Variation in the state's physical geography symbolizes the "mixed values, contradictions, and incongruities making up the Kansas psyche. . . . There is simply no way to express a clear statement of the Kansas concept."

How does the cultural heterogeneity within Kansas in fact compare with that within other states? The most extensive quantitative study of social and economic diversity within American states was published in 1973 by the political scientist John L. Sullivan. He computed a "diversity index" for each state, using sixteen variables drawn from educational, income, occupational, housing, ethnic, and religious categories. Kansas ranked thirty-seventh among the states in diversity, the lowest ranking in the midwestern region. Ten of the states that ranked below Kansas were southern, but race was not included in the index. If it had been, Kansas would have ranked at or near the bottom. (The black, Hispanic, Oriental, native American, and Jewish populations constitute only about 9 percent of the state total.)

Extensive quantitative studies of diversity within states have not been made for earlier periods. But it is clear that from the nineteenth century forward, diversity both within and between states has significantly diminished due to enhanced mobility, increasing economic homogeneity, the development of the mass media, and the reduction in the potency of ethnic and religious groups, among other factors. Thus, distinctiveness has become an increasingly rare commodity in the modern world. In the past, Kansas was more diverse than it is today in most dimensions of life (although not in its feeling of mission or common purpose) in an absolute sense, but almost certainly not in a relative sense—that is, when compared to other states. In other words, Kansas diversity has been and continues to be unremarkable. Modern attempts to make it otherwise are apparently based less on objective criteria than on subjective reactions to the increasing cultural "thinness" and loss of unifying themes in modern state affairs.[15]

The most definitive interpretation of the Kansas experience has been that of Kenneth S. Davis. His 1976 contribution to the series of state histories commemorating the national bicentennial has been called "the best book on the state ever turned out." Davis confirmed the "specialness" of Kansas as a place and the "peculiar intensity of feeling which Kansans have for Kansas." He knew of no other state, except perhaps Texas, "whose citizens are as strongly, intensely, personally identified with it as Kansans are with Kansas."

For Davis, as for his contemporaries, the contrarieties in the Kansas condition loomed large. The state readily evoked "those powerful ambivalences of pride-and-disgust, pleasure-and-exasperation, even passionate love-and-hate." The physical environment—the extremes found in the weather, the skyscapes and landscapes—"encouraged" the contradictory tendencies of the Kansas personality. This could account, Davis suggested, for the admixture "of self-assertion and self-abnegation, of rugged individualism and a passion for conformity, of strong insistence that the human person is free and an equally strong insistence that he act in certain prescribed ways."

Still, Davis found more unity of purpose in the Kansas

story than did most of his contemporaries. The impact of the nineteenth-century experiences on the Kansas character—especially the puritan influence by way of New England—was critical. For Davis, state history was essentially a morality play in which things had turned out badly. The bright flame kindled by the progressive philosophy of the early years had been snuffed out by a puritanism "bereft of common sense and devoid of any true moral intent." Still, if the dream of a "political and cultural renaissance"— which Davis had shared with Milton Eisenhower in the forties—were ever to be realized, it must necessarily enlist the puritan heritage. The core of a revitalized Kansas, Davis insisted, would be "a renewed Puritan emphasis upon moral concerns, a renewed insistence upon individual moral responsibility."[16]

A more distilled statement of Davis's philosophy may be found in his 1979 critique of the meaning of the life and work of William Allen White, published in the widely circulated *American Heritage*. Davis's judgment of White strikingly parallels his assessment of the trends in state history. Davis takes White to task for remaining firmly attached to the Republican party while continuing to espouse liberal causes. White's "sophistry," Davis charged, had consistently benefited conservatives to the detriment of the more liberal-minded. Instead of devoting his life to what Davis vaguely alludes to as "fundamental change," the editor squandered his prodigious talents by "cloaking with sympathetic attractiveness what was nakedly repulsive, [and] making the worse seem the better cause." Davis would have preferred that the Emporia Sage had become a New Deal Democrat or had committed himself "wholly to truth, justice, and beauty." In all, White's story was "a cautionary tale for Americans." But perhaps White only ran true to his Kansas heritage. "His tragedy," Davis tells us, was that "he never quite believed what he said." That, after all, is the classic definition of a hypocrite.[17]

MODERN ARTISTS—those eternal seekers of "truth, justice and beauty"—have struggled to express the meaning of Kansas. For them, as for the historians, the decreasing distinctiveness of the state has posed serious difficulties in the identification of transcendental themes. In recent decades the most valued artistic expressions in Kansas have only rarely been associated with identifiable geographical locales or specific social themes.

Diversity has become the expected characteristic of the work of artists who just happen to live within a circumscribed area. A case in point is the 1987 exhibition of fifty art works by twenty-four leading Kansas artists at the National Museum of Women in the Arts in Washington, D.C. The exhibition juror was "above all . . . struck by the diversity" of the paintings. Expecting wheatfields "peopled with pious farmers recalling . . . Curry's *Baptism* . . . , the viewer will instead find a range of technique and motif that would be at home even in the galleries of New York, London, or Tokyo."[18] The modern Kansas artist can receive no higher praise.

The ongoing nationalization of American culture has encouraged the attitude among state writers that regionally focused work is outmoded, provincial, and inferior— unworthy of the most serious and gifted talent. A 1961 anthology of poetry, plays, and short stories by Kansas writers expressed the modern sentiment more candidly than have most. It contrasts sharply with earlier collections in its attitude toward Kansas as an inspirational source of creative work. Although it was published in the centennial year of statehood, the ironically titled *Kansas Renaissance* fails to even mention that observance. Neither the history nor the physiography of the state, the editors said, had produced the "sense of urgency," the "stirring experiences," or the "wild beauty and picturesqueness" that aroused the writer in other lands. "What has greatly depressed or uplifted the Kansan's soul?" they asked rhetorically. The implied answer was nothing. To even expect a Kansas-flavored literature was "not reasonable." Regional writing, the editors concluded, had "never been popular among the better Kansas writers. Students will not write about life in their home state."[19]

The "decline and fall" of the *Kansas Magazine* serves as a graphic example of the contemporary trend. The magazine had a short-lived but celebrated inception in 1872/73, followed by revivals in the periods 1886 to 1888, 1909 to 1912, and 1933 to 1968. In these several incarnations it served as the principal medium in the state for poets, critics, writers of fiction, and political and social essayists. In the thirties the magazine fairly burst with contributions that were focused like a laser beam on the cultural landscape of the state. Poets, essayists, and creative writers all addressed significant facets of the Kansas milieu. But during the postwar period, the number of items devoted to strictly state themes began to dwindle markedly.

In 1968 the magazine changed its name to *Kansas Quarterly*, pledging its support to the "cultural development of our region." But state-focused items continued to diminish in number, and within a few years they had virtually disappeared. The journal has so totally lost its geographic focus that although it is published in Manhattan, Kansas, it could as well be published in Walla Walla, Washington, or Manhattan, New York. It now publishes articles such as "The Satiric Novels of Thomas Love Peacock" and "A Study of the Influence of Germanic Romantic Folk-Ideology on the Irish Literary Revival." These contributions to this allegedly "Kansas" journal may improve the tenure prospects of assistant professors at Idaho Presbyterian or Northeastern Connecticut State College, but they are questionable vehicles to enhance the cultural cohesiveness of "our region" or the state of Kansas.

For decades and in a steady stream, Kansas artists have left the state for the East Coast, particularly New York City, the nation's cultural capital. For many of those who couldn't leave and for all of those who didn't want to, New York City epitomized Sodom and Gomorrah, the ultimate sin capitals of the world. Back at the turn of the century, ardent Kansas Day speakers were shaking their fists at "the Philistines of New York." The Progressive congressman Victor Murdock (1903–15) once publicly declared that the city of New York "must be destroyed," although he evidently didn't expect that the grand event would occur during his lifetime. In 1978, James E. Jeffries captured the hearts of his constituents and the congressional seat of the Second District in part because of his slashing attacks on the sins of New York City, economic and otherwise. The most cogent indictment ever made by a Kansan about the adverse influence of New York on artistic development in the hinterland came from the Topeka writer-lawyer Gaspar C. Clemens at the turn of the century.

Clemens argued that national cultural centers such as Rome, London, and New York City tended to repress the creative arts in provincial regions such as Tuscany, Scotland, and Kansas. The "ceaseless encroachments" of the national government on the American states had produced "a vast consolidated empire," and in such a centralized system, "genius languishes and dies." Outside of New York, he charged, "no American may hope to win a name in art or literature." All across the country, "genius lies buried in obscurity because New York has not heard of it." Because of these powerful centripetal forces, many men and women were "doomed to die with all their music in them." "Let us restore the independence of the states," Clemens declared, "and we shall not only regain liberty, but rescue genius and have American artists and authors again."[20]

Those creative artists who did emigrate to New York or other "more loving climes" often reacted to more than the "pull" of the opportunity afforded by the national cultural center. They also responded—often with more than a touch of bitterness that later would be expressed in their

111

work—to a real or imagined "push" from the local community. The latter represented a public "difficult to please, dangerous to criticize." For many of the expatriates, critic Jonathan Wesley Bell tells us, the remembered Kansas became "a reminiscence, a place lost in time, the emotion of fading memories and funerals." In many Kansas novels written by such Kansans as Langston Hughes, Joseph Pennell, William Inge, and Kenneth Davis, to name a few, the heroes end up, like their creators before them, leaving the state. This tendency, critic Michael D. Butler has noted, expresses the belief of many writers that in Kansas "the past was dead and the future lay somewhere else."[21]

Modern Kansas poets tend to locate their poems externally in the environment rather more often than internally in the psyche, though the reverse tends to be true of the eastern poet. They differ, however, from their Kansas predecessors in a fundamental way. In earlier periods, Kansas poets often celebrated the struggle for freedom and the conquest of the land—tribal events and pervasive emotions that could be understood and shared by the population as a whole. Their modern counterparts have largely deserted the grand themes—a trend that began in the thirties—and have concentrated instead on "the effect the landscape has on them personally." That is, the focus has shifted from the collective society to the isolated individual. Although "the land and the Puritan myth have been the major guiding forces in Kansas culture and poetry," according to critic Lorrin Leland, the "unifying forces of previous periods . . . are [now] virtually nonexistent. . . . Kansas is, now more than before, in the eye of the beholder."[22]

A strong current that runs through much of modern Kansas literature, both prose and poetry, is the vivid sense of loss of a significant past. To look back is to look up. Reinforcing the interpretation of the historians, Butler says that Kansas writers often portray the state's history as a "degenerative descent from high ideals to base practices:

from moral fervor to moralistic smugness." Contemporary Kansas, they feel, has "betrayed" its nineteenth-century heritage. Kansas fiction often conveys a sense of "frustration and anger at the waning potency, integrity and spirit" of modern Kansas.

A tradition of "grim realism," which yields images that are less than flattering to the state and its inhabitants, has marked the course of Kansas prose literature from Ed Howe's *Story of a Country Town* (1882) through the Haldeman-Juliuses' *Dust* (1921) to John Ise's *Sod and Stubble* (1936). In *The History of Rome Hanks* (1914), Joseph Stanley Pennell fashioned a "realistic" description of the small-town Kansas inhabitant: "They all talked in the same God-dammed flat, nasal voice about the same Goddammed trivial things day-in-day-out year-after-year—eating, sleeping and growing more rustic and pompous and proverbial."

In recent decades the most influential work evoking a realistic sense of Kansas as a significant place has been that of the playwright William Inge. During the 1950s, Inge wrote four plays based on his formative years in Kansas. These catapulted him into the first rank of the American theater: *Come Back, Little Sheba; Picnic; Bus Stop;* and *The Dark at the Top of the Stairs.* Inge's message was more subtle in its social and geographical implications than were its predecessors in the realism genre, but it was powerful nonetheless. The "somber tones" of the plays, Bell says, "remind us of what is frightening about small towns." For Inge, Kansas was an "outback" where lonely people in "backwater towns" struggled for identity and dignity. Typically, the Inge protagonists are intimidated by the demands of modern life. Like Elmer Gantry, overwhelmed by the ante-bellum Virginia mansion, they come to feel that they are inconsequential, that they "don't come from anywhere in particular."[23]

6
FACETS OF
THE MODERN IMAGE

Having traced the broader outlines of the development of the Kansas image, we may now examine the modern landscape in more detail. The image of a population, like that of an individual, is composed of several distinct components. If several observers are asked for their impressions of a complex political entity, the result may very well be as many unique conclusions as there are observers. However, if informed, the opinions will not scatter at random but will suggest dominant themes or facets. When large numbers of such observations are collected, they tend to cluster around a limited number of focal points. Each of these clusters may be more usefully visualized as an amorphous region or zone than as a precise point. As a nodule, or nucleus, in a multidimensional matrix, each element is distinctive yet grades imperceptibly at its margins into other elements of the constellation.

For the past ten years, contemporary images of Kansas and Kansans have been collected in a nonselective fashion from a wide range of media sources. The primary data includes a broad cross section of both local and national opinion, rather than the detailed views of a few political and business leaders.[1] Employing Occam's razor, the images so gained have been found to cluster around five focal points. Each of these facets of the total image may be related to each of the others, though with varying degrees of intensity and relevance. The five facets, identified by a key word, are Rube, Drab, Irrelevant, Puritanical, and Traditional. Each facet has its own history, although these are of differing lengths and saliences. Four of the five subimages are primarily negative. One of these, the Puritanical, has reversed its "charge" over time; that is, it is now surely negative, though it was formerly largely positive. No individual component is unique to Kansas, yet taken as a whole, with their individual intensities, they form a pattern that is not duplicated elsewhere.

The loss of the national prestige that Kansas formerly enjoyed and the progressive nationalization of the American culture may be seen in the changed nature of the message that conveys the state image. Well into the thirties, commentators of a wide range of cultural and political persuasions wrote sober and lengthy essays on the Kansas condition and its relevance to the life of the nation. Although they were often critical, they recognized in Kansas a serious subject for public discourse. Even those who presented their views in a humorous mold—such as Irvin Cobb and Charles Driscoll—expected a serious response from their national readership. But since the Second World War, both the length and the seriousness of the statements have diminished markedly. In the modern period, the one liner of the screenwriter and the fast quip of the stand-up comic have become the standard vehicles for conveying a necessarily superficial message to the American public. The views of Kansas, along with those of its sister states taken individually, are now only infrequently considered a matter of political or social moment in the homogenizing nation.

THE RUBE CLUSTER includes references to hicks, hayseeds, and country bumpkins and to the backwardness of their agrarian culture. It represents the polar opposite of the worldly-wise sophisticate, the urbane cosmopolite. The core notion is that of a simple rural people living in a hinter-land—literally a "behind-land"—semi-isolated from the modern mainstream society. To some extent the image is shared by those in similar circumstances, all the way from Vermont and West Virginia to Arkansas, North Dakota, and Utah.

During the 1890s, Populist farmers were frequently portrayed as untutored "hayseeds." The classical essay broadcasting to the nation the Rube image of Kansas is the 1896 tirade of William Allen White against the Populists. In "What's the Matter with Kansas?" he limned a backward rural state that was rapidly losing population, capital, and respect. Since the ignorant "clodhoppers" had come to power, he wrote, "Kansas just naturally isn't in it. She has traded places with Arkansas and Timbuctoo."

In recent decades it has become more difficult to pin the hick image realistically on anyone. Successful farmers are now often described as managers of an exacting agri-business that utilizes sophisticated equipment and demands a business acumen at least equal to that required of their urban counterparts. As the rural culture wanes, farmers and the small-town inhabitants who are dependent upon them constitute an ever-smaller fraction of the total population. Under these discouraging circumstances, direct attacks on the agrarian culture may be seen as tactless at best, cruel at worst. But a long-term counter-current is also at work. As the state and the nation continue to urbanize, the reservoir of good will for the rural population inevitably diminishes, to be replaced by disinterest or even hostility. For example, in 1986 a former Kansan, writing for the *New Republic*, openly attacked the agrarian life style in a vitriolic article entitled "The Idiocy of Rural Life."

Remarks in the hick genre may lack specific imagery, as evidenced by tourists who complain about the "bucolic wilderness" that, like Zebulon Pike, they have discovered on the plains. Or the comments may be more pointed and picturesque. In Truman Capote's *In Cold Blood*, as the principals cross the state line into Kansas, one of them exclaims (as he farts) that they have just entered the "home of corn, Bibles and natural gas." A writer for the *Washington Post* tells his readers that drinking in Kansas doesn't mean "some lounge lizard with slicked-back hair holding a sissy glass by the stem"; instead, it involves "a bunch of good old boys [getting] a thrill-packed Saturday night [by] watching hair cuts and snooker games [and] chipping in to buy a jug."

Rural humor often takes on a Kansas coloration. Sports writer Kevin Haskin reports that Kansans may be viewed skeptically on foreign turf. On learning the home state of his guest, Haskin's host ordered him to "wipe off your boots and try not to mingle with too many people here. And hey, stay away from the animals." The coach of the Louisiana State basketball team found that he kept running into Kansans on a hotel elevator in New Orleans. "Don't they have elevators in Kansas?" he asked. "Yea, a couple just outside Ottawa," was the answer.

The contemporary Rube image is often conveyed by professional humorists on television and in the movies. After the United States had withdrawn from the 1980 Olympic games in Moscow, U.S.S.R., Tom Snyder produced a television piece that purported to cover the games that had been transferred to Moscow, Kansas (in Stevens County). Visitors flew into the "Moscow International Airport," which consisted of a corrugated metal shed, common on Kansas farms. The most coveted medal of the games went to those who could swim through the town's "sludge pond."

In 1986, the television talk-show host Johnny Carson did a sketch in which yokels were invited to write in for information on breast enhancement to "Boobs for Rubes, Twiggy, Kansas." His competitor, Joan Rivers, has had a

"Two-mules, Kansas" routine for several years. In it, she pretends that she has played the fictitious town; then she proceeds to make a series of remarks centering on the stupidity of the inhabitants. In the popular movie *Vacation*, Chevy Chase takes his Chicago family west for a leisurely vacation. In Kansas a scene parodies the state's penchant for tourist attractions of the "world's largest" variety. Chase is tempted by signs for the House of Mud ("the largest free-standing mud dwelling ever built"). At Coolidge (Hamilton County) they visit his wife's cousin and her family. The entire family is offbeat, but especially the country-bumpkin husband, a beer-drinking, oafish slob.

In both fictional and nonfictional works the uncomplicated, ingenuous Kansas rube has often served as a counterpoint to the sophistication of easterners of power and wealth. In a 1987 television miniseries "The Two Mrs. Grenvilles," which was based on actual events, the contrast was developed as a major theme. A beautiful and ambitious young woman leaves her Kansas home ("she wasn't someone to hang around a town like this") to seek fame and fortune in New York City. She marries the wealthy scion of a leading family, whose haughty mother sniffs that "she's obviously not one of us." At a dinner party a friend remarks that the lavish affair is "a far cry from Kansas." Angry at her anxious and transparent attempts to enter a social circle into which she "doesn't quite fit," her husband exclaims, "If that's what I wanted, I would have married the real thing."

Easterners, especially, seem to expect to find an anachronous culture in Kansas. Westbound travelers often ask turnpike attendants how far the road ahead is paved. A Kansan reports that Chicago friends were amazed to learn that National Public Radio could be heard across the state. But on rare occasions, Kansas receives support on a cultural issue from an unexpected quarter. After an extensive tour of the American hinterland with her play about the life of Gertrude Stein, actress Pat Carroll remarked that "farmers understand a hell of a lot more than we think." Perhaps only a fraction of them had ever heard of Gertrude Stein, she acknowledged, but "in New York I don't think the percentage was any . . . higher than in Kansas."

Ironically, Kansans themselves often join lustily in the national chorus of derision. Outsiders who move to the state are often puzzled by the tendency of the natives to run the place down. For example, the police chief of a rural town announced at a press conference that though "we're a little bit backward . . . we're not altogether stupid." A prominent lawyer, who moved his family from Colorado to Kansas to improve their quality of life, was greeted by an almost universal refrain of "Why would anyone want to . . . ?" In similar cases of voluntary immigration to the state, sanity tests have been suggested.

Local references to the backwardness of the state are ubiquitous. The backwardness dimension of the Rube theme is frequently fused with that of the Puritanical, linking closely these two image facets. "As backward as Kansas is" prefaces many a statement in the letters-to-the-editor column. Kansas must be brought out of the "doldrums," cries one citizen; the "culture Center of the Plains we ain't," rues another. A caller on a Kansas City, Missouri, talk show agrees with the host that Kansas is more backward than Iowa. A sportsman notes that Kansas was "characteristically slow" in stocking the Chinese pheasant in comparison to the other plains states.

The notion that Kansas is "behind" is ever present. "Here in Kansas, we have a tradition of always being four or five years behind national trends," writes a journalist. "We keep at least 20 years behind the rest of the United States," mourns another. Some of their fellow citizens are less generous: they remain unconvinced that the state has entered the twentieth century at all. "You have just entered Kansas, set your watches back 100 years," proclaims a bumper sticker. In a heated "sin issue" debate in the 1985 state legislature, a representative suggested that the name of the state should be changed to The Past. Even with all traces of the sin issues purged from the constitution, the metaphor persists. A concerned citizen in 1987 urged that we should now "get into the 20th century . . . and have two [license] plates for our cars."

Given the stereotype, both Kansans and non-Kansans often find irony in the achievements of the state and its inhabitants. In 1983 a sports writer for the *St. Louis Post-Dispatch* shared the world's amazement that professional football star John Riggins, "from the Flint Hills of Kansas," had brains as well as brawn. "He was *funny*. He was *smart*. To a lot of people, this came as a revelation. Imagine this big lunk out of *Kansas*, of all places. . . . Why he was *really* intelligent. Imagine that."

At the conclusion of the 1985 meeting in Topeka of a national historical society, an officer of the Kansas State Historical Society had difficulty in believing that the state had "shown" so well. "It was really amazing, all the positive comments I heard. So many people think of Kansas as being really backward. But after being here . . . , they've changed their impressions." Kansas native and literary scholar Gary Taylor received a burst of publicity in 1985 for discovering at Oxford University a previously unknown poem by William Shakespeare. Taylor felt that the irony of his Kansas roots made the scholarly find more newsworthy to the eastern press. "The reporter for the *New York Times* felt this made the story all the more interesting, given New Yorkers' notions about Kansas."

A SECOND IMAGE that has a hoary history is characterized by Drab. Descriptors that fall within this cluster include flat, harsh, boring, and plain. From the perception of nineteenth-century explorers such as Zebulon Pike and Stephen Long that the region was an uninhabitable desert to the recently painted panels in the Statehouse rotunda that stress struggle and hardship, Kansas has been perceived predominantly as an inhospitable environment, a land devoid of grace and beauty. And not infrequently the characteristics of the landscape have been imputed to the inhabitants.

Two classics in the Drab mode stand out. In the opening paragraphs of L. Frank Baum's *The Wizard of Oz,* Dorothy surveys a scene of utter drabness. Engulfed by "the great gray prairie" on every side, the lonely farmstead sits amid plowed land "baked . . . into a gray mass" and grassland burnt by the merciless sun into "the same gray color." Indeed the word *gray* appears no less than nine times in the brief description of the high-plains setting. Once a "young pretty wife," Aunt Em has become "thin and gaunt, and never smiled, now." Another victim of the harsh environment, Uncle Henry, looked "stern and solemn, and rarely spoke." The tornado that whisks Dorothy off to Oz furnishes a dramatic counterpoint to the lifeless scene. In the 1939 movie the contrast of the two environments is enhanced by the filming of Oz in color but the Kansas segments in black and white.

In 1965, Truman Capote published his celebrated "nonfiction novel" *In Cold Blood.* A Book-of-the-Month Club selection, it had been previously serialized in the *New Yorker* magazine. The early paragraphs embellish the Oz theme. The "haphazard hamlet" of Holcomb (Finney County) consisted of "an aimless congregation of buildings," set out in "a lonesome area" under "hard blue skies." A "gaunt woman" ran the "falling-apart post office." The depot was "equally melancholy," as was the "meagerly supplied grocery store." After an infrequent rain or snow, the streets, "unnamed, unshaded, unpaved, turn from the thickest dust into the direst mud."

The author personally felt the disdain that these passages convey. As H. L. Mencken would have said, Capote and Holcomb, Kansas, inhabited different solar systems. Years later, Capote recalled that "fantastic period" of "six years" when he had lived "in ghastly motels in the wind-swept plains of western Kansas." In the introduction to the 1985 edition, a New York writer, Mark Singer, points out that for most of those six years, Capote was comfortably ensconced in Europe, writing the book. Singer charitably adds, however, that "his Kansas sojourn must have often felt like a life sentence."

Even during periods in which the overall image was positive, the jejune landscape sometimes received bad reviews. During the modern era, derogatory references to the landscape abound, undiminished in vigor though long in tooth. A high-school student notes that "according to popular opinion, Kansas has no geographic features." One can read most anywhere about the "barren plains" or the "endless wasteland." The *St. Louis Post-Dispatch* speaks of "a terrain as flat as a table top," or yet again of "the endless, treeless, sea-like expanse of stubby wheatfields." On the television series "Portrait of America," narrator Hal Holbrook describes the "infinite," "hostile," and "utterly alien" Kansas prairie where the wind blows "ceaselessly."

Years after a young athlete had been sent from Florida to a Kansas junior college to hone his basketball skills, he remembered most vividly "the bus ride from Coffeyville to Garden City. . . . Man, Kansas just goes on and on forever." An inconvenienced reporter for the London *Times* wrote in early May that he had to drive to the "dreary town" of Abilene in the "summer heat and dust." The Kansas writer Earl Thompson begins a novel with an oft-quoted line: "Love a place like Kansas and you can be content in a garden of raked sand." A guest on the Johnny Carson show says that a plaid suit reminds him of "Kansas from the air." A poem by Robert Penn Warren in the *New York Review of Books*, about a New York family passing through Kansas, echoes the thirties: "Two days behind the dust storm—man's / Fecklessness, God's wrath—and once / Dust on the highway so deep piled / Mules had to drag the car. This / was Kansas. . . . "

On occasion, Kansas has been compared to the more glamorous locales in the nation or the world. In a Hemingway short story, an American couple finds Touraine, France, " a very flat hot country very much like Kansas." An Alaskan promotion claims that "once you've seen Alaska everything else looks like Kansas." After acknowledging that the probability of a devastating earthquake in southern California is quite high, a seismologist remarks that if Californians had to choose between the imminent quakes or having "the country look like Kansas, they'd vote for the earthquakes." In Joseph Millard's science-fiction work *The Gods Hate Kansas*, eleven manned meteors land on "the parched and dusty reaches of the Kansas plains." After that bizarre event, even the midwestern-bred hired man had had enough. "The more I see of Kansas," he says, "the more I wish I'd never left Ioway."

Many of the impressions of the landscape are deposited in the national vault by impatient drivers hurrying across the plains to cool, colorful Colorado. The subspecies has become legendary for its "closed eyes" approach. "It's so boring driving through Kansas!" they wail. For them, the final solution to the "Kansas problem" is to drive through at night in order to be in Colorado in the morning "for the scenery." The dominant perception is enhanced by satiric posters urging the daring to "ski Kansas" and by illustrations, such as that in the *Harvard Lampoon*, which depicts a Kansas license plate with the slogan "Gateway to Nebraska." On the television series "Night Court," New York City newlyweds discuss honeymoon plans. "What about Kansas?" she asks. Whereupon the comedienne Selma Diamond interjects with, "They're overbooked now, it's the high season." A Minnesota journalist put the majority case succinctly: "Kansas is a nice place to stay, but I wouldn't want to visit there."

123

The state receives better reviews from those who settle there or travel its expanses at a more leisurely pace. A new resident enthused that "this is not how I perceived Kansas." A visitor who took the time to smell the flowers on the back roads declared: "It's not boring [or] unendingly flat. . . . Kansas is like other good things in life, things that are looked at but not really seen." The most enthusiastic testimony comes from the bicyclists: "It was just beautiful. I can't explain it. I've always driven through Kansas, and I always thought it was a flat, uninteresting place, but it's really beautiful!"

It is a small, easy, and frequently taken step from the "drab" landscape to its "dull" inhabitants and their "boring" culture. Both L. Frank Baum and Truman Capote made the transition effortlessly. Only a dull folk would tolerate such a dull environment. "Kansas always has had . . . this bad reputation, that it's flat and there is nothing to do," notes journalism professor Rex Buchanan. The historian Alice C. Nichols laments that Kansas has become a synonym for all that is "mediocre in thought and scenery." In the *New York Times Magazine,* Stephen Darst has written about the common perception of the Kansas prairie as "stretching endlessly away into an all-pervading flatness, moral, cultural, social, topographical, political."

The image of a monotonous, culturally deprived hinterland runs continuously from the nineteenth century to the present day. On his 1882 tour of the American West, the English actor Oscar Wilde was asked by a "Griggsville," Kansas, woman how the community could improve its cultural image. "Begin by changing the name of your town," Wilde advised. Modern urban newspapers use a Kansas summer as a calibrating device for "the dry and dull"; others dub the state "dulls-ville with a capital 'D.' " On the network television show "Newhart" the Vermont author contemplates writing a book entitled *Boring Kansas.* The idea is captured in the widely circulated aphorism: "Living in Kansas is a contradiction."

In 1984 this dimension of the image became the focal point of a squabble between Kansas and Michigan. After a Midwestern Governors' Conference, the governor of Michigan reported to his constituents, many of whom were unemployed, that he had found Kansas boring. "Their idea of a fancy hotel," he said, "is a Holiday Inn." The press secretary to the Kansas governor conceded that perhaps there were "a lot of things boring about Kansas." But at least there were jobs in Kansas: "I think most people would rather be bored and working." At the conference the delegates viewed an overly zealous promotional film which claimed that Kansas had more recreational water even than Minnesota. A belated check of the facts produced the final score: Minnesota 4,000,000 acres, Kansas 350,000. Close, but not close enough.

Buried within the Drab cluster is the notion of plainness or ordinariness. It is a first cousin of "typical" or "average," but it carries a more derogatory connotation. Since the Second World War, "plain Jane" Kansas has been considered remarkable only for its "extraordinary ordinariness." In a television commercial a waitress in a greasy-spoon restaurant reports that the customers are complaining about the "shrimp Wichita." In the Neil Simon comedy *The Goodbye Girl*, a struggling New York actor asks the clerk of a liquor store for a bottle of his "finest cheap Chianti." After being quoted a moderate price, the impoverished actor sheepishly inquires if the clerk "has anything from Kansas."

A popular Loretta Lynn song of the 1970s, "One's on the Way," contrasts the prosaic lot of the ordinary Kansas housewife with the glamorous life of the international jet setters:

> They say to have her hair done, Liz flies all the way
> to France,
> And Jackie's seen in a discotheque, doing a brand new
> dance. . . .

But here in Topeka, the rain is a fallin', the faucet is a drippin', and the kids are a bawlin'. . . .

The girls in New York City, they all march for women's lib,
And Better Homes and Gardens shows the modern way to live. . . .
But here in Topeka, the flies are a buzzin', the dog is a barkin', and the floor needs a scrubbin',
One needs a spankin', and one needs a huggin', and one's on the way.

Of course, in Kansas, ordinariness is hardly a political liability. It is worshipped with an egalitarian intensity that would make Henry VIII or Ivan the Terrible weep with despair. After the 1986 gubernatorial election, the new first lady of the state, Patti Hayden, proudly announced that "we're very, very ordinary Kansans. We're very ordinary, and we're very Kansan."

THE IRRELEVANT strand of the state image has only a modern history, but it appears to be growing quite steadily. Apparently a society may become so drab, ordinary, and anachronistic that it becomes virtually invisible—an inconsequential nowhere land. Such a label for Kansas before the Second World War would have been unthinkable, but since then it has become commonplace. The most elaborate statement in this genre is that of Neal Peirce, who in 1973 advanced the notion of the "eclipsed state"—a region of no particular significance to the national life. But given the modern development of the perception, a single line from the 1971 James Bond movie *Diamonds Are Forever* may serve more appropriately as its "type" expression. In it, the Evil Ones want to test a new weapon—a gun that can cause matter to disappear—in some remote area where the experiment will go entirely unnoticed. It is suggested that "if we zap Kansas, the world wouldn't learn about it for a year."

During the early decades of the century, Kansas was characterized but rarely as "way out on the edge of things." As noted in chapter 3, the depiction of Elmer Gantry as from "nowhere in particular" was very uncharacteristic of the period. As late as 1950, a bemused Murdock Pemberton, a native Kansan who had long resided in New York, wondered in a national magazine why things had become so quiet in Kansas. He read regularly about New York, California, Florida, and Texas, he complained, but not of his native state. Did it suffer from an "overdose of modesty"? Perhaps "a good press agent" would help restore the old prestige and prominence. But since that time, the idea of a state of no consequence has only expanded.

A bumper sticker carries the message "Kansas—famous for nothing." A bowler on the women's professional tour rhetorically asks: "Kansas! What goes on in Kansas?" Joan Rivers tells her audience that Kansas is "four hundred miles from nowhere." A caller to a Kansas City, Missouri, talk show reports that he is "in the middle of nowhere." The host correctly guesses that he must be somewhere in Kansas. The *Los Angeles Times* describes Emporia as a town in which "one rarely hears a public argument or a car horn," whose citizens struggle daily to cope with the "vast emptiness" of the surrounding plains. Towns from Kansas City to Topeka, from Wichita to Dodge City decry the fact that they have "no image." Even state boosters refer to Kansas as the nation's "best kept secret."

A sign on an interstate highway in a *New Yorker* cartoon announces: "You are now entering Kansas, or some state very much like it." A wag suggests that the mythical Jayhawk is an appropriate symbol for an invisible state. Topeka columnist Zula Bennington Greene ("Peggy of the Flint Hills") asks a widely traveled man what the American public is saying about Kansas. "Very little," he replies. The Wichita journalist David Awbrey reports that when he worked in the East, Kansas "drew a blank" among his colleagues; they had "few preconceptions of what a Kansan was." A National Merit semifinalist describes Kansas as "a nowhere state. . . . You never hear about anything in Kansas." The baseball statistician Bill James complains in his widely read *Baseball Abstract* that in the national psyche Kansas has come to represent "nowhere—an ugly, barren, empty, square space from which people come but do not return."

In 1985 the television commentator Andy Rooney proposed tongue-in-cheek that one state be sold to pay off the national debt. In the subsequent poll of most-expendable states, Kansas finished ninth. The common reason given by those who selected the state was that "there's nothing there." The status of Kansas as an inconsequential address was underlined in the 1986 satirical television miniseries "Fresno." A mysterious stranger, Torch, suddenly appears at the home of a wealthy California raisin grower. When asked where he is from, Torch shrugs indifferently and indicates that it is a matter of no importance. Years before, his itinerant father had paused in a certain small town "just long enough to have a cup of coffee and me." The town was in Kansas.

Nonspecific, allergic reactions to Kansas are included in the Irrelevant category as "generic" responses. In Ernest Hemingway's *The Sun Also Rises* an American soldier in Paris is warned that he had better shape up or he will end up in the federal penitentiary at Leavenworth. He quickly obeys because "I don't like Kansas." Fifty years later an almost identical exchange occurs on the television series "Mash." On the series "Kate and Allie," poor judgment is defined as "having gone to Oz and preferred Kansas." An eastern mother confesses that when her adult daughter moved to Kansas "we felt a little bit sorry for her." A theatrical set designer from Indiana by way of Montana admits that he had been "afraid of coming to Kansas." While in Los Angeles to appear on the Johnny Carson show, 105-year-old Mildred Holt is asked where she is from. "Oh my goodness," came a response in mock sympathy. ("That made me mad," the feisty centenarian said; "I thought that was awful.") The image makers on both coasts refer to the midsection of the nation as "fly-over country." They are grateful for the invention of television, Kansas author Robert Day writes, so that they don't have to visit awful places "like Kansas."

The dominant public view of Kansas history feeds the Irrelevant conception. In this widely held attitude, Kansas history died on the nineteenth-century frontier with the courageous and picturesque adventures of the Free Staters, pioneers, Populists, cowboys, gunslingers, and whiskey peddlers. Kansas history *was* exciting and colorful, but Kansas history *is* irrelevant to the modern condition. From this perspective it follows that Kansas is not a continuous "community of memory," but is instead alienated from and ignorant of much of its history. The younger generations, especially, are inclined to feel that "nothing ever happened here." Most Kansans, editorialized the *Salina Journal* in 1985, see the state as a "Land of Blahs—blah landscape, blah history and blah people." In 1987 an editor of the *Wichita Eagle-Beacon*, George Neavoll, a relative newcomer to the state, wrote that he had found Kansans "remarkably uninformed" about the "incredibly rich" history of the state. This ignorance, he lamented, was so profound that "it comes close to being a crime."

THE LONGEST-STANDING and most battered image is unquestionably the Puritanical. From the Free State battles that spawned the wild-eyed John Brown and the liquor struggles that produced the irrepressible Carry Nation to the "hypocritical" modern era, Kansas has been seen as the bastion of a repressive, fanatically held morality. The prevailing Kansas position on the emotional, God-driven questions has often made the state appear foolish to a more cynical and secular world. In the latter decades of the twentieth century the "sin issues" have served the state particularly poorly, frequently contributing to the charges of backwardness.

Insightful statements on the Puritanical dimension of the Kansas experience abound. Throughout his life, William Allen White pridefully reminded his fellow Kansans that the ideals of the state derived from Plymouth Rock, that the settlers were "crusaders, intellectual and social pioneers." Throughout the 1920s the image remained, on balance, positive, reflecting the independent and self-confident mood of the populace. But with the cultural collapse of the 1930s, state and national critics of the Puritanical philosophy intensified their attacks. Their judgments have grown increasingly disparaging in tone in recent years, especially those from the more liberal-minded, college-educated segment of society. Given the divergent roles that the Puritanical has played over the course of state history, its type expression should convey a sense of contradiction, of ambivalence. No literary work captures that spirit quite so poignantly as the icon of the frenzied John Brown staring out from the mural on the Statehouse wall. John Steuart Curry's personal relationship with the homeland serves as a haunting and ambivalent echo.

Since the heyday of Mencken, Lewis, and Driscoll, Kansas has been perceived as an especially fervent state in matters religious. In informal religious taxonomies it has often been classified as a Bible Belt state, sometimes even the "buckle" of the belt. Outside newspapers commonly refer to Kansans as "pious" or "deeply religious." In Paul I. Wellman's 1944 novel *The Bowl of Brass*, a land speculator calls his new town Jericho because it had "a Biblical sound and he knew that Kansas people were suckers for the Bible." In their authoritative survey of the

1986 national political scene, the political scientists Michael Barone and Grant Ujifusa describe Kansas as "austere and upright." The "stern morality" of Senator Robert Dole, they assert, is the expected consequence of his having been reared in "straight-arrow Kansas."

But the myth explodes under a more scientific examination. After analyzing data from the 1971 national survey of denominational memberships, the geographer James R. Shortridge concludes that Kansas lies astride a strong band of "liberal" Protestant sentiment that stretches from New England to the far Middle West (the old New England Belt). On an index of religious diversity (the number of different groups), Kansas ranks relatively high; but in religious intensity (church adherents as a percentage of the total population) the state is only at the national average. Shortridge defines the Bible Belt (a term coined by Mencken after the Scopes trial) as a region in which Protestant fundamentalists represent a high percentage of the churched. On this basis he locates the center of the Bible Belt at or near Jackson, Mississippi. Oklahoma City, Oklahoma, is on its northwestern margin, and Kansas is "not in it."[2]

Church statistics notwithstanding, manifestations of the Puritanical spirit continue to occur with some frequency in Kansas and are especially well publicized when they do. "Mention disco dancing in Hiawatha [Brown County] and prepare for an immediate uproar," the *Kansas City Times* said in 1979. But raise the question in Falls City, Nebraska, just over the state line, and "hardly an eyebrow will be raised." In the late 1970s, three ladies from Goodland (Sherman County) questioned the postal service about the propriety of a Christmas stamp that depicted the Madonna holding a naked Christ child. Their priggishness prompted a St. Louis paper to note that we all came into the world that way, "even in Kansas." After screening a segment of a lecture given at Pittsburg (Crawford County) by the sexologist Dr. Ruth Westheimer, a reporter on the television program "60 Minutes" commented that "even in Kansas, talk of explicit sex is accepted without difficulty."

The celebrated trial and conviction for murder conspiracy of the Lutheran minister the Reverend Thomas Bird and his secretary, Lorna Anderson, attracted special media attention because of the irony of its Kansas setting. In the 1987 television miniseries based on the case, the investigating officers come most reluctantly to the conclusion that there has been foul play. After all, as one remarks, "this isn't Chicago or New York, this is Emporia, Kansas." Defense attorneys in the 1970s Kansas trial of New York magazine publishers Larry C. Flynt and Al Goldstein on obscenity charges claimed that the federal trial had been "contrived in Kansas to give the government a better case." The successful prosecution argued that the issue was one of "clean-living Kansas versus morally and financially bankrupt New York." In his emotional "save the children" summation, the prosecutor employed the word *decency* no less than forty-two times.

In the modern period the Puritanical tradition has manifested itself most often in the gambling and alcohol issues. The high-profile antics of Attorney General Vern Miller (1971–75) in raids on prostitution, marijuana, gambling, and liquor activities added spice to the long tradition of "making fun" of "backward" Kansas. In the minds of the urban modern, the image generated by the "archaic" laws seriously impede efforts to further economic development. Acknowledging in 1984 that the state had a serious image problem, Governor John W. Carlin (1979–87) asserted that businessmen from North Carolina to Tokyo sincerely believed that "you couldn't get a drink" in Kansas.

At the governor's urging, the voters approved in 1986 (by about 60 percent majorities) constitutional amendments permitting public liquor by the drink, a state-run lottery, and pari-mutuel wagering. Supporters, especially in the urban areas, are hopeful that these changes in the organic law with respect to the "sin issues" will dull the Puritanical perception of the state. The majority of contemporary Kansans have distilled the lengthy and complex prohibition heritage to two dominant and odious images: religious fanaticism as represented in the stern maternal figure of Carry Nation and hypocrisy as implied in the well-worn aphorism "Kansans will vote dry so long as they can stagger to the polls."

Indeed, when Kansans discuss the sin issues—which is often and heatedly—the word that emerges most frequently, by far, is *hypocrisy*. The "Puritan conscience," it is said, has degenerated into "Puritan hypocrisy." Kansans cheerfully, perhaps some even pridefully, accept their title as the national "capital of hypocrisy." With a wealth of tradition on which to draw, they are able to make distinctions in this field that are denied to other mortals. An otherwise undistinguished schoolchild in Kansas can discourse at length on the subtle nuances to be found among, say, the "basic," "smug," and "sham" varieties of hypocrisy. As one cynic has noted, a hypocritical policy "at least shows that intentions are good."

One of the longest-running debates in the arena of public morality—and the source of much merriment—involves the proper adornment of the capitol dome. The Greek goddess of grain, Ceres, not an inappropriate symbol for the premier wheat state, was first put forward as a serious candidate about 1890. In 1901 the attorney general, the state auditor, and the state architect traveled to Chicago to oversee the production of an appropriate model; the finished statue was to stand sixteen feet tall and cost $6,950. But in response to intense public pressure, the state's Executive Council concluded that the lady's virtue was "not above reproach," so the matter was unceremoniously dropped.

In 1974 the issue was revived, and the legislature appropriated $32,000 for a sculpture of Ceres for the dome.

But those whose sense of virtue was outraged by the "pagan goddess" inundated Governor Robert B. Docking (1967–75) with irate petitions. They claimed that "the true God," not Ceres, had blessed them through the years with abundant crops. The circumspect Docking, deciding that the question was "premature," vetoed the appropriation. The debate continues sporadically to this day, while the dome remains conspicuously unadorned.

Creative writers often find the strait-laced reputation of Kansas an attractive literary vehicle. In such a manner is the Puritanical Myth perpetuated, although it is increasingly at odds with reality. Truman Capote, for instance, reached gratuitously for the puritanical in his *In Cold Blood*. We learn that the murder victim, Herb Clutter, had never tasted spirits and was "inclined to avoid people who did." But this peculiar life style had not impoverished his social life, as might have been the case in a more advanced center of civilization. Most of his Methodist neighbors, it turns out, were "as abstemious as Mr. Clutter could desire."

A more vivid example may be found in the prize-winning novella *A Boy and His Dog*, by the noted science-fiction writer Harlan Ellison. The 1969 story was later made into a movie, starring a Kansas boy who subsequently gained television fame, Don Johnson. After the nuclear devastation of the "Third War," a group of survivors build a city underground. The old-fashioned civilization that they develop is reminiscent of that found in the United States before the First World War. They elect to call their town Topeka.

Ellison presents the simple, conforming culture in a very unflattering light. It is true that there is little crime and the elderly are respected. The citizens fill their days with idle gossip and sidewalk sweeping, cheerfully but mindlessly honoring the puritanical virtues. A champion of economic development proudly announces, "We're growin' and we're prosperin'." But the place has been settled by fundamentalists, law-and-order types, and middle-class conservatives—that is, by "squares of the worst kind." No dissent or unconventionality is tolerated; sex is considered dirty; the movies are "sweet and solid and dull." And polite? "Christ, you could puke from the lying, hypocritical crap they call civility."[3]

IN SPITE OF KANSAS' palpable difficulties and extremely bad press—perhaps in some measure because of them—it has retained a reputation as a land of honest, hard-working, down-to-earth folk who honor the nationally beleaguered Traditional values. Historically, the midwestern region has been seen as the national conservatory of the enduring small-town agrarian values "that have made America great." James R. Shortridge has recently shown that the national public perceives Kansas and Nebraska as the stable core of the Middle West and associates the "pastoral ideal" with the region.[4] The Traditional impulse commonly promotes stability, although under provoking circumstances, it may inspire immoderation. In its most extreme political expression it may manifest itself in radical movements such as those of the Populists and Dr. John R. Brinkley on the Left or the Ku Klux Klan and the Reverend Gerald B. Winrod on the Right.

The Traditional concept in Kansas originated in the image of the rugged, self-reliant pioneer of the nineteenth century, struggling to tame a recalcitrant wilderness. The enduring conflict with nature produced a people close to and shaped by the land. In the Progressive Era, romantic poets such as Vachel Lindsay revitalized the concept, recognizing in the yeomen farmers of Kansas the realization of the Jeffersonian agrarian ideal. In the modern period the Traditional image has been the lens through which most Kansans have preferred to see themselves and to be seen by the world. "Kansas is more than rattlesnakes and prairie winds and things like that," a Barton County woman defiantly declared.

In a 1986 *New Yorker* article, Calvin M. Trillin pictured Kansans in small towns leading a "peaceful front-porch life . . . revolving around family and church and school and service club and neighbors." The rebuttal by Lawrence's mayor David Longhurst to the 1984 charge of the Michigan governor that Kansas was boring may be taken as the type expression. Longhurst argued that the Kansas way of life included "spending time with one's family, playing ball in the park, hearing the laughter of children, living in a community where people care about each other and saying hello to strangers."

References to Kansans, their character, and their life style are peppered with terms such as *decent, caring, friendly, solid, low-key,* and *independent:* Kansans are seen as upholding values that are "articulated in *Reader's Digest* or 1940s movies." The historian Grace E. Muilenburg notes that Flint Hills folk live "as independent as can be, yet as neighborly as all get out." A *Los Angeles Times* sportswriter compares the "regimented, professional" Russian athletes with the Americans who seem like "good, clean boys from Kansas who never took a penny." A Kansas professional observes: "Kansas isn't glitzy. . . . We're kind of like whole wheat bread. Just wholesome and basic." President Ronald Reagan reinforced the theme on his 1987 visit to Kansas on the occasion of Alf Landon's one-hundredth birthday. Reagan declared that for him "the living soul of Kansas" meant "quiet strength and . . . decency."

There is nearly universal agreement that the state is a great place to raise a family. Opponents of liberalization of the gambling and liquor laws hold that changes will diminish the "family atmosphere." Firms that have recently located in Kansas report choosing it because it is "a good place to work and raise children." A physician who emigrated from California was impressed with the "solid families" he found in Kansas. "It was sort of like 'Father Knows Best.' It was Thornton Wilder [*Our Town*] relived."

"Stability" is viewed as a collective virtue, not a community shortcoming. Apparently in recognition of this fact, the 1986 legislature made the box turtle the state reptile. One champion of immutability said that he admired most the "almost pristine primordial" condition of the state. Exotic foods are not well received, it is said, because Kansans "won't eat anything they cannot pronounce or spell." A Topeka accountant admired the state's tendency to "move slowly" and its inclination to be "a little bit provincial." Those who are inclined to a museum mentality see Kansans as "the last true Americans," their values as "survivals of earlier American forms." If "the American way of life" is to survive at all, the pessimists assert, it will be in places like Kansas. After years of studying the rural Kansas culture, author Lyle Alan White wrote in 1986 that "if you dig deep enough . . . , you can reach a level of truth that is authentic and the pure essence of our past."

Despite the attention that the moral issues have received, the only totally unforgivable sin in Kansas is laziness. The Kansas worker is widely advertised as "industrious" and "productive"—a continuing legacy of his agrarian heritage. To symbolize this industry, the honeybee has been adopted as the state insect. A brand of overalls in Denmark is called Kansas because of its ability to stand up to hard work. Elmer Stump, a "straight forward" farmer from Lebanon (Smith County), boasts that he has "some of my dad in me. . . . My dad, he knew every letter of the word *work*—frontwards and backwards." After moving to Garnett (Anderson County), a well-bred Mississippi woman discovered that an alluring manure pile and a knowledge of the proper time to plant oats helped immeasurably in breaking the ice with the neighbors. But she remained puzzled that she rarely received a compliment on her appearance or personality of the type that southern men so routinely bestowed on their womenfolk. For some time she remained ignorant of the fact that

Kansas men employed a very different scale of appreciation of female value. The highest compliment a Kansas
man could pay a woman, she eventually learned, was
"She's a worker!"[5]

In the world of images, diversity is a hallmark, contradiction a commonplace. Aspects of the Traditional
perception may clash directly with other facets of the
image. Can the citizens of the "capital of hypocrisy,"
for example, also be "honest" and "straight-forward"?
The football coach at Kansas State University in the 1960s,
Vince ("we gonna win") Gibson, evidently thought so.
By the 1980s the well-traveled coach could recall only
"good" memories of Kansas: "Let me tell you, Kansas
people are the most down-to-earth and the most genuine people I've ever met. They don't know what it is to
be phony."

Positive references to Kansas in the national media
stress the rural-based, traditional values. In the 1985 television movie *Stark,* a Wichita police officer searches for his
missing chorus-girl sister in the sin capital, Las Vegas. In
the showdown the kidnapper assures his accomplices that
they have no reason to worry because the lawman is "from
Kansas and they trust people." In a 1986 episode of the
television series "Simon and Simon," a sailor stationed at
San Diego, California, tries to save the family farm near
Garden City, Kansas (Finney County). He is portrayed
as decent, naïve, conformist, and very polite. (The military response "Yes sir" seems to come especially naturally from a Kansan's lips.) In the 1987 television movie *An American Harvest*, a Kansas farmer, standing in
his ripening field of wheat, tells his son that "they" can
have their imported oil and Japanese automobiles, but
"we" still grow "the best damn wheat in the world! That's
what gives us our strength, that's what holds America
together." The most famous and indestructible champion
of "truth, justice and the American way" also had a Kansas origin, though that fact has not been widely publi-

cized. Superman learned to honor the traditional values growing to manhood on a farm near "Smallville," Kansas.

Testimonials of expatriates often extol the time-honored Kansas virtues. They declare in a nostalgic and apparently sincere rhetoric that Kansas is, indeed, "a good place to be from." In 1872, at a time when almost no adult Kansans had been born in the state, Senator-to-be John James Ingalls sounded the keynote for the "once a Kansan, always a Kansan" literature. People could physically leave the state, he said, "but no genuine Kansan can emigrate. He may wander. He may roam. He may travel. He may go elsewhere, but no other State can ever claim him as a citizen. Once naturalized the allegiance can never be forsworn."[6]

Although it is far from the universal sentiment that Ingalls proclaimed it to be, many prominent expatriates do recall Kansas fondly. The basketball star Lynette Woodard admitted that after graduating from high school, she had only one desire—"to get out of boring Kansas." But after touring much of the world, she said that she was "happy to return to peaceful, quiet Kansas." The author, photographer, musician, and movie producer Gordon Parks has spoken more directly to the black experience. In the Fort Scott (Bourbon County) of his youth, blacks lived daily in an atmosphere of "fear, hate and violence." It was in Kansas, Parks said, that "I got my drive—I wanted to drive myself out of here." But the years brought a mellower tone, as they tend to do. More recently he has mused that the prairie beauty could be "inspirational," and he cautiously added, the people have "a certain character that ties in with that."

Although he had lived elsewhere for many years, the elderly Milton Eisenhower considered himself "a Kansan by birth and philosophy." The astronaut Ron Evans said that Kansans are "down-to-earth people. There are no pretenses in what they do. They're good, good people." The journalist Bill Kurtis thought that his time in Kansas

provided "a training ground, . . . the most solid foundation a young man could have." The president of Ryder
Trucks, Don Estes, found the "work ethic" strong in a Kansas system which consistently produced "good, honest,
solid people." The CIA official Robert Gates felt that in
Kansas he had acquired "a basic common sense and practicality and general decency. . . . Those are things that
help you in Washington."

"Expatriate" politicians who serve Kansas in Washington are often lavish in their praise of the homespun
virtues of the homeland. The classic statement of this
type, though it was made in 1945 while he was still in
the military, was General Dwight Eisenhower's ringing
declaration that "the proudest thing I can say today is
that I'm from Abilene." For Senator Robert Dole, to be
a true Kansan was to be like Ike, whose heart and soul
"grew out of the richness of the Kansas soil."

In 1983, Fifth District Congressman Robert Whittaker
moved his family out of the "rat race" in the nation's
capital. "For raising a family you can't beat where we are
right here in Kansas," he said in explanation. On the one
hundred and twenty-fifth anniversary of statehood, Second District Congressman Jim Slattery told his fellow
congressmen in Washington that the "pioneer values of
independence, hard work [and] neighbor helping
neighbor are a way of life" in Kansas. In his campaign
for reelection that autumn, Slattery won an award for a
political advertisement that played on the Traditional
theme. A model of simplicity, the full-page ad merely
reproduced a photograph of the congressman and his
elderly mother surveying the sacred acres of their Atchison
County farm. The caption read: "Washington may be
where I do my job, but Kansas is where I learned how."

Closely linked to the Traditional character and its
associated life style are those images that treat positively
of the physical environment. Kansans boast about their
"clean" water, "clean, clear" air, "magnificent" sunsets,

"beautiful" skies, and the "openness" of the prairie. Kansas is "a good place to breathe," a place where "a guy can let his dog run loose." A group of visiting Israelis said that they preferred Kansas to New York City: "There are small buildings and a lot of grass and trees. That's what we'd like to see in Israel."

The features of the landscape are often ascribed to the character of the natives. The El Dorado newspaperman Rolla Clymer frequently wrote about the effect of his beloved Flint Hills on the area's inhabitants. "The Hills are peopled by a sturdy breed," he said, "whose natures have absorbed some of the region's rugged strength." In a profile of Senator Dole a *Wall Street Journal* reporter wrote from Dole's hometown that there is "a hardness to this land, and it shows in Russell's native son." For Dole's part, he prides himself on his "open" style—"What you see is what you get." But above all else, Dole declares, "I'm a survivor." Interestingly, the historian Homer E. Socolofsky has suggested that if the historical character of Kansans were to be distilled to a single word, that word would most appropriately be *survivor.*[7]

Over the past two decades, poets, painters, and photographers have begun to celebrate once again the beauty of the Kansas landscape—following a lonely trail blazed by pioneers such as the internationally recognized Birger Sandzen of Lindsborg. Kansans now have "permission" to appreciate their physical environment, although the "drab" assessment of the short-term visitor continues unabated. In 1985, for the first time ever, a photograph of a Kansas scene (the Konza Prairie near Manhattan) appeared in the prestigious Sierra Club calendar. "There's an appreciation of what is good and rural and indigenous to Kansas," arts director Don Lambert said. Introducing a popular book of photographs, *Kansas in Color,* editor Andrea Glenn stated that her goal had been "quite simply to make the reader feel good about Kansas."

Kansas has a beauty, though it is a subtle beauty—

141

one that reveals itself only slowly, almost shyly, to the newcomer. The photographer Frank Gohlke has written perceptively that it took some time on the prairie for him to feel "the presence of space rather than the absence of things." A stanza in a poem by Jani Sherrard captures the spirit:

> Kansas does not shout
> or whisper
> She sings.
> Though only to herself.[8]

Although the long-term urbanizing trend continues unabated, Kansans show an unequivocal preference for the rural over the urban landscape. In 1986, the Kansas State geographers Roxane Fridirici and Stephen E. White studied systematically Kansans' reactions to "commonly viewed" landscapes. They found that their respondents preferred skycapes and those landscapes in which the human presence was in harmony with nature, as opposed to urban environments and landscapes reflecting a disharmony. Of thirty-five scenes shown to observers, the two most popular were a canyon setting in the Gypsum Hills and a stormy sky over the Flint Hills. The two judged least appealing featured automobile traffic in congested Johnson County.[9]

When Kansans, young and old, are asked what they like best about the state, they almost invariably give their highest priority to the relatively unpolluted environment and those behavioral attributes—such as friendly people and low crime rates—that are closely associated with the small-town ethos.[10] That is, they value most those factors that are dependent upon a low-density population. This poses in bold relief the "growth paradox." While cherishing most highly those values that require a relatively sparse population, the state tends to consider growth in both the economic and demographic spheres as a full synonym for "progress." A town, regardless of its current size, that is not growing must be "stagnating." The more culturally and environmentally sensitive have misgivings. "I struggle a lot with what we reap from progress," photographer Carol Schmidt confesses. "Is economic development our only goal?" asks the *Washington County News*.

THE NEGATIVITY that flows continually from the image fount has not been without its psychological impact on the population. Whatever else the collective Kansan may or may not be, he is imprinted by and self-consciously aware of the "image problem." According to a 1986 public-opinion survey conducted by the University of Kansas, only 7 percent of the respondents felt that the state had an "excellent" image across the country. In other low-image states, such as New Jersey and Mississippi, at least 30 percent gave this response. Awareness of the ambience occurs early in life. Over 50 percent of a large group of high-school students who wrote essays solely concerned with "state pride" volunteered a recognition of the negative perceptions of the state. These occurred nearly twice as frequently as references to the pioneer heritage.[11] "Changing the image" has become a state obsession—a pastime indulged alike by precocious children, disquieted politicians, and the idle rich.

The adverse impact of the image on economic development has increasingly concerned academic, business, and political leaders. *Ks. Magazine* was started in 1984, its editor later said, because Kansans "had an image problem." The influential economic-development study by the economists Anthony Redwood and Charles Krider recommended to the 1986 legislature that improvements in the image "should be made." At major 1986 economic-development conferences in Emporia and Salina the "image problem" loomed large. In 1987 the city of Wichita launched a five-year, $2.7 million campaign "to develop Wichita's image." A community task force created to improve Topeka's image sends its members out of state to learn the niceties of "image development." In 1987 the Southwestern Bell Telephone Company loaned one of its top executives to the state Department of Commerce for eighteen months to further the business climate and to "improve Kansas' image, both at home and outside the state." Sensitivity to image has even carried over to the design of automobile license plates. Introducing a new format in 1986, state officials explained that a state that was not on the "cutting edge" of advances in this field could expect to "suffer in the image race." But with the sleek new design, scheduled for release in 1988, Kansas would soon shed its ancient reputation as a "rural backwater."[12]

A controversy over the speech and style of candidate Mike Hayden during the 1986 gubernatorial campaign carried both economic and psychological overtones. Several prominent Republican businessmen defected to the enemy camp because Hayden's pronounced nasal twang and his "rough-hewn mannerisms" weren't "urbane enough." "Imagine the image people in New York would get of Kansas," a Wichita executive said. After the election the *Manhattan Mercury* urged that Governor-elect Hayden attend a speech school "to control" his Kansas twang. A supporter of the proposal acknowledged that President John F. Kennedy also had had a pronounced accent, but in his case that charming imperfection had been muted by "his wit and charisma."

The collective complex surfaces in numerous enterprises, not least in those that advertise the state to the world. Promotional slogans are frequently employed that do not derive from the state heritage but, instead, from distant symbols and exotic cultures. "Midway USA" appeared on the automobile license plate from 1965 to 1970 and is still to be found on official highway signs at points of entry. The "Land of Ah's" tourist promotion masochistically keeps alive the exotic "Oz" theme, which portrays Kansas in a very unflattering light. A 1987 tourist campaign promotes the state as America's Central Park. Manhattan dubs itself the Little Apple, apparently to bask in the reflected glory of the Big Apple fifteen hundred miles to the east. To celebrate the one hundred and twenty-fifth anniversary of statehood, Governor Carlin introduced perhaps the most self-deprecating slogan in the annals of American advertising: "125 and Coming Alive!" Mixing his metaphors, Carlin explained that "we've been asleep for awhile." The implied locus of morbidity contrasts sharply with the contemporary Missouri promotion: "Wake up to Missouri!"

The reaction of the Kansas media to the "big boys"—that is, New York and California—yields significant clues regarding the state's self-esteem. The 1987 claim by the *Wichita Eagle-Beacon* that "what is happening in this city is only beginning to happen in New York, Chicago [and] Los Angeles" stands in stark contrast to the usual meekness of Kansans. Although significant local events go underreported, the local media—no doubt in response to local pressures and priorities—cover coastal events and personalities extravagantly. The influence on the developing perceptions and priorities of the young has yet to be studied.

A major Kansas newspaper devoted fifteen column inches to a story about two Kansans who were entirely anonymous among the thousands participating in the Rose Bowl Parade. The trials and tribulations of a young Kansan who managed to become a "gofer" and an extra in the movies after only six months in Hollywood merited an even longer story. A television station ran a series of no less than three lengthy installments on the career of the Kansas-bred movie star Don Johnson. Another held a contest for soap-opera fans. Winners would have the opportunity to dine with "live" stars, flown in—like lobsters—from their coastal lairs, thus affording an unparal-

leled opportunity to learn "about life in New York and
Los Angeles." In announcing an Academy Awards contest, a newspaper entices its readership with: "If you've
ever dreamed of flying off to the West Coast, . . . here's
your chance to make your dream a reality." When two
New Yorkers walked off with the $12,000 prize in a public
song contest to improve the image of Wichita, cynics claimed that the "Kansas hicks" had been had again. The
Chamber of Commerce, they charged, had tried "to buy
a New York image for Wichita."

The attitude of individual Kansans would seem to jus-
tify the fawning, "other-directed" posture of the media
toward the coastal cultures. A high-school student remarks
that her Kansas friends think that "I'm crazy for wanting to
live here and not in California." Another notes that before
coming to Kansas, she had lived only in states that "had
a name." A school-district superintendent urges his board
to endorse a new educational program because it is "really
big back East." A businessman reports that on a trip to New
York City, he and his Wichita colleagues had made "ex-
cuses" about their geographic origin. The developer of
an upper-income housing project in Topeka boasts that
his plans will be very "progressive," of the type that "you
might find in California and Florida."

A young man is "pissed off" that his friends refuse
to believe that some sports figures actually prefer to live
in Kansas, instead of on the coasts. It is suggested that
the sunflower is an especially appropriate symbol for Kansas because it is perpetually bowing to the East. An airport lounge displays photographs of the prominent people
who have stopped over in Topeka. The two visages that
inaugurate the gallery are Mayor Edward I. Koch of New
York City and the California comedian Pat Harrington.
Even the archaeologists have conspired to deflate the Kansas balloon. Their literature fairly teems with references
to "higher cultures," grandly ensconced for millennia
on the eastern flank of the plains region.

The love/hate relationship of modern Kansans with their state differs importantly from the intermittent malaise of the nineteenth-century pioneer. The "hate" of the latter could quickly turn to "love" after a good soaking rain that saved the corn crop. But the decades of adverse propaganda, emanating from local, but especially national, sources, have produced in the modern citizen a much more deep-seated ambivalence. The result may be similar to, though probably less profound than, the mind set of the "self-hating Jew" immersed in a Christian culture. In a 1980 study of the geographical perceptions of Kansas college students, Shortridge found that negative cultural references (such as *boondocks* and *sticks*) occurred more than six times as frequently as negative physical ones (such as *desert* and *tornado alley*). After comparing the responses of young Kansans with those of young Texans, he concluded that "the Texas self-perceptions are much more positive."[13] In the Age of Communication it could hardly be otherwise.

The similarities and contrasts between Kansas and Texas are revealing. Like Kansas, Texas is a largely rural, "drab" Great Plains state with an economy that depends primarily on agriculture and oil. Both states had unusual, dramatic, and highly mythologized prestatehood experiences. Both have prided themselves on a hardiness and an independence of character that derives from the wresting of the land from primitive savages and a recalcitrant nature. Historically, both regions have been viewed by the eastern establishment as part of a large, undifferentiated, and dismal hinterland. But Texas has parlayed this heritage and landscape into a swaggering, larger-than-life image, a "media-made mental map" that is honored by emulation the world over. Powered by the extravagant and the superlative—a hype that would make the contemporary Kansan (though not his Progressive ancestors) blush with shame—the Texas mystique stubbornly persists in an ever-more-homogeneous world. With

147

the recent shift of affluence and influence to the Sun Belt, the Lone Star State has even begun to challenge the image-generating power of New York and California, as a "third coast." Although the physical and cultural diversity of Texas is much greater than that of Kansas, Texas nonetheless projects an integrated picture to the world. The state conveys an image of "tight cohesiveness," John Steinbeck has written, of being "one thing."[14]

"Why can't we be more like Texas?" plaintively asks the title of an article in the now-defunct *Ks. Magazine.* Similar expressions of Kansas diffidence and self-deprecation are ubiquitous. A Wichitan claims that if you live very long in Kansas "you start to carry a chip on your shoulder." A high-school student observes that "many people are embarrassed because they are from Kansas." A semifinalist for a National Merit scholarship wonders whether, as a Kansan, she should aspire to "the far-off glamour spots . . . like Harvard." A Rotarian who is leaving the state tells his fellow club members that Kansas is "the best place in the world, but it has an inferiority complex." A former director of tourism concedes that the question most frequently asked of Kansans returning to the state is "Why did you come back?" At an economic conference a successful businessman chastises his colleagues because "We don't like ourselves. . . . We kind of [think] we [are] hicksville." The Australian-reared economist Anthony Redwood at Kansas University has summed up the phenomenon concisely, though in a non-Kansan vernacular. "Kansans," he said, "are a denigrating lot."

In recent years an increasing number of Kansans, from the most humble to the governor, have publicly expressed their resentment and frustration at the ceaseless stream of adverse publicity. In the words of a Shawnee County housewife: "We're so tired of Kansas being run down by so many people." Jill Docking, the wife of the 1986 Democratic gubernatorial candidate Tom Docking, said that "he really gets mad when he . . . tells people he's from Kansas and hears them snicker."

During his eight years in office (1979–87) Governor John Carlin struggled almost continuously with the frustrating image problem and its possible solutions. He warned of economic decline as a result of the "brain drain," which for decades has siphoned off the "best and brightest" among the young, leaving by inference only the "worst and dullest." The view portrayed by a 1984 episode of a syndicated comic strip "The Wizard of Id" made the governor "sick." In it, a character takes steps to prevent landing in a Kansas wheatfield and making a trip similar to that of Dorothy in the *Wizard of Oz.* "We [have] an image that is not the best for growth and development, for keeping the best of our talent in the state," Carlin said. "We're labeled in a way that's going to make it very difficult to have the success we'd all like."

Many Kansans have come to share the governor's pessimistic assessment. Whatever the fit between image and reality under any given circumstances, progress for Kansans, individually and collectively, economically and culturally, seems ineluctably bound to at least partial solutions to the decades-old image problem. The Drab facet, tied to an unchangeable feature of the landscape, is fated to change slowly, if at all, especially in the eyes of the short-term visitor. The Rube and Puritanical facets, and their hybrid offspring "backward," are slowly but surely edging in the positive direction. The Traditional facet remains positive, although it includes conservative elements that may drift uncomfortably close to backward in the swiftly changing future. The Irrelevant label will wane only after the populace begins to insist on a more distinctive and creative public agenda, one of sufficient novelty to capture the national imagination.[15]

7

HEARTLAND OR HINTERLAND?

FROM THE BEGINNING, the friends of Kansas have attached a special significance to her geographical position. For human beings generally, centrality has carried a spiritual connotation since the dawn of time. In preliterate societies the homeland was viewed typically as the literal center of the universe. For modern man, the midland position could mean—or could be claimed to mean—a nation's vital center, a heartland.

On May 19, 1856, at the height of the Free State struggle, Senator Charles Sumner of Massachusetts delivered his famous address "The Crime against Kansas"—one of the most memorable speeches ever heard in the Senate chamber. "Take down your map, Sir," he addressed the Senate's president, "and you will find that the Territory of Kansas . . . occupies the middle spot of North America, equally distant from the Atlantic on the east, and the Pacific on the west: from the frozen waters of Hudson's Bay on the north, and the tepid Gulf stream on the south, constituting the precise territorial centre of the whole vast continent. To such advantages of situation, on the very highway between two oceans, are added a soil of unsurpassed richness, . . . calculated to nurture a powerful and

150

generous people, worthy to be a central pivot of American Institutions."[1]

It was an idea that would fascinate and inspire Kansans for generations to come. In 1875 the journalist Daniel W. Wilder suggested that by folding a United States map in both directions "you will know that Kansas is the centre and heart of America." In 1888 the writer W. M. Thayer prophesied that "the time will come when this State will be the powerful centre of the most powerful nation on earth." In 1896 the former Senator John J. Ingalls said that Kansas is "the navel of the nation. Diagonals drawn from Duluth to Galveston; from Washington to San Francisco; from Tallahassee to Olympia; from Sacramento to Augusta; intersect at its center. Kansas is the nucleus of our political system . . . the focus of freedom . . . the core and kernel of the country."

Not surprisingly, the idea blossomed during the prideful Progressive Era. Poems and novels often carried a heartland theme. Secretary of Agriculture Coburn embellished the image with his characteristic restraint. He announced in 1901 that Kansas was situated "in the favored parallel—a district that controls the destinies of the globe." As the "core of the continent," it was destined to be at the center of things "for all time," the spot where Western civilization would realize "its strongest and grandest climax." A 1907 pamphlet sponsored by the Rock Island Railroad claimed that as the hub of the United States, Kansas stood at the very "heart of things." Reflecting the ebullient spirit of the age, Virginia King Frye wrote in 1910 that Kansas was "the true and exact geographical centre of the United States, and, naturally, the centre of attraction as well, drawing all eyes first to her own achievements and possibilities—the advance agent . . . [of] the United States of America."

With the deterioration of the image during the twenties and its almost total collapse during the thirties, the centrality motif decreased in popularity, although it did not entirely disappear. In 1923, Dr. John R. Brinkley's pioneer radio station KFKB (Kansas First, Kansas Best) advertised itself as "The Sunshine Station in the Heart of the Nation." In 1929, Governor Clyde M. Reed entitled a promotional article "Kansas, Heart of the Continent." In 1932 a General Motors broadside accurately identified Kansas as "the exact center of the United States," but in the next breath unrealistically referred to it as "the real heart of America's economic life."

In the immediate postwar years the sentiment began to show signs of rejuvenation. In 1947, John Gunther described Kansas as the "heart" of the nation in the "strict topographical sense" and "a kind of gravity point for American democracy" as well. Kenneth Davis speculated that the midcontinent position might well have inclined Kansans to "middle positions generally." But Milton Eisenhower found in the concept of centrality the greatest political potentiality for the state. The stability and common sense of a Kansas that embraced the traditional values of the heartland, he said, would enable it to serve as the "firm core of the American culture and the vital center of creative compromise." During the postwar era the United States had assumed the role of the Atlas of the free world. "And Kansas is the heart of Atlas! . . . Geographically and spiritually, Kansas is at the heart of our continental power."

While others only talked about the real or imagined advantage that flowed from the central geographical position, a wealthy economist from Massachusetts, who had been the 1940 presidential candidate of the Prohibition party, did something about it. For a short time after the Second World War, inland sites seemed especially attractive for development because of their presumed greater security from atomic attack. Employing one hundred statisticians, Roger Ward Babson (1875–1967) determined to his satisfaction that an area of 400,000 square miles in the "heartland" included all of life's necessities and afforded the greatest protection from enemy bombers. He was delighted to discover Utopia (Greenwood County) at the dead center of his "Magic Circle." When he found that Utopia had become a ghost town, he turned his attention to nearby Eureka.

In 1946, Babson made extensive purchases of land and buildings in Eureka and established Utopia College. Renamed the Midwest Institute of Business Administration a few years later, the tiny school attracted primarily the scions of well-to-do eastern families. Babson boomed the area within the Magic Circle as the last best hope of all North America. In addition to its rich natural resources, it had a location "central for all U.S. and foreign markets" and possessed a climate that produced "hardy animals" and caused "hardy children" to develop to a "strong manhood." Given the region's material advantages and the possibility of a Third World War, Babson urged Americans to "seriously consider living in some small community within the Circle."

Fortune magazine called Babson's attempts to trumpet the Magic Circle "the most extraordinary campaign in the history of United States boosting." But by the mid 1960s the college had closed and the visionary plan had collapsed. The largest extant relief map of the United States (65 feet by 45 feet) is housed in a specially designed building at Babson College, in Wellesley, Massachusetts—a tangible remnant of Babson's dream. Until it received a facelift in 1980, the huge map highlighted the Magic Circle with the small but "safe" town of Eureka at its epicenter.[2]

Kansas as a place to survive a nuclear attack has fueled the imagination of a number of science-fiction writers, in addition to Roger Babson. In Paul Cook's well-received *Duende Meadow* (1985) a sealed biosphere is sunk deep into the earth outside of Salina (Saline County). The clandestine operations required an isolated inland locality which the Russians would have difficulty in detecting.

After six hundred years of nuclear winter after the Third World War, the biosphere is brought cautiously back to the surface. The hopeful inhabitants scramble out, only to find horizon-to-horizon wheat that is being harvested by combines with CCCP stamped on their sides.[3]

In recent years the notion of a centrality of significance seems to have grown as the state reaches for a modern identity. Kinsley (Edwards County) proclaims that it is precisely 1,561 miles from both New York City and San Francisco. In 1986 the names of sixty-seven Topeka businesses included some reference to centrality such as Mid-America, Mid-Continent, Midway, or Midwest. The most evocative terms, *Heart* and *Heartland,* are waxing in popularity. Winfield advertises itself as the Heartland of America. An interstate billboard promises that a weary traveler will find "Heartland Hospitality" in Salina. Topeka hosts the Heartland Health Fair and the Heart of America accordion festival. A museum exhibition sponsored by the Kansas State Historical Society bears the title "Voices from the Heartland." A line in a popular song by Bill Post declares that "When God made Kansas, he used the heart of the USA." A successful 1986 historical novel by Robert Douglas Mead—in which settler Isaac Pride helps tame the wild Kansas frontier—is entitled *Heartland.*

The linkage between central location and specific character traits has often been made explicit. Playwright William Inge once suggested that because his hometown of Independence (Montgomery County) was "in the very heart of our country," perhaps its people had "more heart in human affairs." Lyle Alan White has written about the "special energy" to be found in the "very soul of America." Marlin Fitzwater, press secretary to President Ronald Reagan, has stated that Kansas instilled in him "family values from the heartland." A 1986 Republican gubernatorial candidate, Barbara Pomeroy, declared that Kansas was "heartland both in the geographical sense and as the keeper of the [traditional] values for the nation."

A high-school student has seen a mediating role for the central state: "We are the difference in the equation which keeps both sides equal." The notion of equilibrium surfaced again in the 1987 television series "Portrait of America." Situated at the "exact center" of the United States, Kansas is conceived as a "balance place," a region in which the "steady, reliable pulse" of the national corpus can be found.

Some interpreters have seen a causal relationship between central location and the proclivity of modern Kansas politicians to take the middle path, the middle way. In 1976, Kenneth Davis proposed that Dwight D. Eisenhower's affinity for "middleness"—his tendency to reject the extremes in life—was organically related to the fact that he came from Abilene, "near the center of the most central state in the Union." The proximity of the family home to the geographical center meant that the "physical environment of the boy's growth to manhood was balanced precisely halfway between every pair of national geographical extremes."[4] Davis left unremarked the hoary tradition of Kansas extremism in social and political affairs.

Separating the unadorned geographical facts from their romantic derivatives is a relatively easy, though perhaps painful, exercise. Kansas has two solid factual claims to centrality, both of which are value neutral in their raw geographical context. The geographical center of the conterminous forty-eight states is near Lebanon in Smith County—"smack-dab in the heart of America," according to the farmer who donated the land. (The geographical center of the fifty states is at Castle Rock, South Dakota; of North America, at Rugby, North Dakota. The population center of the United States is thirty miles south of St. Louis.) The more functional geodetic datum is located in southern Osborne County. This small, mushroomed-shaped marker is the ultimate reference point for every legal description of property, public and private, in the United States, Canada, and Mexico.

It is seductively easy to pass from the physical sense of centrality to its more primitive and irrational overtones. The heart of an enterprise is that "vital or essential part" which confers significance and meaning on the other components. A heartland is an area of "decisive importance" to the political and cultural unit in its entirety. Athens, Rome, and London, during their halcyon days of empire, are classic examples. *Heartland* is the polar opposite of *backward* and *irrelevant*. Geographic center is that which is conferred upon you by blind nature; heartland is something that you must earn.

A comparison with the more diagrammatic Australian configuration may be useful. The island continent is roughly the size and shape of the United States, but its population is concentrated in a narrow band on its eastern, southern, and western margins. The distribution of people and power suggests the American pattern, although in an exaggerated form. The great interior region, the Outback, averages less than two people per square mile; over large areas it is totally uninhabited. Near the exact geographical center of the continent is Alice Springs, which has recently been described as a "sweltering, arid outback town." Australians would regard as preposterous a suggestion that Alice Springs represented the heart of the nation in anything other than the narrow geographical sense. Kansans reflect the same attitude when they contemplate the geography of their own state. Who knows or cares that the "heart" of Kansas is a cow pasture fifteen miles northeast of Great Bend?

With the advent of modern transportation and communications, being "the heart" has never been less consequential. For years, Kansas has promoted its central location as a major economic asset, though with indifferent results. But economist Anthony Redwood has concluded recently that its location is actually a disadvantage for economic development because it is so removed from the "primary markets" on the coasts. And the percentage of

Americans who live within an hour's drive of a coast is expected to increase from its current 67 percent to 80 percent by the year 2000.

The hold of the nation's central section—the Middle West—on the national imagination has diminished steadily since the 1920s. The political scientist Daniel J. Elazar has described the prairie-plains regions as "the last bastions of the old agrarian ethic." An eastern protagonist in a John Updike novel speaks of the depression evoked in him by the "stale pieties," the "old prohibitions," and the "complacent mediocrity" of the heartland. In an extensive 1985 survey of American perceptions, James R. Shortridge found that the Middle West had shrunk in the national eye from the time-honored twelve-state region to a five-state remnant (including only about 6 percent of the population), with Kansas, Nebraska, and Iowa at its core. Americans continued to associate the diminished region with a traditional rural society. Words that connote an aging, declining culture were volunteered as descriptors of the region ten times more frequently than were antonyms such as *progressive* and *modern*.[5]

In contrast, the coastal culture is almost universally perceived as the locus of advanced thought and the avant-garde. The coastal bias of the media has become notorious. *USA Today* ("the nation's newspaper") locates all six of its editorial offices on the nation's periphery. Television network specials that deal with universal topics such as drug abuse, teenage pregnancy, and weight control draw their examples, experts, and conclusions from coastal samples. Foreign audiences receive a steady diet of "national" news framed by a California or New York angle.

The midcontinental repository of the "traditional" values is increasingly viewed as a national museum piece. The little old lady from Dubuque, Iowa, or her counterpart in Great Bend, Kansas, have become quaint reminders of the tribal past, symbols of a culture that has gone from exemplary to reassuring to irrelevant and is now threatened with extinction. In the media heavens the Middle West, or its remaining remnant, functions more like the moon than like the sun. That is, its activities are illuminated by light that is dependent upon an external source, rather than being generated from within.

THE KANSAS CITY metropolitan area is perhaps even more fascinated with its central location than is Kansas. In 1986, no less than 632 business firms in the greater Kansas City area included a central-locational reference in their names. *Midwest* led in popularity with 310, followed by *Mid-America*, with 146. From time to time, Chambers of Commerce from the upper reaches of the Ohio River to the eastern slopes of the Sierra Nevada have evinced a commercial interest in the concept of heartland. But Kansas City has pressed its claim with the most unrelenting vigor, undergirded by a certain compelling logic. In the "Heart of America" you can begin your day with a "heartland omelette," cross over the Heart of America Bridge to do business with the Heartland Market, the Heartlands Fiction Collective, the Heartland Presbytery Peacemaking Committee, or the Heart of America Bolt and Nut Company—and end it in the Heartland Suite of the American Heartland Theatre.

Throughout their mutual lives, the state of Kansas and the metropolitan area have been intimately entangled in both cultural image and economic interest. Because no large city developed in Kansas, at an early date Kansas began to look to Kansas City for economic, social, and cultural leadership. In years gone by, the influence that the *Kansas City* (Mo.) *Star* and its Kansas correspondents exerted on the political affairs of Kansas has been considerable. Visiting pundits have often discovered for their readers that the "real capital" of the state was the city named after it, though the city (one of them) was in a different state.

To the present day, even well-educated outsiders are apt to confuse the state with its "real" capital. Airline stewardesses, Arab terrorists, and just plain folk may believe that the city is part of the state, or vice versa. (Some unkind easterners have claimed that "Kansas City" is an oxymoron.) Disappointingly, the carefully edited *Wall Street Journal*—which loves to publish offbeat stories about Kansas eccentricities—is no exception. It regularly indexes under "Kansas," not under "Missouri," stories that have a totally Missouri focus, such as those dealing with the development of Crown Center, the 1981 tragedy at the Hyatt Regency Hotel, activities at the Board of Trade, and Missouri school-desegregation cases.

Kansas City, Missouri, suffers from some of the same negative stereotypes as Kansas, and for some of the same reasons. Beneath the brave talk of heartland lurks the fear of being second-rate, of being "the gizzard of America." A local talk-show host, new to the area, declares that the city suffers a massive inferiority complex. The sports writer Bill James calls it a "world class" complex. The syndicated columnist Andy Rooney writes that he was "surprised at what a pleasant and thoroughly civilized place" he found the city to be. In 1970 the writer Richard L. Rhodes, a native of the area, plumbed the depths of his own and the metropolitan's psyche. He admitted that he had grown to manhood looking longingly at *New Yorker* ads and that he had become "ashamed" of his hometown. Later he found nothing to apologize for except his own rejection of Kansas City. Like the citizens of Kansas, Kansas Citians are frequently found to be on the defensive in matters cultural. A local drama critic asserted that the city had been a symbol of "yokeldom" for years: " 'Kansas City' *sounds* so bad. It commends itself to a nasal tone of voice."[6]

During the 1970s, Kansas City tried to become a "hot city," modeling itself after the "glamour cities" of the 1960s such as Dallas, Houston, and Atlanta. Upon the advice of its public-relations consultant (in New York), the city made a concerted effort to shed its "cow-town" image. By the late 1970s, interest in the hot-city image had waned, however, and the city fathers returned to the agriculturally based notion of "World Food Capital." But throughout these several promotional cycles, the native-born Calvin Trillin writes in the *New Yorker*, an all-consuming fear has persisted in the deep recesses of the mind of the Kansas Citian—namely, "rubophobia," the fear of being taken for a rube. In the early 1980s the Russians made a documentary film about Kansas City in which former President Harry S. Truman is portrayed as a crook and a mass murderer. But the utterance that upset the natives far more than the aspersion on the character of the hometown president, Trillin reports, was the bald assertion that they were "provincial."[7]

For the past several decades the metropolitan area has sprawled amorphously over the region, totally oblivious to the state line. More than one hundred thousand commuters puncture the invisible line daily, an increasing number (40 percent in 1980) headed west in the morning. The boundary that in the early nineteenth century represented the western edge of the United States and, later, separated slave from free soil is becoming an irrelevancy. Nearly everyone finds it an irritation, and some feel that it may hamper economic growth.

Thousands of the area's residents have forsaken forever the Missouri side for the greener lawns, better schools, and lower crime rate of Johnson County, just over the line to the west. The most prestigious address in all Kansas is Mission Hills, an upper-class neighborhood that helps Johnson County achieve one of the highest per capita income averages in the nation. The go-getters of the area often grow impatient with "backward" Kansas and its puritanical heritage. They prefer to think of themselves as Kansas Citians or cosmopolites, rather than as Kansans. "We really don't fit in with Kansas," they say. "People have a terrible impression of Kansas . . . especially in the East," said Henry W. Bloch, the millionaire tax consultant who resides in a Mission Hills mansion. Bloch and his Johnson County neighbors make up over one-half of the Civic Council of Greater Kansas City, an influential group of corporate executives who provide the civic leadership for the metropolitan area. Appropriately, when Governor Mike Hayden signed the 1987 liquor-by-the-drink bill into law, he did so at a ceremony in "progressive" Johnson County.

To outsiders, place names such as Shawnee Mission and Prairie Village may conjure up images of Plains Indians, mountain men, and the Santa Fe Trail; but Johnson County in reality is the "yuppie haven" of Kansas. Its "dizzying" growth and "advanced" culture are light-years removed from those of the hundreds of dying rural communities that dot the nearby Kansas landscape. Its economic heart is Overland Park, which was not incorporated until 1960 but which now boasts the fourth-largest population in Kansas and sends as many sons and daughters to Greek houses at Kansas University as do Topeka and Wichita combined. Its "Wall Street" is College Boulevard—where yuppies in Gucci loafers drive BMWs to work and think deep thoughts in plastic-walled cubicles inside dark glass-and-steel boxes. The secretary of the state Department of Commerce accurately boasts that "you can't tell an office on College Boulevard from a board room in Dallas." Nearby hotels, beckoning the citizenry to spend the weekend "in the country," have introduced a novel dimension to the "rural" experience in Kansas.

The anxieties found in the public square of Johnson County are those of any wealthy, rapidly growing suburb intent on controlling its own destiny. Unfortunately, the affluence is matched by the impermanence of young, upwardly mobile residents, so that continuity, though not a dearth of ideas, has threatened to become a major civic problem. Fast-food restaurants find that willing teenage workers are in such short supply that the restaurants are reduced to importing their employees in buses from the Missouri side. The local teenagers received some additional unwelcome attention from the national press when they confused the peace symbol with the logo of the more familiar—to them—Mercedes-Benz automobile. But overall, life is good in Yuppie Land—so good, in fact, that a touch of guilt sometimes creeps in. "It's difficult to be so blessed . . . really," confesses an Overland Park official.

A LONG AND ROCKY, though hardly drab, road has marked the official efforts of Kansas to attract tourists to the state. From the outset, two facets of the national perception have handicapped promotional activities. The lack of breathtaking scenery and a moderating climate has put the state at a decided disadvantage in competition with such "destination states" as Colorado, Florida, and Minnesota, which attract short-term vacationers in large numbers. The puritanical culture, translated into restrictive sumptuary laws, has been neither understood nor appreciated by the more sophisticated traveling public. The visual image of drabness has fused with the cultural one of backwardness to produce a hybrid perception of Kansas as a tourist hinterland—a region to be avoided or, failing that, to be hurried through as quickly as possible. These conditions have encouraged national journalists, often themselves expatriates, to ridicule the state's efforts to promote tourism, an indoor sport that has increased in both intensity and volume in recent years.

As Senator Charles Sumner noted in 1856, Kansas is indeed "on the very highway between two oceans." During the nineteenth century, Indian, military, commercial, and cattle trails crisscrossed the state in every direction. Transportation remains a major industry in the twentieth century. But Kansans have always tended to public apology about the absence of certain features from their physical environment. In the first issue of the fabled *Kansas Magazine* in 1872, its editor, Henry King, wondered if "these vast monotonous, sparsely-peopled prairies" could support a literary enterprise that hadn't been "besprinkled with salt-water from either Ocean. . . . It has no roar of huge waves, and no shadows of mighty mountains" to sustain it. One hundred and twelve years and many apologies later, in the premier issue of *Ks. Magazine*, the publisher dutifully developed the same theme. "Kansas is OK with us, " she said; "unquestionably we know what it *doesn't* have (mountains, oceans, forests, canyons, skyscrapers)."

Although the volume of through traffic grew to substantial proportions over the years, the feeling developed that Kansas wasn't benefiting from it as much as it could have. As early as 1905 a concerned citizen compared the state to "the middle of an hourglass; travel east and west has gone directly through and we have profited little by it." What was needed, he said, was a campaign to advertise to the world "the material, industrial and moral advantage" of Kansas.

In 1914 a major promotional effort attempted to do just that. A booster tour, designed to carry the sacred word to the pagan East, originated in Montgomery County in southeastern Kansas. An eleven-car train, which carried oil, minerals, grain, a marching band, and 120 businessmen, visited several eastern cities on a two-week sojourn. Their avowed purpose, reported a New York paper, was "to demonstrate what a considerable position [the] region occupies on the map, and how things are hustling thereabouts." The moment the train came to a halt in New York City, the leader told the press that "a little parade" ought to be organized, because "we have one of the finest bands between New York and the Pacific Coast." He then began to reel off to the glassy-eyed easterners a long string of Coburn-generated statistics:

"Last year, in spite of droughts, we turned out 72 million bushels of wheat and. . . ."

In 1915 the state legislature appropriated $10,000, which was matched by state newspapers, to establish the Central Newspaper Bureau under the guidance of the School of Journalism of Kansas University. One of the first organized efforts in the West designed to attract the attention of eastern manufacturers, the novel idea furnished the manufacturer with detailed information on the demographics and economics of Kansas in exchange for advertisements placed in Kansas newspapers. In 1925, Miss Vada Watson, the winner of a state beauty contest, which was euphemistically called a "popularity" contest, toured the East "to gain publicity for her State." In New York City she had lunch with the Kansas Society of that city. During her White House visit, President Calvin Coolidge enhanced his already-enormous popularity in the state by declaring that Kansas grew not only the best wheat but the "best-looking girls" as well.

It was as first-hand, if ephemeral, observers, however, that thousands upon thousands of Americans, as automobile tourists, began to make the acquaintance of Kansas. The interest of the public in the automobile developed rapidly after Henry Ford began to mass produce his inexpensive and dependable Model T in 1908. In 1914 his famous $5-a-day wage helped to place the vehicle within the grasp of many and the dream of all—a democratizing process that ultimately produced the celebrated marriage of Americans with their automobiles.

In 1924, Irvin S. Cobb voiced the considered opinion of the transcontinental motorist about the newly discovered western landscape. From a car window, he said, Kansas seemed to be "a dismalish interlude between the Mississippi Bottoms and the Raton Pass [Colorado], a sort of dull-toned anteroom through which you must pass to reach the sun parlors of New Mexico and the great corridor of painted glory that is Arizona." A *New York Times* editorial in 1925 echoed the sentiment. Many motorists, it said, viewed Kansas "with the pseudo-sophistication of the professional critics for whom the very name connotes sun-bleached Nordic drabness. They cross its four hundred miles impatiently counting off the distance to the border."

The increasing mobility of Americans brought another major embarrassment to Kansas. The development of the automobile had created a strong public demand for good roads. In the beginning, the roads were impossible everywhere. For instance, in 1916 the author of the Tarzan novels, Edgar Rice Burroughs, with the most advanced automotive equipment, took six weeks to travel from Chicago to Los Angeles (ten long days of which were spent traversing Kansas). But by the mid twenties the condition of Kansas highways had become notorious across the country. The noted journalist Bruce Bliven complained of the many "long and weary" hours spent on the "washboardy" roads. As late as the early 1930s, when most of the nation was enjoying all-weather roads, the intrepid traveler on the major highways of Kansas often ended up spending the night in a local farmer's spare bedroom.

Many motorists simply detoured around "the mudhole state." The American Automobile Association "pulled out" of Kansas in disgust and routed its members in other directions, a rupture that was not healed until the late 1940s. In 1929 a strong state booster, the editor of the *Jayhawk* magazine, said that he found life in Kansas infinitely preferable to that in eastern industrial states such as New Jersey. But when it came to roads, he admitted that he would take "New Jersey or any other state." Not everyone agreed that muddy roads were undesirable. A drouth-conscious farmer wrote a local newspaper that he was "tired of reading things belittling our good state. . . . If there is anything that will put a smile on our [farmers'] faces, it is to know the roads are muddy."

The unhappy condition of the roads has been attributed to the state's prohibition policy and its absence of liquor-generated revenues. But Kansas fell seriously behind the nation in road-building during the tenure of the Eighteenth Amendment. Highway construction became a victim of the general reluctance of the fiscally conservative population to allow the government to engage in "internal improvements." In 1920, Kansas voted to liberalize the constitutional provision that had permitted the government to borrow for internal improvements only "to repel invasion, suppress insurrection, or defend the state in time of war." The amended law permitted the state to defray the costs of 25 percent of county-road construction, but the locus of control remained at the local level. This arrangement precluded the development of an integrated state highway system and brought down the wrath of the federal government, which threatened to cut off its highway funds.

Beginning in 1924, business and professional organizations, led by an energetic state Chamber of Commerce, mounted a good-roads campaign designed "to get Kansas out of the mud." Improved roads, the Chamber argued, would remove "much of the present prejudice against the state from a tourist standpoint." In 1928 a special session of the legislature passed a highway amendment that permitted the building of a modern system of state highways. The now-frustrated and embarrassed electorate ratified the amendment by a whopping 81 percent—and, by 76 percent, the companion measure, which permitted the use of gasoline and motor-vehicle taxes for road purposes. Thus, Kansas began to try to catch up with the rest of the country in road building and tourist accommodations.

The state Chamber of Commerce combined its call for highway improvement with campaigns to promote the industrial and agricultural interests of the state. In 1927 it announced a plan to raise $1.2 million to advertise the state's natural resources "to the world at large." Another campaign, launched in 1929, sought to enhance industrial development while dispelling the image of an "undeveloped, raw frontier State with the Indian and buffalo hunter still in evidence." The Chamber also detected the initial stages of a truth that would become axiomatic in the modern period: the ironic need "to sell Kansas to Kansans."

In 1931, when the state image, like the stock market, was plunging to record lows, the Chamber recognized that Kansas was developing "an inferiority complex concerning its historical background." To correct the situation it called for an increased emphasis on Kansas history in the public schools and launched its own weekly series of radio broadcasts on state historical themes. But by the close of the decade the Chamber, along with the rest of Kansas, had significantly lowered its expectations. One should be thankful that things hadn't gotten any worse, the Chamber's president said in 1939. And there was one small glimmer of hope: he thought that he had detected among the state's citizens "a new inclination . . . to see the good in Kansas rather than the bad."

The status of Kansas in the tourism industry was sketched vividly in a 1934 *Fortune* survey of the rapidly expanding field. The "happy marriage" of Americans with their automobiles, the business magazine said, had produced the "restive" tourist with spendthrift habits. For the alert entrepreneur, there were "ten thousand little ways [to] cash in on him en route." The delights of the "Great American Road" were many and diverse, but unhappily, across Kansas, the highway degenerated into "a rigorous lattice of country dirt . . . the smell of hot wheat . . . and this summer a blindness and a strangulation of lifted dust."

On the center-fold map—which had been drawn by John Steuart Curry—the major migration routes of the touring public were noted. The most attractive destinations ("lodestones" such as California, Florida, and New England) could be found along the periphery, while "The Transient Belt"—the "middle vacuum" that the motorist "crosses but abhors"—marked the central hinterland. A "bone-dry" label on the map further stigmatized Kansas in the tourist's eye, an undeserved defamation, because beer had enjoyed a quasi-legal status in the state for more than a year. The damage wrought by the alcohol policy was mitigated somewhat by the designation of a Carry Nation "hatchetation" site as the sole tourist spot worthy of note in the entire state.[8]

In 1934, Roy F. Bailey, the editor of the *Salina Journal* and the president of the state Chamber of Commerce, initiated a drive to erect roadside markers at major historical sites in the state. He had been moved to action on a trip to historical sites in the East, when his twelve-year-old daughter had asked, "Daddy, does Kansas have any history?" Stung by this remark, Bailey persuaded the Chamber to establish a committee to identify potential Kansas sites. One hundred were soon identified, but Bailey failed repeatedly in his efforts to convince a governor that the project deserved funding.

Finally, in 1940, as planning moved forward for the celebration of the four-hundredth anniversary of the Coronado expedition, Governor Payne Ratner (1939–43) approved the project. He recognized that increased tourist travel could result in more revenue from the gasoline tax, better roads, and "the cash crop that would be harvested by hotels, eating places, drug stores and similar businesses." In 1942, with fifty-seven markers in place, Bailey reminded Kansans that the appreciation of historical traditions helped to create "the state pride which is essential to the development of any commonwealth." Perhaps as a belated response to *Elmer Gantry*, he added that Kansans did not need to "take a back seat for the First Families of Virginia, or the citizens of any of the other states of the Union."[9]

AT THE BEHEST of the Chamber of Commerce, the 1939 legislature created the Kansas Industrial Development Commission (KIDC) as a "promotive" agency for both industrial development and tourist travel, with an annual budget of $60,000. In 1963 the agency became the Kansas Economic Development Commission, and in 1987 it became the Department of Commerce, a cabinet-level department. In November 1945 the KIDC launched a monthly promotional magazine, *To the Stars*. The name was changed to *KANSAS!* in 1957 to eliminate the difficulty that out-of-state subscribers had with the allusion to the state's motto.

The very first issue of *To the Stars* declared that tourist travel would be "a major peace industry" in the postwar world and that the KIDC was planning accordingly. If Kansas were to grow industrially and achieve the proper balance with agriculture, it needed the right kind of advertising and "lots of it." To this end the KIDC announced a $1-million fund drive to tell the nation about "all the fine qualities" that could be found within the state's borders. Although late to the field, the agency moved rapidly to overtake the competition. After visiting all forty-eight states, John Gunther wrote in 1947 that in no other state had the promotional material ("propaganda") been so "handsomely prepared" as that issued by the KIDC. Even the hypercritical Neal Peirce had some good words for the Economic Development Commission in his 1973 announcement of the "Eclipsed State." He lauded the agency and the legislature for having avoided a helter-skelter approach to economic development by having encouraged only those industries that would "match Kansan needs and not harm the Kansan environment."

As the postwar years unfolded, both tourism and industrial development loomed ever larger in the state's profile. The development of the interstate-highway system during the Eisenhower years (1953–61) and the proliferation of recreational reservoirs made both Kansans and non-Kansans more aware of tourism possibilities in the state. The many public events that marked the centennial of statehood in 1961 were inspired, Kansan Charles C. Howes said in *Travel Magazine,* by a combination of state pride and a "profitable" tourist business. Increasing urbanization and the continuing outmigration of the young elevated industrial development of the middling-sized communities into a major political issue. The Hutchinson journalist Jack Harris declared that "the yearning for industry has become almost an hysteria." The major cultural and economic concern of Kansans as they approached the centennial of statehood, John Bird reported in the *Saturday Evening Post,* was the image projected to the rest of the nation.

In recent decades the subject of Kansas tourism has not infrequently evoked a loud guffaw from the rest of the nation. Rarely does a serious or positive report on the subject emanate from the nation's journalists. In *Dateline America,* Charles Kuralt advises motorists heading west from Kansas City to stock up on peanut-butter sandwiches, because there is "nothing to eat until one reaches Denver. Kansas is the gastronomic wasteland of America." The state's "peculiar" liquor laws are often mocked in the national press. "If you own a whistle," the *Wall Street Journal* advised in 1973, "don't try to wet it in the State of Kansas." "If Kansas Is So Dry, Why Are the People Staggering So Much?" asks a front-page *Journal* headline in 1978. In that article a pious Winfield woman declares that liquor is "a tool of Satan," and a fellow townsperson explains that the town is so dry because "the hypocrites gotta keep their halos lit."

Former Kansans seem especially anxious to join in the fun. Trying to make Kansas a tourist state, mused Bill Farmer of the *St. Paul* (Minn.) *Pioneer Press,* was something like trying to make Hawaii "the Wheat State." Kansas should be content with its image as "a gray, tornado-ravaged frump of a state," patronizingly advised Jack Kisling of the *Denver Post.* "The life of a hustler [Colorado] isn't as much fun as you might imagine."

A former Kansan on the staff of the *Washington Post* expounded on the image of Kansas as a tourist mecca, as portrayed, for example, in the movie *Vacation.* Kansas may be woefully deficient in the standard enticements for tourists, Alex Heard wrote in the *Post* and the *New Republic,* but it leads the nation in "pitiful-yet-lovable" attractions of the "World's Largest" variety. These include the cement prairie dog (in Russell), the Jello memorabilia (Lakin), the free outdoor concrete municipal swimming pool (Garden City), and the exact replica of the Liberty Bell woven from turkey-red wheat straw (Goessel). Kansas, Heard counseled, should quit trying to be something that it is not. It should stick with the "yokelrific" attractions that serve as "inspiring-though-pathetic monuments to the state's eternal, fruitless quest to get people to plan their vacations around it."[10]

The classic in this genre appeared on the front page of the *Wall Street Journal* on July 18, 1973, while the Watergate scandal was absorbing much of the nation's political interest. Written by the former Kansan Eric Morgenthaler, the first sentence set the tone: "It isn't too late to change your vacation plans and come to Kansas. [Laughter.]" He proceeds to extol the virtues of tourist attractions such as the world's deepest hand-dug well (Greensburg) and the world's largest ball of twine (Cawker City). (The twine would unravel all the way to Carrollton, Missouri, on the east, the locals said; but the western limit was unknown, because the ball was "too heavy to roll uphill.") Morgenthaler reported the results of an "unsettling" survey by the Department of Economic Development. Most of the travelers were "pass-throughs" and so passive about the state that criticisms such as "dead animals on the roadways" seemed almost welcome. "Kansas is trying to promote tourism," Morgenthaler concluded, "but it really doesn't have a heck of a lot to promote."

Cries of outrage could be heard from the Hugoton gas fields to the apple orchards of Doniphan County. Governor Robert Docking (1967–75) led the hosts, though his indignation had to be tempered somewhat by an embarrassing fact. He had recently vetoed a bill that would have established tourist-information centers, with the gratuitous suggestion that such activity could be handled adequately at the truck-weighing stations. Docking rebutted the devilish article by ticking off Kansas' enviable positions in regard to wheat, mental health, light aircraft, and "uncluttered" environments. He reminded the *Journal's* editor that the natives still held to "such 'antiquated' concepts as patriotism, honesty and the work ethic."

Other irate correspondents labeled the *Journal* article "slanted" at best, "twisted and malicious" at worst. The *Pittsburg Headlight-Sun* thought that it had given the state its blackest eye since the *Wizard of Oz*. But the *Iola Register* acknowledged that Kansas was "no place to sight see. . . . Kansas, like the girl with the dumpy figure and the plain face, will just have to concentrate on building a wonderful personality." Probably the solemn assessment of Jerry Holley, president of the Kansas Association of Broadcasters, came closest to the mark: "The damage done by Mr. Morgenthaler's article cannot be measured."[11]

Twenty-three-year-old Phil McLaughlin of the *Miami (County) Republican* in Paola took a completely different approach. He suggested that Kansans were still suffering from a collective inferiority complex—"a state-wide sensitivity to its rank on a national opinion scale of state worth." Many of the reactions of Kansans, including the governor's, seemed more "a justification for Kansas' existence . . . than an appeal for tourism." The little county seat of Paola couldn't offer "sea breezes" to vacationers or a "Rocky Mountain High. . . . It is just a pleasant place to live for a small number of people who believe life shouldn't be an accelerating kaleidoscope of regimented events. Its justification, if it needs one, lies there." A year later, members of the International Society of Weekly Newspaper Editors conferred on young McLaughlin their Golden Quill Award for the best editorial of the year.[12]

In 1977 the state commissioned a Tulsa firm to conduct the first-ever in-depth study to help the state reach "its optimum potential in tourism." In their six-volume report the consultants elaborated on themes that had been known or suspected for decades. In a phone survey conducted among potential vacationers in a nine-state midwestern area, Kansas finished last in a preference listing of destinations for pleasure trips. The respondents most often cited the weather, "poor scenery," or "nothing to do" as justification for their assignment. The dominant images were those of "drabness" and irrelevancy ("no definitive image"). About 75 percent of the approximately 40 percent who had never been in Kansas indicated that they had no desire to visit it. Among those who had visited the state, only 8 percent were attracted by the scenery. Seven times as many had another destination, confirming the historic role as a pass-through state. The consultants also rediscovered the venerable truth that Kansans themselves held a low opinion of the state "as a place to visit."[13]

To help remove that disturbing obstacle to the modern El Dorado, Governor Robert F. Bennett (1975–79) and Larry Montgomery, the director of tourism, launched a systematic campaign in 1977/78 to "talk up" Kansas among those who apparently needed it most—Kansans. The effort was stimulated by reports of "negative criticism" of the state's image by "visitors, many of our youth and some of our fellow Kansans." To counteract such subversive talk, the *Topeka Capital* editorialized that the state at the heart of the nation had a "thrilling story to tell." Kansas represented "the wave of the future, with a central location, relatively uncrowded cities and unpolluted air and water." In the spring of 1978 the "Kansans Talk Kansas!" tour made stops in all 105 counties. A central feature of the promotional material was a list of fifteen state rankings, ranging from oil production (seventh) and railroad miles (fifth) to mobile-home production (third) and helium production (first). Phil McLaughlin's reactions are not recorded, but they may readily be surmised.

In recent years, official efforts to attract tourists and industry to the state have often met with futility or embarrassment. In a 1985 national survey the travel editor of the *Kansas City Star* stated that Kansas promotional materials dwelt excessively on trying to convince tourists that Kansas should be "visited, not just endured" and didn't "succeed too well at that." A 1986 Rand McNally book that rated the "best vacation places in America " included not a single location in Kansas—not even a Carry Nation hatchetation site. And a 1987 promotion that urged outsiders to "open your eyes" to the "Real Kansas" had to be withdrawn by the Department of Commerce after members of the press noticed that it included pictures of a sixty-story skyscraper (the state's tallest building has twenty-two stories) and an elk (elks were exterminated in Kansas in the nineteenth century).

Since the 1960s a not inconsiderable fraction of the national perception of Kansas in tourism and otherwise has been refracted through the improbable prism of an old movie which had been made from an even older children's fairy tale. Over the years the state's image has been reflected in and shaped by movies to only a moderate extent. Because films developed as a full-fledged medium only since the late 1920s, they have conveyed a negative perception of Kansas much more often than not. Westerns, such as *Dodge City* (1939), *The Kansan* (1943), and *Wichita* (1955), portray the stereotypic violence and mayhem of the frontier town of the late nineteenth century. In *Picnic* (1955), *The Learning Tree* (1969), and *Paper Moon* (1973), the small-town milieu of twentieth-century Kansas is characterized respectively as stultifying, racist, and excessively pietistical. But no movie about Kansas has approached the image-generating power of the *Wizard of Oz*.

When the popular book was published in 1900 at the dawn of the Progressive Era, the gray tones of its opening scenes did not stick on the up-and-coming, reform-minded state. The 1939 movie, starring the adolescent Judy Garland, met with limited success; it was overshadowed by *Gone with the Wind* and, soon thereafter, the Second World War. Kansas came to be only weakly linked with the film in the public mind, in much the same marginal manner that at a later date the state was associated with *Superman*. But in 1956 a sagacious television-network executive retrieved *Oz* from archival oblivion to make of it a perennial springtime event, rivaling in popularity crimson tulips and the Easter bunny. In the reincarnation the identification with Kansas has been close, continuous, and controversial.

Contemporary Kansans are incessantly reminded of *Oz* both at home and abroad. Posters, postcards, paintings, stationery, greeting cards, and T-shirts—all bear icons of *Oz* characters, most frequently Dorothy or her dog, Toto. The formal opening of an exhibit on symbols and images at the Kansas State Historical Society employs the *Oz* theme. Corporate-jet travelers to Topeka are feted with cuisine from "Auntie Em's kitchen." Kansans abroad may be solicited for health reports on Aunty Em or Uncle Henry. A group of high-school seniors, while touring Chicago, are greeted with "That's where Dorothy is from!" after they reveal their home state. A Kansas University student declares that in the East, "all they know of Kansas is the Wizard of Oz and [basketball star] Danny Manning." A journalist reports that his former eastern colleagues knew little of Kansas "except for Dorothy and the Wizard." At her first public appearance in Washington, D.C., in 1979, the newly elected Senator Nancy Landon Kassebaum quipped, "Toto, I have a feeling we're not in Kansas anymore."

Some literary critics have argued that *Oz* should be read as a serious political allegory in a Populist setting. Perhaps so. But generations of children and adults have delighted in the exciting fairyland where magical things happen repeatedly and the roads are paved with golden bricks. The Land of Oz is the polar opposite of a "drab" Kansas—a veritable anti-Kansas—a place where one's imagination may escape the dull grayness of a tornado-ravaged country.

In 1979, Governor John Carlin took a calculated risk by deciding that "instead of fighting the image, we would use it to our benefit." The Travel and Tourism Division launched an aggressive promotional campaign which played on the *Oz* theme. Over the next several years the slogan appeared in permutations such as "Kansas, Land of Ah's!" "Ah! Kansas . . . Coming Alive," and "Ah Kansas . . . 125 and Coming Alive!" The 1983 legislature designated a federal highway, U.S. 54, as the Yellow Brick Road. Carlin declared that Dorothy's House in Liberal (Seward County) was "the Gateway to the Land of Ahs and Oz." The advertising agency of record purred that the tourist promotion would "position Kansas as the progressive, forward-looking state that it is."

Not surprisingly, the governor's gamble stirred up a great deal of controversy. Still another derisive article on the front page of the *Wall Street Journal* in 1983 by yet another former Kansan, Kevin P. Helliker, added further fuel to the flame. Reactions to the article, which disparaged the state's efforts to exploit the Oz theme, were as varied as they were predictable. Arthur S. Brisbane, writing in the *Kansas City Times,* charged that the flint-hearted *Journal,* chock full of "East Coast cynicism," encouraged Americans to accumulate material goods "rapaciously." On the other hand, in Kansas, one found few "rapacious magnates"—only the wide open spaces and a lot of "nice folks" with a consuming desire to alter their image as "Dullsville." Governor Carlin responded that

Kansas had "clean air, low unemployment, a good industrial climate . . . and a high quality of life." He repeated the egregious claim that the state had more surface water than Minnesota (this was before the Kansas "watergate").

This time around, Secretary of State Jack H. Brier performed the statistical duties. In a letter to the *Journal*, Brier asked Americans to remember at breakfast that Kansas was first in wheat; at dinner, that it was fourth in cattle; and all day long, that "almost 60% of the free world's aircraft is produced in whole or in part by Kansas." Nor should they forget that "we rank 16th in per capita income, 10th in percent of students completing high school, sixth in longevity, and second lowest in unemployment."[14] F. D. Coburn would have been proud.

The most useful insight into the Kansas psyche that the "Ahs" campaign affords is not that the contrived message may suggest grayness to some or conjure up visions of tornadoes to others. But that—like the "Midway USA" and "America's Central Park" slogans—it accepts as its core the perception of the external agent instead of building on local notions of self-worth. Kansans lack the self-confidence of, say, Vermonters, who proudly push the slogan "Vermont is the way America used to be." Only an "other-directed" commonwealth—one whose confidence in itself has been shaken by decades of adverse publicity—would incorporate so anxiously the extraneous view in what amounts to an exercise in self-definition.

IN RECENT YEARS, cultural geographers, led by Peter Gould, have constructed "mental maps" from place preferences expressed by young adults in various regions of the country. Respondents tend to rank their own areas more highly than the average, but their images of more distant locales as living sites are remarkably similar. Thus, maps of the nation drawn from the preferences of college students in, say, California, North Dakota, Pennsylvania, and Alabama resemble one another closely, except for the home region. The coastal areas, appearing on the mental relief maps as "highs," are generally perceived as the most desirable. Kansas lies in the center of an elongated north-south trough of undesirability which runs through the nation's midsection. Just to the west of the Great Plains depression sits a prominent Colorado "high."

According to Gould's studies, a given geographical area and its associated culture tend to be assigned by respondents to a rather narrow range among the possibilities, whether the region is evaluated on a physical or on a social scale. Thus, Kansas (and the Great Plains generally) tends to be viewed as physically unattractive, economically disadvantaged, and culturally backward. It is the image of a land from which the young and the most talented flee at the earliest possible opportunity.

The attractiveness of a region tends to be highly correlated with the amount of information held about it by the respondent. Thus, an "information surface" looks much like a "preference surface." On national informational tests, Kansas is confused most often with Nebraska and Arkansas. Knowledge of a region is, in turn, a function of the population density and the cultural visibility of the perceived region, in addition to its distance from the perceiver. For example, Pennsylvanians strongly prefer California to Kansas; indeed, in their eyes, Kansas occupies the penultimate position among the fifty states, narrowly edging out Iowa for that honor. On information tests, Pennsylvanians demonstrate a knowledge level of California about twenty times greater than that of Kansas (and the other plains states).

In the absence of massive social or environmental changes, one's perceptions of the national landscape remain relatively stable throughout life. The mental maps of Gould in the 1980s correspond closely to the tourists' perception of America portrayed by *Fortune* magazine in the 1930s. From childhood, the regions that are valued most highly are the home areas but also prominent cultural centers such as New York, Boston, and Los Angeles. Such inherent inclinations in the Age of the Mass Media may help explain the powerful attraction of the urban centers for those in the rural districts of the United States, Latin America, Scandinavia, Africa—indeed, for provincials of the entire globe.[15]

To a not inconsiderable extent the plains region has been viewed nationally as a homogeneous unit; however, important differences are to be found within the region. Systematic analyses of broad cultural differences between Kansas and its neighboring states have rarely been made. Political scientist Daniel J. Elazar has examined the qualitative differences in the cultural patterns among the plains states as associated with political style and moralistic attitude. He finds that Kansas "differs substantially" from all the adjacent states in these dimensions. The southern and eastern borders were so pronounced as to delineate "a cultural fault line."

In an extensive quantitative study based on data from the 1940 federal census, the sociologist Margaret Jarman Hagood developed a Coefficient of Similarity to facilitate comparisons among the forty-eight states. Her coefficient represented the correlation of 104 demographic, economic, and social factors between pairs of states. For Kansas, the highest correlation was with Nebraska (.77). It was followed, at a considerable distance, by Iowa (.52), Oklahoma (.48), Missouri (.28), and Colorado (.25). The rank order of the correlations supports a great deal of other, more impressionistic evidence regarding cultural similarities.[16]

From the inception of the United States, there have been hostility, mistrust, and jealousy between the so-called larger and smaller states. The distribution of power and influence has always been asymmetrical, tending to favor the coastal areas over the hinterland. The role of the ten largest states, or megastates, seven of which are coastal, was assessed in 1972 by Neal R. Peirce. Here, he asserts, are the sites of "essential action," the "centers of advanced thinking," the "capitals of the arts," and the headquarters of the "powerful corporations." Collectively, the ten mega-states contain over 50 percent of the population and account for over 60 percent of state and local governmental spending. (A parallel phenomenon occurs within the state of Kansas. The 10 "megacounties" [of 105] account for 53 percent of the population; just four [Sedgwick, Johnson, Shawnee, and Wyandotte] account for 40 percent.) In a 1982 study of cultural trends ("megatrends"), the futurist John Naisbitt identifies five bellwether states which generate a disproportionate number of cultural and political innovations. Of these, four are coastal: California, Washington, Florida, and Connecticut; the other is Colorado.[17]

Regional studies of well-being present a picture that is the inverse of those dealing with power and influence. In a 1982 study of "psychological well-being," the social scientist Carin Rubenstein found that the West Central Region, which includes Kansas, ranked the highest among eight regions in the nation. Here the modal preference was for the simpler and more stable life centered on the family and traditional values. Although highest in material well-being, the Pacific Region was characterized as restless, disgruntled, and most prone to suicide and chemical dependency. The Middle Atlantic Region (New York, New Jersey, Pennsylvania) scored the lowest on the overall index. Residents of the "Miserable Metropolis" reported the greatest stress, the fewest friends, and the least satisfaction with employment and local neighborhoods.[18]

These results are compatible with several American studies that report a relatively low correlation between material affluence and the sense of well-being or perceived quality of life. In an extensive quantitative study in 1981, the social scientist Angus Campbell could account for less than one-half of the total variation among individual Americans' psychological sense of well-being by analyzing the "objective" factors of income, occupation, education, and so forth. The sense of well-being was found to be heavily dependent upon such "subjective" factors as family relationships, job satisfaction, interpersonal trust, leisure-time activities, and group belongingness.[19]

Recent evidence suggests that the cultural homogeneity of a state may play a critical role in the shaping of the sense of well-being of its residents. In 1987 the political scientists Earl and Merle Black reported an extremely high statistical correlation between satisfaction with one's state and local community and Sullivan's Diversity Index (p. 106) in a thirteen-state sample (which did not include Kansas). The correlation (-0.94) accounted for 88 percent of the variance in the scores. The more homogeneous the state, the more likely the populace is to view it in a benign manner. Residents of the more diverse (and affluent) states, such as New York, Massachusetts, and Illinois, expressed much less satisfaction with their locales than did those of the more homogeneous (and less affluent), such as North Carolina and Alabama.[20]

Over the past several decades, quality-of-life indices have been generated by investigators who were seeking to compare the overall livability of the several states. These "objective" parameters typically measure critical social factors, such as education, crime, income, and the like. The index so produced may or may not be positively correlated with the widely accepted reputation, or image, of a state as a desirable place to live. Kansas almost always ranks in the upper 50 percent, occasionally in the upper 10 percent, of the states on such indices.

The first comprehensive study designed to identify the "best" and the "worst" states in overall livability was conducted by H. L. Mencken and Charles Angoff in 1931. In this pioneering work, which was based on data derived from the *Statistical Abstract,* Kansas ranked twentieth overall. Evidently somewhat dismayed by this showing of his "favorite" state, Mencken couldn't resist noting that the statistical evidence notwithstanding, many Americans regarded Kansas as "almost barbaric."[21]

In another 1931 quality-of-life study, Kansas ranked nineteenth; in a 1967 study, twenty-sixth; in a 1972 study, twenty-third; in one 1973 study, twenty-third; and in another, fourteenth. In the most recent comprehensive study available, the Iowa Development Commission in 1985 analyzed twenty-three factors distributed over eight categories (education, public safety, personal economics, taxes, health care, environment, stress, and work-related). The Kansas rankings ranged from first (debt per capita) to thirty-sixth (environmental controls). On twenty of the twenty-three scales, Kansas ranked in the upper 50 percent; on eight scales, in the upper 20 percent. On the overall quality-of-life index, the state ranked fifth.[22]

Many national surveys have reported that Americans, if given the economic opportunity, would prefer to live in rural areas or small-to-moderate-sized towns. This is nearly as true for residents of large cities as for those in more thinly populated areas. In a 1980 study of Kansans' preferences, Stephen B. Bollman found that 68 percent of the urbanites in his sample and 98 percent of those in a more rural environment preferred to live in areas with low population densities.

Despite the persistence of the negative images and the relatively low self-esteem of Kansans, most residents continue to think highly of the state as a place to live. In a 1986 scientific survey sponsored by Kansas University, 84 percent considered Kansas excellent or good as a place to live. In a 1980 survey sponsored by Kansas State University, Bollman found that from 75 to 89 percent of the families that were sampled expressed a basic satisfaction with the quality of their life in Kansas, depending upon the dimension analyzed. The urban respondents showed more concern for personal safety; the rural, for employment opportunities. Both groups expressed the least satisfaction in the political realm—with the effectiveness of elected officials and with the perceived return on their tax dollars.

In a 1987 scientific poll the *Wichita Eagle-Beacon* asked Kansas respondents if they would "prefer to live in Kansas or some other state?" Sixty-nine percent preferred Kansas (from ages 18 to 24, the percentage was 45; over age 65, the percentage was 90). The East apparently holds little attraction for Kansans as an alternative place of residence. The most popular "other" states, in order, were Colorado, California, Arizona, and Texas. These results compare favorably with the "most satisfied" regions of the country (North Carolina scored 70 percent on a similar question; New York, 29 percent). Given the high level of homogeneity within the state, the results are not surprising.[23]

"TYPICAL' KANSANS do retain some emotional attachment to their state, even though they are increasingly confused about what, if anything, their "Kansasness" means. Part of their self-concept also derives from their residency in the Middle West and on the Great Plains. The images associated historically with these regions have tended to be somewhat more formless than those attached to an individual state. But in recent years the concepts that are most prominently coupled with these regions are decidedly negative. To the extent that Kansans identify with these broader areas, they only add to their already burdensome problem of image.

Whether Kansas is viewed as a heartland or a hinterland is, of course, largely in the eye of the beholder. Most of the recent claims to heartland, by both commercial and governmental interests, are mere assertion or vainglorious flatulence. Perhaps the "progressive" coastal cultures have tossed the midsection a harmless bone on which to chew, as they in fact lead the nation into the promising future. Kansas will have to raise much less corn and a great deal more hell in the public arena in order to be taken seriously as "the vital part" or true heartland of the nation. Neither raw biology (sex, race, age) nor unadorned geography (center, periphery) will determine the fate of the individual or the population in the twenty-first century.

8

PROSPECTS

THE HISTORY of the images of Kansas, as well as the implications for the collective psyche and the common purpose, may be placed in a broader context. The tendency of human beings to identify profoundly with a particular place and culture is deeply rooted in the history of the species. The psychologist Abraham H. Maslow has identified "belongingness" as a basic human need equal to other fundamental drives, such as those for safety and respect. Although the "image crisis" of Kansas has been most often framed in terms of economic development, the cultural ramifications run far deeper than the mere acquisition of material goods. A brief consideration of the more cosmic implications may usefully illuminate the state's past as well as its prospects for the future.

Over nearly the entire span of its long history *Homo sapiens* has evolved in small, tightly integrated groups. These semi-isolated, cohesive bands developed elaborate rules, rituals, and customs that encouraged group stability and solidarity. The emphasis was much less on the welfare of the individual than on the harmony and survival of the whole. The individual made few meaningful life choices or decisions, obtaining his satisfaction and identity instead from the fulfillment of the cultural norms. The preeminent guide for both individual and group behavior was an unquestioned and unexamined tradition. Whatever was, was right. It was a taken-for-granted existence in a world that, for the individual, was essentially a "one-possibility thing."[1]

In these preliterate communities, religion was supreme and all-pervasive, the ultimate source of legitimacy of the laws, the leaders, and the institutions. There was no separation of the sacred and the profane, to say nothing of church and state. Following the time-honored customs, leaders both prescribed and proscribed particular moral behaviors, often in great detail. The modern canard that "you can't legislate morality" is dismaying to the cultural anthropologist.

The early societies almost universally developed a strong emotional bond to place. The land was particular and inviolable—a trust. It was the central and sacred feature of their known universe—the geographical handmaiden of the tribal inclination to ethnocentrism. Ancestor worship was strong ("My dead are not powerless"). The burial grounds and, by extension, the home range became holy ground, bestowing a transcendental function on the physical landscape. The geographer Yi-fu Tuan has defined place as "a center of meaning constructed by experience." Thus, man, the "meaning-seeking" animal, has conferred a religious significance on his geographical setting.

Under such circumstances, it was impossible to know your identity outside a geographical context. Throughout human history it has been important to be from "somewhere in particular." José Ortega y Gasset has said that if you "tell me the landscape in which you live, I will tell you who you are." In the traditional world, permanent relocation could be traumatic. The Nuer tribe of Sudan carry soil from the old living site to the new one. For a period of weeks they drink a solution in which new soil is gradually substituted for the old, thus symbolically abating the anxiety generated by dislocation. In our oldest historical documents the sense of rootedness is pervasive. In the famous funeral oration of Pericles to his fellow Greeks in 430 B.C. and the "great speech" of Camillus, beseeching the Romans not to abandon their capital city in 386 B.C., the leaders of these ancient civilizations made stirring appeals to their countrymen's patriotism—to their conjoined sense of place, religion, and tradition.

About five centuries, or twenty generations, ago the Renaissance and Reformation ushered in profound changes in the traditional patterns. Europeans, especially, began to explore the globe and to initiate a long-term trend toward rootlessness. A new social type, the "individual," arose in the Old World and eventually populated the New. Freeing himself from most of the bonds of the conventional society, this mutant form of *Homo sapiens* vigorously pursued "self-fulfillment" in addition to economic, social, and political equality. The development of the contemporary individual is marked by the widespread use of such technological innovations as mirrors, cosmetics, chairs (replacing benches) and electronic headphones, and by modern social attitudes that promote psychotherapy, autobiography, genealogy, single-issue politics, the attenuated childhood, and universal literacy and salvation. Modern Western man is guided less by secular or religious authority than by his own talents, ambition, opportunities, and blind luck. Increasingly divorced from his historical moorings and energetically protecting his hard-earned individual freedoms, he constantly strives for answers to the very modern question "Who am I?"—an improbable incertitude in the more primitive societies.

Increased mobility and the elevation of the individual at the expense of the community has produced a long-term trend toward cultural homogenization. One hundred and fifty years ago the widely traveled French observer

Alexis de Tocqueville remarked that "variety is disappearing from the human race: the same ways of acting, thinking, and feeling are to be met with all over the world." Since Tocqueville's time, the rate of loss of the local and the distinctive has accelerated enormously. Cultural regions around the globe are less appreciated for their unique traditions than—like a molting reptile—for their progress in shedding the old and adopting the new. The rate of loss of cultural richness and variety rivals that of plant and animal species that are being doomed to extinction. As mankind converges on the global village, the "one-possibility thing" that characterized preliterate societies may return in the guise of a world-wide monoculture. Never has humankind's relationship to particular place been more fragile or ephemeral.

As the American nation matures, uniformity proceeds apace in the economic, political, and social realms. A national orthodoxy is progressively supplanting the unique state and regional cultures. In this "blenderized" American world, everyplace is becoming anyplace. As the historian Daniel J. Boorstin has noted: "The more we move about, the more difficult it becomes not to remain in the same place."

The United States is in the process of assimilating a remarkable range of cultures, ethnicities, and religions on a scale quite unprecedented in human history. It is a very different world from that of the Kansas pioneer of the 1870s who declared that her Geary County neighbors had been "of all nationalities—English, Scotch, Welsh, Irish [and] German." In the new order, diversity of consequence becomes suspect, while uniformity grows ever more comfortable and nonthreatening. The ethnic multiformities that remain, humanist Allan Bloom has said, are but "decaying reminiscences" of differences that once "caused our ancestors to kill one another."

Paradoxically, as ethnic and religious groups decline in power and function in the public arena, they tend to be celebrated in an ever-more-visible and sentimental manner. Since the Second World War, several hundred ethnic and county historical societies have sprung up in Kansas. Ethnic observances, such as the Fasching Ball, Polski Day, Columbus Day, St. Patrick's Day, the Exoduster celebration, and the Fiesta Mexicana, grow more numerous and more popular each year. Instead of representing a firm and possibly threatening political statement—a Gay parade or a Ku Klux Klan rally, for example—these observances offer light-hearted, festive occasions to which all segments of society are warmly welcomed. They represent a nostalgic salute to what was—not to what is or will be. The vitality of the corpse can't be inferred from the number who attend the funeral.

Nominal religious affinity remains high, but the impact of religious doctrine on the secular behavior of the faithful continues to erode. After preparing a tribal dish for a religious ceremony in Wichita, a Native American leader confided to the press that "if you want to know the truth, I like McDonald's better." American Jewish leaders anxiously record the heavy inroads of agnosticism and intermarriage on the viability of the ancient faith. The authority of the mainline Protestant and Roman Catholic churches over their communicants is well illustrated by their influence—or lack thereof—on the "sin" and reproductive issues, respectively.

In the Age of Information the citizen of whatever ethnicity or religion receives a rich and constant diet of "nonactionable" news emanating from the four corners of the globe. While important community-enhancing local events go unreported, a staccato barrage of global minutiae noisily intrudes into his living room. In thirty-second bursts he learns about a hotel fire in Baden-Baden, a windstorm in Bangkok, the collapse of a rowboat in Bangladesh (with 2.6 Americans aboard), and the unhappiness of Fiji Island teenagers with the quality of the sandwiches in their school lunches. In a world that is becoming addicted to the distant and the exotic, the local and familiar must necessarily deteriorate in priority.

The process of cultural entropy also can be seen at work in the economy with the advent of national franchising, advertising, and production. Branch managers, Peter Gould has remarked, are but "lapdogs at the end of a long electronic leash." As more jobs are created in the service area, the uniqueness of the local economy diminishes to the vanishing point. In Kansas the number of those who sit on wheat combines, compared to the number working at the ubiquitous computer terminal, shifts rapidly toward the latter.

As the established sources of community cohesiveness evaporate, the hiatus is partially being filled by the enhanced visibility of the marketplace. Increasingly the glue that holds the state and the nation together is composed of economic "stuff," rather than a shared tradition of values, visions, achievements, and historical legends. The mass media feed the bewildered public a steady stream of technical economic reports on a daily basis. One no longer needs to subscribe to the *Wall Street Journal* to learn, at regular intervals, about the secular trends in everything from the sales of automobiles and durable goods through the wholesale price index and the prime interest rate to new housing starts and the value of the dollar against the yen and the Deutsche mark.

The quintessential public purpose of modern Kansas society—to which all else is held hostage—is, apparently, the development of the economy, an economy that increasingly looks like everyone else's economy. An enhanced knowledge of the past is touted so that citizens "can talk to visitors about the state's history and so encourage tourism." Greater support for the institutions of higher education, it is stated, "will ring cash registers across Kansas." Benefactors of the arts and the humanities contribute, they publicly proclaim, not because of the inherent worth of the patronized enterprises, but because they "play a big role in economic development." The marketplace grows crowded, affluent, and arrogant; the public square becomes lonely, impoverished, and diffident.

In no segment of public life is the trend toward homogeneity more manifest or consequential than in the relationship of the states to the central government. Contrary to widespread belief, federalism is not a managerial concept embracing the familiar pyramid of administrative power found in religious, educational, and business organizations. Rather, it is a structural theory of shared, noncentralized government based upon the notion of covenant or mutual obligation. (The best-known covenant in the Judeo-Christian tradition is, of course, that made by Jehovah with Abraham some four thousand years ago.) In this concept, formalized in the Constitution, the individual states are not contingent creatures of the general government but, like the general government itself, derive their being and legitimacy directly from the people.

In the constitutional debates circa 1787, even the staunchest Federalists envisioned a central government that would be limited primarily to its enumerated or "expressed" powers. The "father" of the Constitution, James Madison, wrote that "the powers delegated by the proposed Constitution to the Federal Government are few and defined. Those which are to remain in the State Governments are numerous and indefinite." Seventy-five years later, at the time when Kansas entered the Union, the general government remained a weak and distant force in the lives of most Americans. The Civil War, referred to in the South as the War between the States, could appropriately be called the War against the States, because it forcibly resolved the question of the right of an individual state to leave the Union peacefully. In the aftermath of that conflict, Chief Justice Salmon P. Chase wrote reassuringly that the Constitution guaranteed "an indestructible Union, composed of indestructible States."

By the middle decades of the twentieth century the

locus of power had shifted dramatically in the centralized direction. Aggressive legislative and executive branches, reinforced by an activist judiciary and with broad public support, had preempted a host of roles and functions that had long been considered the prerogatives of the states. (Interestingly, until the 1930s the word *state* was capitalized regularly in informal contexts, but now it almost never is.) Even in policy areas that address such social issues as speed limits, drinking age, chemical dependency, child support, and sexual behavior, the central government rules supreme. The states are being relegated steadily and surely to the submissive role of middle management in a centralized bureaucratic system. They tend to function more as "lapdog franchises" of a distant, all-powerful corporate home office than as quasi-autonomous commonwealths of significance. As the attrition of state authority continues at full bore, the very existence of federalism qua covenant is being threatened.[2]

As the locus of political control recedes from the local community and as the traditional sources of metaphysical meaning continue to weaken, the individual feels progressively more helpless in a world dominated by a remote government, big business, and the mass media. It has been a basic tenet of the American dream that an improvement in socioeconomic conditions would lead willy-nilly to an increase in that illusive condition called happiness. But the collective experience of the past few decades forces us to conclude quite otherwise. The forces of modernity that have brought an unprecedented material well-being have also produced a pervasive malaise, or poverty of the spirit. Hope is replaced by fear; participation, by fatalism; belongingness, by alienation. The corroding effects of an unremitting materialism suffuses all dimensions of life, both public and private. The Kansas historian James C. Malin once asked if "the genius of democracy [was] limited solely to the attainment of physical comfort." The economist Robert L. Heilbroner has written that the national malaise "reflects the inability of a civilization directed to material improvement . . . to satisfy the human spirit." Nearly two thousand years ago, Jesus of Nazareth reminded us that "man does not live by bread alone."

THE STATE of Kansas, of course, has not remained immune from the global currents sweeping toward individuality and homogeneity and the consequent cultural thinness. These have been manifest unmistakably in the artistic, social, and political histories of the culture. In 1944, at the time of the death of William Allen White, who was a vigorous champion of a distinctive state culture, *Life* magazine noted that the state and the nation had both entered an "age of declining localism." That trend is now sufficiently advanced to threaten a condition undreamt of by White and other Kansas patriots—a world without a singular Kansas psyche and culture.

As the Imperfect Rectangle positions itself for the twenty-first century, an overview of the twentieth reveals a dramatic rise and fall in the image, prestige, and self-esteem of the state. The twin epics of the nineteenth century—the territorial struggle for freedom and the settling of the harsh prairie environment—do not sustain and inspire the modern citizen. He retains no sense of high public purpose apart from the economic realm. He feels little or no connectedness with either the ancient or the unfolding heritage of his state. Kansas is no longer a "community of memory"; it has neither a "living" history nor a "usable past." Consciously or subconsciously, Kansans have largely internalized the dominant national view that the state is a hinterland, a land of no consequence.

For decades, well-intentioned prophets have urged the "backward" state to "catch up" with the modern world. As a result, the young have been forced to mature in an unnecessarily self-deprecating environment as their elders have scrambled to embrace a degrading program of "me-tooism"—a policy that necessarily poisons the wells of local creativity. Will Kansans be content forever to chase mindlessly the national norm while they assimilate passively the latest economic, social, and moral innovations to drift in from New York, California, or North Dakota?

If the Kansas agenda were more focused and imaginative, it could attract with cultural as well as economic lures. Although American mobility has been a major culprit in reducing the peculiarity of place, it can also serve as a vehicle to reestablish it. Increasingly, "voluntary communities" that have a distinctive focus are being formed through differential migration. The process of self-selection, the geographer Wilbur Zelinsky notes, is correcting the "lottery of birth," thus enabling those with congenial life styles and philosophies to join together. More Americans are working where they want to live rather than living where they have to work. The environmentally sensitive have been attracted to the Pacific Northwest; computer wizards, to the Silicon Valley; country music hopefuls, to Nashville; homosexuals, to San Francisco; Cuban exiles, to Miami.[3]

A new and exciting public program for Kansas must spring from diverse sources. At its core, however, it should draw on the state's historic strengths, not on the national perceptions of its weaknesses. This implies a stress on family values, moral concerns, respect for the physical environment, aggressive support of the rural agrarian culture, and an expansion of the role of women and seniors in society. Perhaps a postpuritan morality could be forged, one that would reconnect historic concerns in areas such as chemical dependency with modern, innovative practices.

A more creative Kansas agenda would simultaneously arrest the trend toward bland homogeneity, restore self-confidence, revest the public purpose, and encourage economic development. The agenda-setting debate itself could serve as a force for renewal and for communal cohesiveness. If the state were to reestablish its innovative reputation and if it were to rekindle the righteous indignation for which it was widely known, the celebrated brain drain on the economy would soon cease to be. Many of the best and the brightest, of any age and locale, are less interested in the promise of a subsistence existence ("a job") than in an intellectual and moral challenge, the opportunity to be a part of a stirring and meaningful enterprise. A healthy economy may be a necessary condition, but it is hardly a sufficient one, to satisfy either the requirements of a positive image or the basic human drives for meaning and belongingness.

In the past, students of American politics have celebrated the state line as one of the "great inventions" of the nation. In the original federal conception the states were expected to serve as "experimental plots" on social, political, and economic issues for the ultimate edification of the entire nation. For decades, Kansas served as just such a national exemplar. The whole was stronger because of the vigor and the diversity of its parts. The best government was that closest to the governed. At the state level, the world that the average citizen saw outside the kitchen window and the levers of power that controlled that world were in an acceptable proximity. It was a scale of government, population, and diversity that human beings—with their ancient heritage of living in small, tightly integrated groups—found manageable, even comfortable.

Although the prerogatives of the states have been severely reduced, they continue to serve numerous public functions, and they continue to serve as foci, albeit fading ones, of inspiration and personal identity. Kansans, of course, have not entirely lost their sense of peoplehood. Many citizens can still resonate to the Progressive Era sentiments of Peggy Greene's father, who "talked about Kansas with the tenderness of a man remembering his first love." And to the 1930s declaration of Paul Jones, who exclaimed that there was "something magnetic, fascinating and beautiful about the name, Kansas."

The ultimate distinguishing characteristic of a culture—whether it be Pawnee, Roman, British, or Kansan—is not its technology, its military, or its budget; rather, it is the perspective that it brings to the manifold dimensions of the human condition. The greatest challenge for Kansas is to rediscover her perspective, her soul, if you will—to recapture the position that she formerly enjoyed as a major source of identity for her citizens and a significant fount of ideas for the nation. The greatest sin—the modern equivalent of "The Crime against Kansas"—is the perpetuation of the aimless drift toward uniformity, mediocrity, and irrelevancy. If the course can be altered, future generations need not record that on their journey to the stars, Kansans became extinct.

NOTES

ACRONYMS USED IN THE NOTES

KH   *Kansas History*
KHC   *Kansas Historical Collections*
KHQ   *Kansas Historical Quarterly*
KSHS Kansas State Historical Society

CHAPTER 2. THE PROGRESSIVE ERA

1. William Allen White, "Will White on Kansas" (broadside, 1897), KSHS.
2. G. W. Ogden, "Lifting the Curse from Kansas," *Hampton's Magazine* 23 (1909): 371–80.
3. Editor, *Kansas Magazine*, January 1909, p. 58.
4. Charles Moreau Harger, "The Kansas of To-day," *Atlantic Monthly* 90 (1902): 361–70.
5. (James Barton Adams), "Sneakin' Back to Kansas," *Independence* (Kans.) *Tribune*, 24 July 1901.
6. H. J. Allen, "A Civilization of Fifty Years," *Kansas Magazine*, Jan. 1909, p. 49.
7. George W. Martin, "Kansas Fifty Years Ago," *Emporia* (Kans.) *Gazette*, 4 July 1907.
8. *New York Times*, 28 June 1905; Walter R. Stubbs to Florence E. Ringle, 1 Apr. 1909, Stubbs gubernatorial papers, KSHS.

9. Carl Becker, "Kansas," in *The Heritage of Kansas: Selected Commentaries on Past Times*, ed. Everett Rich (Lawrence: University of Kansas Press, 1960), pp. 340–59.

10. *Kansas Magazine*, May and July 1909.

11. Barton W. Currie, "Kansas, U.S.A.," *Country Gentleman* 81 (1916): 438.

12. Charles Moreau Harger, "The Kansan of Tomorrow," *Graduate Magazine, University of Kansas* 2 (1903): 2.

13. Julian Street, *Abroad at Home: American Ramblings, Observations, and Adventures* (New York: Century Co., 1914), pp. 308, 337, 338, 350, 366, 375.

14. Nicholas Vachel Lindsay, *Adventures: Rhymes and Designs* (New York: Eakins Press, 1968).

15. Willard Wattles, ed., *Sunflowers: A Book of Kansas Poems* (Lawrence, Kans.: World Co., 1914).

16. "Doc" Divilbiss, "Kansas," *Kansas Magazine*, Aug. 1909, p. 62.

17. George P. Morehouse, "Kansas as a State of Extremes, and Its Attitude during This World War," *KHC* 15 (1923): 20.

18. *Topeka Capital*, 28 Oct. 1905.

19. Anne E. Bingham, "Sixteen Years on a Kansas Farm, 1870–1886," *KHC* 15 (1923): 510, 516.

20. Morehouse, "Kansas as a State of Extremes," pp. 15, 16; *KH* 1 (1978): 65; John James Ingalls, "Kansas, 1541–1891," *Harper's Monthly*, Apr. 1893, p. 707.

21. James H. Nottage and Floyd R. Thomas, Jr., " 'There's No Place Like Home': Symbols and Images of Kansas," *KH* 8 (1985): 146–47; James P. Callahan, "Kansas in the American Novel and Short Story," *KHC* 17 (1928): 139–88.

22. *New York Times*, 2 Feb. and 30 Mar. 1916.

23. Albert Jay Nock, "Prohibition and Civilization," *North American Review* 204 (1916): 407, 409; *New York Times*, 10 Sept. 1916.

24. *Topeka Capital*, 3 Feb. 1916.

25. Morehouse, "Kansas as a State of Extremes," p. 27.

CHAPTER 3. THE TWENTIES

1. W. G. Clugston, "Kansas the Essence of Typical America," *Current History* 25 (1926): 14–20.

2. *Emporia Gazette*, 25 Apr. and 25 Aug. 1922.

3. Irvin S. Cobb, *Kansas: Shall We Civilize Her or Let Her Civilize Us?* (New York: George H. Doran Co., 1924).

4. William Allen White, "Emporia and New York," *American Magazine* 63 (1907): 258–64, and "What's the Matter with America," *Collier's Weekly*, 1 July 1922.

5. Alfred A. Knopf, ed., *Menckeniana: A Schimpflexikon* (New York: Alfred A. Knopf, 1928).

6. H. L. Mencken, "Business," *Smart Set* 54 (1918): 138.

7. H. L. Mencken, "The Last of the Victorians," *Smart Set* 29 (1909): 153–55.

8. Charles B. Driscoll, "Why Men Leave Kansas," *American Mercury* 3 (1924): 175–78.

9. Charles B. Driscoll, "Major Prophets of Holy Kansas," *American Mercury* 8 (1926): 18–26.

10. H. L. Mencken, "Elmer Gantry," *American Mercury* 10 (1927): 507.

11. Sinclair Lewis, *Elmer Gantry* (New York: Harcourt, Brace & Co., 1927). In 1934 Lewis published a second novel, *Work of Art*, in which Kansas plays a symbolic role, albeit a greatly diminished one. After an up-and-down career of hotel keeping in the East, the protagonist ends up (in the last dozen pages) running a "hick" hotel in Kansas.

12. William Allen White, "These United States: Kansas, a Puritan Survival," *Nation* 114 (1922): 460–62.

13. Helen Rhoda Hoopes, ed., *Contemporary Kansas Poetry* (Lawrence, Kans.: Franklin Watts, 1927).

14. *New York Times*, 4 Nov. 1928.

15. M. Sue Kendall, *Rethinking Regionalism: John Steuart Curry and the Kansas Mural Controversy* (Washington, D.C.: Smithsonian Institution Press, 1986). My interpretation of Curry's relationship to the state in this and the next chapter draws extensively on Kendall's analysis.

16. Herbert Asbury, *The Great Illusion: An Informal History of Prohibition* (New York: Greenwood Press, 1968), p. 332.

17. Heywood Broun, "It Seems to Heywood Broun," *Nation*, 12 Oct. 1927.

18. Charles B. Driscoll, "Kansas in Labor," *American Mercury* 16 (1929): 339–46.

19. Herbert Asbury, *Carry Nation* (New York: Alfred A. Knopf, 1929), p. xv.

20. *Chicago Tribune*, 23, 25, 28, and 29 Apr. 1929.

21. *New York Times*, 8 Mar. 1929.

CHAPTER 4. THE THIRTIES

1. Meridel LeSueur, "Corn Village," *Scribner's Magazine* 90 (1931): 133–40.

2. Maureen McKernan, "In Defense of Kansas," *Scribner's Magazine* 92 (1932): 106–8.

3. William Allen White, "Just Wondering," *Kansas Magazine*, 1934, pp. 86–88.

4. Frederick Simpich, "Speaking of Kansas," *National Geographic*, Aug. 1937, pp. 135–82.

5. Karl A. Menninger, "Bleeding Kansas," *Kansas Magazine*, 1939, pp. 3–6.

6. *Chicago Tribune*, 20 Aug. 1933.

7. "Isms in Kansas," *Newsweek*, 1 Aug. 1938, pp. 11–12.

8. Bruce Bliven, "Bleeding Kansas and Points West," *New Republic* 85 (1935): 96.

9. Martyn J. Bowden, "The Great American Desert in the American Mind," in *Geographies of the Mind*, ed. David Lowenthal and Martyn J. Bowden (New York: Oxford University Press, 1976), pp. 119–38.

10. Paul Jones, *Kansas the Beautiful* (Topeka: Kansas Chamber of Commerce, [1931]); Ruth Hale, "A Personal," *Literary Digest*, 28 Apr. 1923, p. 36.

11. *New York Times*, 29 Dec. 1936.

12. Paul A. Jones, *Coronado and Quivira* (Lyons, Kans.: Lyons Publishing Co., 1937), p. 1.

13. R. I. Thackrey, "Editor's Quarters," *Kansas Magazine*, 1935, p. 101.

14. Raymond Clapper, "The Kansas Spirit in Politics," *Kansas Magazine*, 1938, pp. 8–11.

15. Alfred Haworth Jones, "The Search for a Usable American Past in the New Deal Era," *American Quarterly* 23 (1971): 710–24; Joseph Wood Krutch, "The Usable Past," *Nation* 138 (1934): 191–92.

16. William Allen White, "Kansas in Need of Ideals and Ideas," *Chanute* (Kans.) *Tribune*, 30 Jan. 1932.

17. Nelson Antrim Crawford, "A Note on the Kansas Language," *Kansas Magazine*, 1934, pp. 9–12.

18. W. G. Clugston, "A Kansas Prose Review," *Kansas Magazine*, 1938, pp. 65–69.

19. Kenneth Porter, "Anthology of Kansas Verse," *Kansas Magazine*, 1937, pp. 35–37.

20. Lorrin Leland, ed., *The Kansas Experience in Poetry*

(Lawrence: Division of Continuing Education, University of Kansas, 1982), pp. 63–84.

21. Kendall, *Rethinking Regionalism*; Vertical File—Artist, Curry, KSHS; *New York Times*, 7 Dec. 1930; *Time*, 24 Dec. 1934; *Topeka Capital*, 4 and 10 Feb. 1935; *Emporia Gazette*, 30 Sept. 1936; *Life*, 23 Nov. 1936; Thomas Craven, "Art and Propaganda," *Scribner's Magazine* 95 (1934): 189–94; idem, "Kansas Refuses Curry," *Kansas Magazine*, 1937, pp. 85–87; idem, "John Steuart Curry," *Scribner's Magazine* 103 (1938): 37–41, 96, 98; Bret Waller, "Curry and the Critics," *Kansas Quarterly* 2 (1970): 42–55; Calder M. Pickett, "John Steuart Curry and the Topeka Murals Controversy," *Kansas Quarterly* 2 (1970): 30–41.

CHAPTER 5. THE MODERN ERA

1. Debs Myers, "The Exciting Story of Kansas," *Holiday*, June 1951, pp. 53–63, 166–68; Clyde M. Reed, Jr., "Once Kansas Was—Young, Daring, Venturesome!" *Kansas Teacher* 59 (Mar. 1951): 12–13.

2. Nelson Antrim Crawford, "The State of Kansas," *American Mercury* 70 (1950): 465–72.

3. John Ise, *The American Way* (Lawrence, Kans.: Allen Press, 1955), pp. v–vi.

4. Milton S. Eisenhower, "The Strength of Kansas," *Kansas Magazine*, 1950, pp. 9–13; Stephen E. Ambrose and Richard H. Immerman, *Milton S. Eisenhower: Educational Statesman* (Baltimore, Md.: Johns Hopkins University Press, 1983), pp. 26, 31, 80, 83, 93.

5. Kenneth S. Davis, "That Strange State of Mind Called Kansas," *New York Times Magazine*, 26 June 1949; idem, "What's the Matter with Kansas? *New York Times Magazine*, 27 June 1954.

6. Clarence Woodbury, "What Happened to Kansas," *American Magazine* 147 (Jan. 1949): 20–21, 115–19. Kansas maintained a constitutional prohibition against the "open saloon"— i.e., public liquor by the drink—until the restriction was removed by public referendum in 1986.

7. Jack Lait and Lee Mortimer, *U.S.A. Confidential* (New York: Crown Publishers, 1952), pp. 277–80.

8. John Gunther, *Inside U.S.A.* (New York: Harper & Brothers, 1947), pp. 256–69.

9. Allan Nevins, "Ad Astra per Aspera," in *Kansas: The First*

Century, ed. John D. Bright (New York: Lewis Historical Publishing Co., 1956), vol. 2, pp. 503–15.

10. *Life*, 14 Feb. 1944.

11. *New York Times*, 20 June 1945.

12. Erskine Caldwell, *Afternoons in Mid-America: Observations and Impressions* (New York: Dodd, Mead & Co., 1976); Evan Jones, ed., *The Plains States* (New York: Time-Life Books, 1968), pp. 132–36; *Wichita Eagle-Beacon*, 12 Oct. 1986.

13. Berton Roueche, *Sea to Shining Sea: People, Travels, Places* (New York: Avon Books, 1987).

14. Neal R. Peirce, *The Great Plains States of America: People, Politics, and Power in the Nine Great Plains States* (New York: W. W. Norton & Co., 1973), pp. 221–45; idem and Jerry Hagstrom, *The Book of America: Inside Fifty States Today* (New York: W. W. Norton & Co., 1983), pp. 585–92.

15. John L. Sullivan, "Political Correlates of Social, Economic, and Religious Diversity in the American States," *Journal of Politics* 35 (1973): 70–84.

16. Kenneth S. Davis, *Kansas: A Bicentennial History* (New York: W. W. Norton & Co., 1976); idem, "Portrait of a Changing Kansas," *KHQ* 42 (1976): 24–47.

17. Kenneth S. Davis, "The Sage of Emporia," *American Heritage* 30 (1979): 81–96.

18. Dodge Thompson, "Juror's Statement," in *A Kansas Collection* (Topeka: Kansas Arts Commission, 1987).

19. Warren Kliewer and Stanley J. Solomon, eds., *Kansas Renaissance* ([Lawrence, Kans.]: Coronado Publications, 1961).

20. G. C. Clemens, "Repressed by New York," Kansas Biographical Scrapbook, vol. 27, p. 25, 21 Aug. 1897, KSHS.

21. Jonathan Wesley Bell, ed., *The Kansas Art Reader* (Lawrence: Independent Study, University of Kansas, 1976).

22. Leland, *The Kansas Experience in Poetry*.

23. Bell, *Kansas Art Reader*; Leland, *The Kansas Experience in Poetry*; Bill Myers, *Prairie, People, and Stars: The Literature of Kansas* (Topeka, Kans.: School of Applied and Continuing Education, Washburn University, 1986); Thomas Fox Averill, *Kansas Literature* (Lawrence: University of Kansas Extension, 1983).

CHAPTER 6. FACETS OF THE MODERN IMAGE

1. The clippings and notes furnishing the source material for this chapter have been collected in a 200-page scrapbook

entitled "Modern Images of Kansas." It is on deposit in the Library of the Kansas State Historical Society, Topeka.

2. James R. Shortridge, "Patterns of Religion in the United States," *Geographical Review* 66 (1976): 420–34.

3. Harlan Ellison, "A Boy and His Dog," in *The Beast That Shouted Love at the Heart of the World* (New York: Bluejay Books, Inc., 1969).

4. James R. Shortridge, "The Vernacular Middle West," *Annals of the Association of American Geographers* 75 (1985): 48–57.

5. Monna McGill, "What I Learned from Kansas," *Kansas Magazine*, 1959, pp. 98–99.

6. John James Ingalls, "Albert Dean Richardson," *Kansas Magazine* 1 (1872): 19.

7. In 1986, conferences of business and educational leaders at Manhattan, Emporia, and Salina considered the several dimensions of the composite state character, especially as it related to economic development. Most of the traits that several hundred participants suggested could readily be assigned to one of the five image categories identified in this work. Only the Irrelevant facet went unrecognized.

8. Bell, *Kansas Art Reader*.

9. Roxane Fridirici and Stephen E. White, "Kansas through the Eyes of Kansans: Preferences for Commonly Viewed Landscapes," *Great Plains Quarterly* 6 (1986): 44–58.

10. The statement is supported by a great deal of anecdotal evidence, although it has not been systematically studied for adults. For adolescent opinions the author has analyzed themes submitted to the Mamie Boyd High School Essay Contest, "Kansas! Say It above a Whisper," sponsored annually by the Native Sons and Daughters of Kansas. The theme for the 250-word essays is "state pride"; no more detailed instructions are given to the contestants. I examined two hundred essays selected at random from those submitted during the interval 1983–87. About 10 percent of the sample came from each of the towns of Pittsburg, Hiawatha, Lindsborg, and Hays. The remaining 60 percent came from scattered localities across the state, although the metropolitan areas of Wichita, Kansas City, and Topeka were definitely underrepresented. Each essay was examined to see if it at least mentioned any of eleven specific topics. The results are as follows:

Low-density related factors	*Percentage*
Physical environment (landscape, skyscape, small-town milieu)	65

Traditional values (friendly, caring, hard-working)	53
Agriculture (breadbasket)	65
Other economic activities	
Aircraft	17
Energy (oil, gas, minerals)	12
Heritage	
Pioneers, settlers	28
Bleeding Kansas (slavery controversy)	9
Defensiveness	
General awareness of negative image of state	52
Wizard of Oz	22
Geographic center (heartland, midway, hub)	15
Individuals mentioned	21

Names appearing more than once, in descending order of frequency: Dwight Eisenhower, Amelia Earhart, Robert Dole, Wild Bill Hickok, Jim Ryun, William Allen White, Bernard Rogers, Alf Landon, Wyatt Earp, John Brown, Carry Nation, Francisco Coronado, Karl Menninger, Bat Masterson, Nancy Kassebaum, Joe Engle, Walter Chrysler, John Riggins, Glenn Cunningham, Clyde Cessna.

11. Steven Maynard-Moody and Jerry Mitchell, *The Second Annual Public Opinion Survey of Kansas: 1986* (Lawrence: Institute of Public Policy and Business Research, University of Kansas, 1986); for essays by high-school students see note 10.

12. Kansas was one of fourteen states (in 1986) that did not carry a slogan on its license plate. "The Wheat State" appeared on the plate from 1949 through 1959; "Centennial 1961" in 1960/61; "Midway USA" from 1965 to 1970; "Wheat Centennial" in 1974/75.

13. James R. Shortridge, "Vernacular Regions in Kansas," *American Studies* 21 (1980): 73-94.

14. Gene Burd, "Texas: A State of Mind and Media," *Heritage of the Great Plains* 19 (Summer 1986): 17-34; D. W. Meinig, *Imperial Texas: An Interpretive Essay in Cultural Geography* (Austin: University of Texas Press, 1969); John Steinbeck, *Travels with Charley: In Search of America* (New York: Viking Press, 1962), p. 304.

15. On 13/14 Sept. 1987, while this book was in production, the *Wichita Eagle-Beacon* published the results of a "statistically reliable" telephone poll of non-Kansans about their images of Kansas. The results reinforce the major conclusions of this study. The dominant images were those of agriculture (Rube, Tradi-

tional), the Wizard of Oz (Drab), and no image (Irrelevant). Other common responses included flatland, desert, tornadoes (Drab), and Kansas City. The highest quality-of-life scores were given for "friendly people" and "good family life." About one-half of the respondents said that their image of the state had been formed principally by the mass media.

CHAPTER 7. HEARTLAND OR HINTERLAND?

1. Charles Sumner, "The Kansas Question" (Cincinnati, Ohio: Geo. S. Blanchard, 1856), pamphlet, KSHS. Except as otherwise noted, the sources for this chapter are included in the Bader scrapbook "Modern Images of Kansas," on deposit at the Kansas State Historical Society, Topeka.

2. Roger Ward Babson, "How I Found Eureka," *Eureka* (Kans.) *Herald*, 1957, in Greenwood County clippings, vol. 1, p. 284, KSHS; Horace B. Powell, "A Date with Destiny?" *Kansas Teacher* 58 (Nov. 1949): 6–7, 25–27; Roger Ward Babson, "The Magic Circle," pamphlet, KSHS.

3. Paul Cook, *Duende Meadow* (New York: Bantam Books, 1985).

4. Davis, *Kansas: A Bicentennial History*, pp. 203–4.

5. Shortridge, "The Vernacular Middle West," pp. 48–57.

6. Richard Rhodes, *The Inland Ground* (New York: Atheneum, 1970).

7. Calvin Trillin, "U.S. Journal: Kansas City, Missouri," *New Yorker*, 8 Apr. 1974, pp. 94–101; idem, "American Royal," *New Yorker*, 26 Sept. 1983, pp. 57–125; idem, "Department of Amplification," *New Yorker*, 19 Mar. 1984, pp. 118–22.

8. "The Great American Roadside," *Fortune* 10 (Sept. 1934): 53–63, 172, 174, 177.

9. Roy F. Bailey, " 'To the Stars through Difficulties': Accomplishments of Kansas Shown by Historical Markers," *Kansas Teacher* 50 (May 1942): 28–29.

10. Alex Heard, "Homage to Jello," *New Republic* 192 (1985): 10–12; idem, "In Praise of Kansas Corn," *Washington Post Magazine*, 18 Jan. 1987.

11. Eric Morganthaler, "Hey, You. Wanna See a Big Ball of Twine? Or a Hand-Dug Well?" *Wall Street Journal*, 18 July 1973; *Kansas City Star*, 26 July 1973.

12. Phil McLaughlin, "Tourism Blues," *Miami* (County, Kans.) *Republican*, 26 July 1973; reprinted on 25 July 1974.

13. Welling, Minton and Vanderslice, Inc., *Technical Assistance for the State of Kansas in Reaching Its Optimum Potential in Tourism*, 6 vols., 1977, KSHS.

14. Kevin P. Helliker, "A Yellow Brick Road Minus Yellow Bricks Stirs Kansas Storm," *Wall Street Journal*, 9 and 23 Mar. 1983; *Kansas City Times*, 23 Mar. 1983.

15. Peter Gould and Rodney White, *Mental Maps* (Baltimore, Md.: Penguin Books, 1974); Peter Gould, *The Geographer at Work* (Boston, Mass.: Routledge & Kegan Paul, 1985).

16. Daniel J. Elazar, "Political Culture on the Plains," *Western Historical Quarterly* 11 (1980): 261–83; Margaret Jarman Hagood, "Statistical Methods for Delineation of Regions Applied to Data on Agriculture and Population," *Social Forces* 21 (1943): 287–97.

17. Neal R. Peirce, *The Megastates of America: People, Politics, and Power in the Ten Great States* (New York: W. W. Norton, 1972); John Naisbitt, *Megatrends: Ten New Directions Transforming Our Lives* (New York: Warner Books, 1982).

18. Carin Rubenstein, "Regional States of Mind," *Psychology Today* 16 (Feb. 1982): 22–30.

19. Angus Campbell, *The Sense of Well-Being in America: Recent Patterns and Trends* (New York: McGraw-Hill Book Co., 1981); Frank M. Andrews and Stephen B. Withey, *Social Indicators of Well-Being: Americans' Perceptions of Life Quality* (New York: Plenum Press, 1976).

20. Earl Black and Merle Black, *Politics and Society in the South* (Cambridge, Mass.: Harvard University Press, 1987).

21. Charles Angoff and H. L. Mencken, "The Worst American States," *American Mercury* 24 (1931): 1–16, 175–88, 355–71.

22. Ben-Chieh Liu, *The Quality of Life in the United States, 1970: Index, Rating, and Statistics* (Kansas City, Mo.: Midwest Research Institute, 1973); David M. Smith, *The Geography of Social Well-Being in the United States* (New York: McGraw-Hill, 1973); Jack Bailey, *Iowa's Quality of Life as Compared to the Nation* (Des Moines: Iowa Development Commission, 1985); Albert H. Bowker, "Quality and Quantity in Higher Education," *Journal of the American Statistical Association* 60 (1965): 1–15.

23. Stephen R. Bollman, ed., "Kansas: The Quality of Life," *Agricultural Experiment Station, Bulletin*, no. 632 (1980), pp. 1–17; Maynard-Moody and Mitchell, *Second Annual Public Opinion Survey of Kansas*; *Wichita Eagle-Beacon*, 29 Mar. 1987; Black and Black, *Politics and Society*, pp. 221–22. In the Blacks' sample, respondents were asked about their satisfaction with both the

state and the local community; the Kansas data apply only to the state.

CHAPTER 8. PROSPECTS

1. The principal secondary sources that I consulted as background for this chapter are listed in the Selected Bibliography under General.

2. The New Federalism championed by the Reagan administration is less a constitutional recovery of lost state prerogatives than an administrative shift along the centralization/decentralization axis. With the 1985 decision of the Supreme Court in *Garcia* v. *San Antonio Metropolitan Transit Authority* (469 U.S. 528), much of the remaining remnant of state sovereignty appears to have disappeared through a black hole in the Commerce Clause.

3. Wilbur Zelinsky, *The Cultural Geography of the United States* (Englewood Cliffs, N.J.: Prentice-Hall, Inc., 1973).

SELECTED
BIBLIOGRAPHY

The principal sources that I consulted have been divided into Kansas and General (non-Kansas) lists. The latter includes principally the sources relevant to chapters 7 and 8.

KANSAS

Abbott, Ernest Hamlin. "Religious Life in America, VIII: Kansas. *Outlook* 70 (1902): 968–72.
Allen, Frederick Lewis. "These Disillusioned Highbrows." *Independent* 118 (1927): 378–79.
———. "There, There Little Highbrow, Don't Cry!" *Independent* 118 (1927): 587–88.
———. *Only Yesterday: An Informal History of the Nineteen Twenties*. New York: Harper & Brothers, 1931.
Allen, H. J. "A Civilization of Fifty Years." *Kansas Magazine*, Jan. 1909, pp. 49–52.
Ambrose, Stephen E., and Richard H. Immerman. *Milton S. Eisenhower: Educational Statesman*. Baltimore, Md.: Johns Hopkins University Press, 1983.
Anderson, George L., and Terry H. Harmon. *History of Kansas*. Lawrence: Division of Continuing Education, University of Kansas, 1974.
———, eds. *History of Kansas: Selected Readings*. Lawrence: Division of Continuing Education, University of Kansas, 1974.

Angoff, Charles, and H. L. Mencken. "The Worst American State." *American Mercury* 24 (1931): 1–16, 175–88, 355–71.

Anonymous. "What's the Matter with Kansas?" *Western Teacher* 24 (1915): 123.

Anonymous. "Why Kansas Bans the Klan." *Literary Digest* 75 (11 Nov. 1922): 13.

Anonymous. "The Truth about Kansas—A Scofflaw's Confession." *McNaught's Monthly* 3 (1925): 42–44.

Asbury, Herbert. *Carry Nation*. New York: Alfred A. Knopf, 1929.

———. *The Great Illusion: An Informal History of Prohibition*. New York: Greenwood Press, 1968.

Averill, Thomas Fox. *Kansas Literature*. Lawrence: University of Kansas Extension, 1983.

Babson, Roger Ward. "How I Found Eureka." *Eureka Herald*, centennial edition, 1957. In Greenwood County clippings, vol. 1, p. 284, KSHS.

———. "The Magic Circle." Pamphlet, KSHS.

Bader, Robert Smith. *The Great Kansas Bond Scandal*. Lawrence: University Press of Kansas, 1982.

———. *Prohibition in Kansas: A History*. Lawrence: University Press of Kansas, 1986.

———. "Modern Images of Kansas." Scrapbook, 1987, KSHS.

Bailey, Roy R. " 'To the Stars through Difficulties': Accomplishments of Kansas Shown by Historical Markers." *Kansas Teacher* 50 (May 1942): 28–29.

Barone, Michael, and Grant Ujifusa. "Kansas." In *The Almanac of American Politics: 1986*, pp. 498–503. Washington, D.C.: National Journal, 1985.

Beals, Carleton. "Kansas at the World's Fair." *Kansas Magazine*, 1942, pp. 19–24.

Becker, Carl. "Kansas." In *The Heritage of Kansas: Selected Commentaries on Past Times*, edited by Everett Rich, pp. 340–59. Lawrence: University of Kansas Press, 1960.

Bell, Jonathan Wesley, ed. *The Kansas Art Reader*. Lawrence: Independent Study, University of Kansas, 1976.

Bertsch, Wilhelmina F. "Native Sons and Daughters of Kansas." *Jayhawk* 2 (1929): 45–46.

Bingham, Anne E. "Sixteen Years on a Kansas Farm," 1870–1886." *KHC* 15 (1923): 501–23.

Bird, John. "Kansas, My Kansas." *Saturday Evening Post*, 29 Apr. 1961: 20–21, 81–84.

Birkhead, L. M. *Is "Elmer Gantry" True?* Girard, Kans.: Haldeman-Julius Publications, 1928.

Blackburn, Forrest R., ed. "Bypaths of Kansas History." *KH* 1 (1978): 65.

Bliven, Bruce. "Bleeding Kansas and Points West." *New Republic* 85 (1935): 96.

Bode, Carl. *Mencken.* Carbondale: University of Southern Illinois Press, 1969.

Bollman, Stephen R., ed. "Kansas: The Quality of Life." *Agricultural Experiment Station, Bulletin, no. 632 (1980), pp. 1–17.*

Bracke, William B. *Wheat Country.* New York: Duell, Sloan & Pearce, 1950.

Broun, Heywood. "It Seems to Heywood Broun." *Nation,* 12 Oct. 1927.

Burd, Gene. "Texas: A State of Mind and Media." *Heritage of the Great Plains* 19 (Summer 1986): 17–34.

Caldwell, Erskine. *Afternoons in Mid-America: Observations and Impressions.* New York: Dodd, Mead & Co., 1976.

Callahan, James P. "Kansas in the American Novel and Short Story." *KHC* 17 (1928): 139–88.

Capote, Truman. *In Cold Blood.* New York: Random House, 1965.

Carruth, William Herbert, ed. *Kansas in Literature.* 2 vols. Topeka: Crane & Co., 1900.

Clapper, Raymond. "The Kansas Spirit in Politics." *Kansas Magazine,* 1938, pp. 8–11.

Clark, Carroll D., and Roy L. Roberts. *People of Kansas: A Demographic and Sociological Study.* Topeka: Kansas State Planning Board, 1936.

Clark, Esther M. "The Call of Kansas." *Kansas Magazine,* Sept./Oct. 1910, p. 1.

Clark, Norman H. *Deliver Us from Evil: An Interpretation of American Prohibition.* New York: W. W. Norton & Co., 1976.

Clemens, G. C. "Repressed by New York." Kansas Biographical Scrapbook, vol. 27, p. 25, 21 Aug. 1897, KSHS.

Clugston, W. G. "Kansas the Essence of Typical America." *Current History* 25 (1926): 14–20.

————. "A Kansas Prose Review." *Kansas Magazine,* 1938, pp. 65–69.

Cobb, Irvin S. *Kansas: Shall We Civilize Her or Let Her Civilize Us?* New York: George H. Doran Co., 1924.

Coburn, F. D. "Why Kansas Is Loved." *Independence* (Kans.) *Tribune,* 24 July 1901, p. 37.

_____. *Kansas and Her Resources*. N.p.: Atchison, Topeka & Santa Fe Railway Co., 1902.

_____. *Points Kansans May Well Emphasize*. Topeka: W. J. Rickenbacher, 1913.

Cook, Paul. *Duende Meadow*. New York: Bantam Books, 1985.

Cornish, Dudley T. "Carl Becker's Kansas: The Power of Endurance." *KHQ* 41 (1975): 1–13.

Cowgill, Donald O. "Cultural Values in Kansas." *University of Wichita Alumni Magazine* 9 (1961): 6–7, 12.

Craven, Thomas. "Art and Propaganda." *Scribner's Magazine* 95 (1934): 189–94.

_____. "Kansas Refuses Curry." *Kansas Magazine*, 1937, pp. 85–87.

_____. "John Steuart Curry." *Scribner's Magazine* 103 (1938): 37–41, 96, 98.

Crawford, Nelson Antrim. "A Note on the Kansas Language." *Kansas Magazine*, 1934, pp. 9–12.

_____. "The State of Kansas." *American Mercury* 70 (1950): 465–72.

Current, Richard N. "Tarheels and Badgers: A Comparative History of Their Reputations." *Journal of Southern History* 42 (1976): 3–30.

Currie, Barton W. "The Backbone of America." *Country Gentleman* 80 (1915): 770–71.

_____. "Kansas, U.S.A." *Country Gentleman* 81 (1916): 311–12, 352, 438–39, 476–77.

Darst, Stephen. "How It Is Playing in Emporia." *New York Times Magazine*, 20 Oct. 1974.

Davis, Elmer. "Mr. Lewis Attacks the Clergy." *New York Times*, 13 Mar. 1927.

Davis, Kenneth S. "That Strange State of Mind Called Kansas." *New York Times Magazine*, 26 June 1949.

_____. "What's the Matter with Kansas?" *New York Times Magazine*, 27 June 1954.

_____. "Portrait of a Changing Kansas." *KHQ* 42 (1976): 24–47.

_____. *Kansas: A Bicentennial History*. New York: W. W. Norton & Co., 1976.

_____. "The Sage of Emporia." *American Heritage* 30 (1979): 81–96.

Dewey, Ernest A. "Cocktails in Kansas." *Commonweal* 11 (1930): 384–86.

Doran, Thomas F. "Kansas Sixty Years Ago." *KHC* 15 (1923): 482–501.

Driscoll, Charles B. "Kansas Cleans up Governor Allen's Mess." *Nation* 115 (1922): 600–601.

_____. "Why Men Leave Kansas." *American Mercury* 3 (1924): 175–78.

_____. "Major Prophets of Holy Kansas." *American Mercury* 8 (1926): 18–26.

_____. "Kansas in Labor." *American Mercury* 16 (1929): 339–46.

Duffus, R. L. "Ruggedly Kansas Holds to Her Course." *Kansas Magazine*, 1935, pp. 67–71.

_____. "In Kansas the Old Traditions Echo." *New York Times Magazine*, 5 July 1936, pp. 4–5, 19.

Eisenhower, Milton S. "The Strength of Kansas." *Kansas Magazine*, 1950, pp. 9–13.

Ellison, Harlan. "A Boy and His Dog." In *The Beast That Shouted Love at the Heart of the World*. New York: Bluejay Books, Inc., 1969.

Emmons, David M. "Richard Smith Elliott, Kansas Promoter." *KHQ* 36 (1970): 390–401.

Farnham, Mateel Howe. *Rebellion*. New York: Dodd, Mead & Co., 1927.

Fecher, Charles A. *Mencken: A Study of His Thought*. New York: Alfred A. Knopf, 1978.

Fedder, Norman J. "The Kansas Character." Unpublished play, 1976.

Flentje, H. Edward, ed. *Kansas Policy Choices: Report of the Special Commission on a Public Agenda for Kansas*. Lawrence: University Press of Kansas, 1986.

Fridirici, Roxane, and Stephen E. White. "Kansas through the Eyes of Kansans: Preferences for Commonly Viewed Landscapes." *Great Plains Quarterly* 6 (1986): 44–58.

Frye, Virginia King. " 'O.K.'—Of Kansas." *Kansas Magazine*, Jan. 1910, pp. 3–8.

Galloway, Grace. "Kansas: As Seen through a Girl's Letter Box." *Kansas Magazine*, 1888, pp. 596–597.

Garwood, Alfred N., ed. *Almanac of the Fifty States: Basic Data Profiles with Comparative Tables*. Burlington, Vt.: Information Publications, 1985.

General Motors. "A Tribute to Kansas." N.p.: n.p., 1932. Broadside, KSHS.

Giddens, Paul H. "News from Kansas in 1870." *KHQ* 7 (1938): 170–82.

Gleed, J. W. "Is New York More Civilized Than Kansas?" *Forum* 17 (1894): 217–34.

_____. "Eastern Kansas in 1869–1870." *KHQ* 9 (1940): 371–83.

Glenn, Andrea, ed. Introduction by Zula Bennington Greene. *Kansas in Color*. Lawrence: University Press of Kansas, 1982.

Graham, I. D. *Kansas: "She Is the Heart of the Continent."* Topeka: Hall Lithographing Co., [1919?]. Pamphlet, KSHS.

"The Great American Roadside." *Fortune* 10 (Sept. 1934): 53–63, 172, 174, 177.

Gunther, John. *Inside U.S.A.* New York: Harper & Brothers, 1947.

Hale, Ruth. "A Personal." *Literary Digest*, 28 Apr. 1923, p. 36.

Hanna, Frank A. *State Income Differentials, 1919–1954*. Durham, N.C.: Duke University Press, 1959.

Harger, Charles Moreau. "The Kansas of To-day." *Atlantic Monthly* 90 (1902): 361–70.

_____. "The Kansan of Tomorrow." *Graduate Magazine, University of Kansas* 2 (1903): 1–9.

_____. "Kansas Is Building Citizenship." *Kansas Magazine*, 1933, pp. 21–22.

Harris, L. David. "Dear Old Kansas: Looking Backwards at Future." *Wichitan* 2 (Jan. 1980): 54–59.

Harrison, Henry, ed. *Kansas Poets*. New York: House of Henry Harrison, 1935.

Haywood, C. Robert. "Kansas as a State of Mind." In *The Washburn Reader, 1865–1915*, edited by Robert D. Stein. Topeka, Kans.: Woodley Memorial Press, 1984.

_____. "What Happened to Kansas?" *Humanities* [Kans.] 10 (Winter 1985).

Heard, Alex. "Homage to Jello." *New Republic* 192 (1985): 10–12.

_____. "In Praise of Kansas Corn." *Washington Post Magazine*, 18 Jan. 1987.

Helliker, Kevin P. "A Yellow Brick Road Minus Yellow Bricks Stirs Kansas Storm." *Wall Street Journal*, 9 and 23 Mar. 1983.

Hill, Charles E. "Progressive Legislation in Kansas." *KHC* 12 (1912): 69–77.

Hoopes, Helen Rhoda, ed. *Contemporary Kansas Poetry*. Lawrence, Kans.: Franklin Watts, 1927.

Hope, Clifford R., Sr. "Kansas in the 1930's." *KHQ* 36 (1970): 1–12.

Howe, Ed. "Kansas—Past and Present." *Country Gentleman* 84 (4 Oct. 1919): 3–4, 26.

Howes, Charles C. *This Place Called Kansas*. Norman: University of Oklahoma Press, 1952.

_____. "Kansas Centennial." *Travel*, Jan. 1961, pp. 28–31.

Hubbard, Elbert. "Kansas in One Sentence." *Jayhawk* 1 (1928): 32.

Ingalls, John James. "Albert Dean Richardson." *Kansas Magazine* 1 (1872): 15–19.

———. "Catfish Aristocracy." *Kansas Magazine*, 1872, pp. 173–79.

———. "Kansas, 1541–1891." *Harper's Monthly*, Apr. 1893, pp. 697–713.

Ise, John. *The American Way*. Lawrence, Kans.: Allen Press, 1955.

Isely, Bliss, and W. M. Richards. *Four Centuries in Kansas*. Topeka: State of Kansas, 1937.

"Isms in Kansas." *Newsweek*, 1 Aug. 1938, pp. 11–12.

James, Bill. *Bill James Baseball Abstract*. New York: Ballantine Books, 1986.

Jones, Evan, ed. *The Plains States*. New York: Time-Life Books, 1968.

Jones, Paul A. *Kansas the Beautiful*. Topeka: Kansas Chamber of Commerce, [1931].

———. "On Being Our Brother's Keeper." *Kansas Magazine*, 1933, pp. 33–35.

———. "Concerning Kansas." *Kansas Magazine*, 1934, pp. 38–40.

———. *Coronado and Quivira*. Lyons, Kans.: Lyons Publishing Co., 1937.

———. "The Truth about Kansas." *Lyons Daily News*, n.d., KSHS.

Juhnke, James C. "Mob Violence and Kansas Mennonites in 1918." *KHQ* 43 (1977): 334–50.

Kansas Semi-Centennial, 1911. Clippings, KSHS.

Kellogg, Paul U., ed. "Social Legislation, Kansas." *Survey* 34 (1915): 453.

Kendall, M. Sue. *Rethinking Regionalism: John Steuart Curry and the Kansas Mural Controversy*. Washington, D.C.: Smithsonian Institution Press, 1986.

King, Henry. "Editor's Quarters." *Kansas Magazine*, 1872, p. 89.

Kliewer, Warren, and Stanley J. Solomon, eds. *Kansas Renaissance*. N.p. [Lawrence, Kans.]: Coronado Publications, 1961.

Knopf, Alfred A., ed. *Menckeniana: A Schimpflexikon*. New York: Alfred A. Knopf, 1928.

Knox, Carleton Everett. *Kansas Land*. N.p.: Author, 1917.

Kuralt, Charles. *Dateline America*. New York: Harcourt Brace Jovanovich, 1979.

Lait, Jack, and Lee Mortimer. *U.S.A. Confidential*. New York: Crown Publishers, 1952.

Landis, J. M. "By the Artificial Reason of Law." *Survey* 54 (1925): 213–14.

Lapham, Jim. "For Map Makers It All Begins in Kansas." *Kansas City Star* (magazine), 3 May 1970.

Leland, Lorrin, ed. *The Kansas Experience in Poetry.* Lawrence: Division of Continuing Education, University of Kansas, 1982.

LeSueur, Meridel. "Corn Village." *Scribner's Magazine* 90 (1931): 133–40.

Leuchtenburg, William E. *The Perils of Prosperity, 1914–32.* Chicago: University of Chicago Press, 1958.

Lewis, Sinclair. *Elmer Gantry.* New York: Harcourt, Brace & Co., 1927.

_____. *Work of Art.* Doubleday, Doran & Co., 1935.

Liggett, Walter W. "Holy Hypocritical Kansas." *Plain Talk* 6 (1930): 129–42.

Lindquist, Emory K. "Kansas: A Centennial Portrait." *KHQ* 27 (1961): 22–66.

Lindsay, Nicholas Vachel. "Adventures While Preaching the Gospel of Beauty." *Forum* 50 (1913): 296–307.

_____. *Adventures: Rhymes and Designs.* New York: Eakins Press, 1968.

Lippmann, Walter. *Men of Destiny.* New York: Macmillan Co. 1927.

Lombard, Frank L. "The Program of the Kansas State Chamber of Commerce—as Viewed by Its President." *Kansas Business Review* 15 (June 1962): 2–7.

Low, Denise, ed. *Thirty Kansas Poets.* Lawrence, Kans.: Cottonwood Review Press, 1979.

Lowenthal, David, and Martyn J. Bowden, eds. *Geographies of the Mind.* New York: Oxford University Press, 1976.

Luskin, John. *Lippmann, Liberty, and the Press.* University: University of Alabama Press, 1972.

Lynn, Kenneth S. "Only Yesterday." *American Scholar* 49 (1980): 513–18.

MacDonald, William. "The New United States, IV: Kansas in Reaction." *Nation* 108 (1919): 393–94.

McGill, Monna. "What I Learned from Kansas." *Kansas Magazine*, 1959, pp. 98–99.

McKernan, Maureen. "In Defense of Kansas." *Scribner's Magazine* 92 (1932): 106–8.

McLaughlin, Phil. "Tourism Blues." *Miami* (County, Kans.) *Republican*, 26 July 1973.

McNeal, T. A. "Kansas." *Earth* 26 (Nov. 1929): 5.

Malin, James C. "The Kinsley Boom of the Late Eighties." *KHQ* 4 (1935): 23–49, 164–87.

_____. "Kansas: Some Reflections on Cultural Inheritance and Originality." *Journal of the Central Mississippi Valley American Studies Association* 2 (1961): 3–19.

Manchester, William. *The Sage of Baltimore: The Life and Riotous Times of H. L. Mencken.* New York: Andrew Melrose, 1952.

Maranell, Gary M. "Regional Patterns of Fundamentalistic Attitude Configurations." *Kansas Journal of Sociology* 4 (1968): 159–74.

Martin, Edward A. *H. L. Mencken and the Debunkers.* Athens: University of Georgia Press, 1984.

Martin, George W. "Early Days in Kansas." *KHC* 9 (1906): 126–43.

_____. "Kansas Fifty Years Ago." *Emporia* (Kans.) *Gazette*, 4 July 1907.

Maynard-Moody, Steven, and Jerry Mitchell. *The Second Annual Public Opinion Survey of Kansas: 1986.* Lawrence: Institute of Public Policy and Business Research, University of Kansas, 1986.

Meinig, D. W. *Imperial Texas: An Interpretive Essay in Cultural Geography.* Austin: University of Texas Press, 1969.

Mencken, H. L. "The Last of the Victorians." *Smart Set* 29 (1909): 153–55.

Menninger, Karl A. "Bleeding Kansans." *Kansas Magazine*, 1939, pp. 3–6.

Messner, Ruth Ann. "Publisher's Notes." *KS Magazine* 1 (Fall 1984): 6.

Meyer, Richard, ed. *Kansas Communities: Changes, Challenges, Choices.* Lawrence: University of Kansas, 1986.

Millard, Joseph. *The Gods Hate Kansas.* Derby, Conn.: Monarch Books, 1964.

Miner, Craig. *West of Wichita: Settling the High Plains of Kansas, 1865–1890.* Lawrence: University Press of Kansas, 1986.

Morehouse, George P. "Kansas as a State of Extremes, and Its Attitude during This World War." *KHC* 15 (1923): 15–28.

Morgenthaler, Eric. "Hey, You. Wanna See a Big Ball of Twine? Or a Hand-Dug Well? *Wall Street Journal*, 18 July 1973.

Morrison, Richard. "It Has Kansas." *Kansas Magazine*, 1966, pp. 73–77.

Morrow, Marco. *A Glimpse into the World's Greatest Farm Market.* N.p.: n.p., 1920.

Moyers, Bill. *Listening to America: A Traveler Rediscovers His Country.* New York: Harper & Row, 1971.

Muilenburg, Grace E. "Where East Meets West—In Kansas." *Prairie Scout* 5 (1985): 37–61.

Myers, Bill. *Prairie, People, and Stars: The Literature of Kansas.* Topeka, Kans.: School of Applied and Continuing Education, Washburn University, 1986.

Myers, Debs. "The Exciting Story of Kansas." *Holiday,* June 1951, pp. 53–63, 166–68.

_____. "Kansas." In *American Panorama,* edited by the editors of *Holiday Magazine,* pp. 339–54. New York: Doubleday & Co., 1960.

Napier, Rita, ed. *History of the Peoples of Kansas: An Anthology.* Lawrence: Division of Continuing Education, University of Kansas, 1985.

Nevins, Allan. "Ad Astra per Aspera." In *Kansas: The First Century,* edited by John D. Bright, vol. 2, pp. 503–15. New York: Lewis Historical Publishing Co., 1956.

Nichols, Roy F. "Kansas Historiography: The Technique of Cultural Analysis." *American Quarterly* 9 (1957): 85–91.

Nock, Albert Jay. "Prohibition and Civilization." *North American Review* 204 (1916): 407–12.

Nottage, James H., and Floyd R. Thomas, Jr. " 'There's No Place Like Home': Symbols and Images of Kansas." *KH* 8 (1985): 138–61.

Ogden, G. W. "Lifting the Curse from Kansas." *Hampton's Magazine* 23 (1909): 371–80.

Ogrizek, Dore, ed. *The United States.* New York: Whittlesey House, 1950.

Overmyer, David. *The Spirit of Kansas.* Topeka: Crane & Co., 1904.

Pasley, Jeffrey L. "The Idiocy of Rural Life." *New Republic,* 8 Dec. 1986, pp. 24–27.

Paulen, Ben S. "Kansas—By One Who Knows It." *Union Pacific Magazine* 6 (Nov. 1927): 5, 30–35.

Peirce, Neal R. "Kansas: The Eclipsed State." In *The Great Plains States of America: People, Politics, and Power in the Nine Great Plains States,* pp. 221–45. New York: W. W. Norton & Co., 1973.

_____, and Jerry Hagstrom. "Kansas: The Eclipsed State." In *The Book of America: Inside Fifty States Today,* pp. 585–92. New York: W. W. Norton & Co., 1983.

Pemberton, Murdock. "Town without a Sage." *New Yorker,* 5 July 1947, pp. 53–56.

_____. "Everybody Comes from Kansas." *Pageant* 5 (May 1950): 100–104.

Pickett, Calder M. *Ed Howe: Country Town Philosopher.* Lawrence: University Press of Kansas, 1968.

———. "John Steuart Curry and the Topeka Murals Controversy." *Kansas Quarterly* 2 (1970): 30–41.

Porter, Kenneth. "Anthology of Kansas Verse." *Kansas Magazine,* 1937, pp. 35–37.

Powell, Horace B. "A Date with Destiny?" *Kansas Teacher* 58 (Nov. 1949): 6–7, 25–27.

Queen, Stuart A. "Kansas: Proud but Puzzled." *Survey* 54 (1925): 613–14, 641.

Ratner, Payne. *Kansas, the Different State.* Topeka: Kansas Industrial Development Commission, 1941.

Redwood, Anthony, and Charles Krider. *Kansas Economic Development Study: Interim Report and Recommendations.* Lawrence: Institute of Public Policy and Business Research, University of Kansas, 1986.

Reed, Clyde M. "Kansas, Heart of the Continent." *Earth* 26 (Sept. 1929): 1.

Reed, Clyde M., Jr. "Once Kansas Was—Young, Daring, Venturesome!" *Kansas Teacher* 59 (Mar. 1951): 12–13.

Rhodes, Richard. "Death All Day in Kansas." *Esquire,* Nov. 1969, pp. 146, 189–98.

———. *The Inland Ground.* New York: Atheneum, 1970.

Richmond, Robert W. *Kansas: A Land of Contrasts.* St. Charles, Mo.: Forum Press, 1974.

Riley, Glenda. "Kansas Frontierswomen Viewed through Their Writings." *KH* 9 (1986): 2–9.

Rock Island Railroad. *Kansas, the Bountiful.* Chicago: Rock Island Lines, 1907.

Roueche, Berton. *Sea to Shining Sea: People, Travels, Places.* New York: Avon Books, 1987.

Sackett, S. J. "Reaction and Reform in Kansas Literature of the Nineteenth Century." *Kansas Magazine,* 1959, pp. 73–83.

Schiller, Ronald. "America's Dying Small Towns: Tragedy or Opportunity?" *Reader's Digest,* July 1972, pp. 199–204.

Schorer, Mark. *Sinclair Lewis: An American Life.* New York: McGraw-Hill, 1961.

Schruben, Francis W. *Kansas in Turmoil, 1930–1936.* Columbia: University of Missouri Press, 1969.

Seiler, William H. "Magazine Writers Look at Kansas, 1854–1904." *KHQ* 38 (1972): 1–42.

Seward, C. A. "The Millet of the Prairies." *Kansas Magazine,* Aug. 1909, pp. 1–5.

Sheldon, Charles M. "Why I Prefer to Live in Kansas." *Topeka Capital*, 15 Mar. 1931.

Shepherd, William G. "Kansas, the Beer State." *Collier's*, 26 Jan. 1929.

Shortridge, James R. "Patterns of Religion in the United States." *Geographical Review* 66 (1976): 420–34.

———. *Kaw Valley Landscapes: A Guide to Eastern Kansas.* Lawrence, Kans.: Coronado Press, 1977.

———. "Vernacular Regions in Kansas." *American Studies* 21 (1980): 73–94.

———, and Barbara G. Shortridge. "Patterns of American Rice Consumption 1955 and 1980." *Geographical Review* 73 (1983): 417–29.

Shumaker, K. A. "A State Wide Enterprise." *Kansas Magazine*, Mar. 1909, pp. 46–48.

Siegfried, André. *America Comes of Age.* New York: Harcourt, Brace & Co., 1927.

Simpich, Frederick. "Speaking of Kansas." *National Geographic*, Aug. 1937, pp. 135–82.

Singleton, M. K. *H. L. Mencken and the American Mercury Adventure.* Durham, N.C.: Duke University Press, 1962.

Smith, William R. "Solicitor for Santa Fe Urges New State Seal." *Topeka State Journal*, 16 July 1921.

Socolofsky, Homer E. "Kansas in 1876." *KHQ* 43 (1977): 1–43.

Sojka, Gregory S. "Hollywood Comes to Terms with Kansas." *Kansas Business News* 6 (May 1985): 46–51.

Souders, Floyd R. "The Small Town and Its Future." *KHQ* 35 (1969): 1–12.

Spillman, Patricia R. "The Kansas Ethos in the Last Three Decades of the Nineteenth Century." *Emporia State Research Studies* 30 (1980): 1–47.

Stearns, Harold E. *Civilization in the United States.* New York: Harcourt, Brace & Co., 1922.

Steinbeck, John. *Travels with Charley: In Search of America.* New York: Viking Press, 1962.

Street, Julian. *Abroad at Home: American Ramblings, Observations, and Adventures.* New York: Century Co., 1914.

Sumner, Charles. "The Kansas Question." Cincinnati, Ohio: Geo. S. Blanchard, 1856. Pamphlet, KSHS.

Tarpy, Cliff. "Home to Kansas." *National Geographic*, Sept. 1985, pp. 352–83.

Thompson, Dodge. "Juror's Statement." In *A Kansas Collection.* Topeka: Kansas Arts Commission, 1987.

Travis, Paul. "Changing Climate in Kansas: A Late Nineteenth-Century Myth." *KH* 1 (1978): 48–58.

Trillin, Calvin. "U.S. Journal: Kansas City, Missouri." *New Yorker*, 8 Apr. 1974, pp. 94–101.

———. "American Royal." *New Yorker*, 26 Sept. 1983, pp. 57–125.

———. "Department of Amplification." *New Yorker*, 19 Mar. 1984, pp. 118–22.

Vawter, Parke. "Some Revelations about Famous State of Kansas." *Topeka State Journal*, 18 July 1931.

Waller, Bret. "Curry and the Critics." *Kansas Quarterly* 2 (1970): 42–55.

Walsh, Richard J. "Kansas from Exile." *Kansas Magazine*, 1940, pp. 3–5.

Watson, Jo-Shipley. "Through Kansas on the Limited." *Kansas Magazine*, June 1910, pp. 19–20.

Wattles, Willard, ed. *Sunflowers: A Book of Kansas Poems.* Lawrence, Kans.: World Co., 1914.

Welling, Minton and Vanderslice, Inc. *Technical Assistance for the State of Kansas in Reaching Its Optimum Potential in Tourism.* 6 vols. Technical report, 1977, KSHS.

Welsh, Orville A. "Government by Yokel." *American Mercury* 3 (1924): 199–205.

White, Gilbert F. "The Future of the Great Plains Re-visited." *Great Plains Quarterly* 6 (1986): 84–93.

White, Lyle Alan. *The Pioneer Spirit: A Prairie Portrait.* Kansas City, Mo.: Walter Publications, 1986.

White, William Allen. "What's the Matter with Kansas?" *Emporia* (Kans.) *Gazette*, 15 Aug. 1896.

———. "Kansas: Its Present and Its Future." *Forum* 23 (1897): 75–83.

———. "A Typical Kansas Community." *Atlantic Monthly* 80 (1897): 171–77.

———. "Will White on Kansas." N.p., [1897]. Broadside, KSHS.

———. "Fifty Years of Kansas." *World's Work* 8 (1904): 4870–72.

———. "The Kansas Conscience." *Reader Magazine* 6 (1905): 488–93.

———. "Emporia and New York." *American Magazine* 63 (1907): 258–64.

———. "Certain Voices in the Wilderness." *Kansas Magazine*, Jan. 1909, pp. 1–5.

———. "Free Kansas: Where the People Rule the People." *Outlook* 100 (1912): 407–14.

_____. "The Glory of the States: Kansas." *American Magazine* 81 (1916): 41.

_____. "Two Famous Questions." *Emporia Gazette*, 25 Apr. 1922.

_____. "What's the Matter with America." *Collier's Weekly*, 1 July 1922.

_____. "These United States: Kansas, a Puritan Survival." *Nation* 114 (1922): 460–62.

_____. "Kansas in Need of Ideals and Ideas." *Chanute* (Kans.) *Tribune*, 30 Jan. 1932.

_____. "Just Wondering." *Kansas Magazine*, 1934, pp. 86–88.

_____. "Address of the President." *KHQ* 8 (1939): 72–82.

_____. "Kansas on the Move." *Kansas Magazine*, 1942, pp. 5–7.

Whitehead, Fred. "The Kansas Response to the Haymarket Affair." *KH* 9 (1986): 72–82.

Wilder, Daniel W. "Facts in Relation to Kansas." *Report of the State Board of Agriculture for 1875* (1876), pp. 5–17. Topeka: State of Kansas, 1876.

Williams, Burton J. "Kansas: A Conglomerate of Contradictory Conceptions." *Heritage of the Great Plains* 19 (Summer 1986): 3–11.

Wilson, Samuel. "Development for Kansas." *Progress in Kansas* 5 (1939): 359–60.

Woner, Bruce J. "Pride in Kansas." Broadside distributed by Beech Aircraft, 1972, KSHS.

Woodbury, Clarence. "What Happened to Kansas." *American Magazine* 147 (Jan. 1949): 20–21, 115–19.

Zornow, William Frank. *Kansas: A History of the Jayhawk State.* Norman: University of Oklahoma Press, 1957.

GENERAL

Andrews, Frank M., and Stephen B. Withey. *Social Indicators of Well-Being: Americans' Perceptions of Life Quality.* New York: Plenum Press, 1976.

Bailey, Jack. *Iowa's Quality of Life as Compared to the Nation.* Des Moines: Iowa Development Commission, 1985.

Bellah, Robert N.; Richard Madsen; William M. Sullivan; Ann Swidler; and Steven M. Tipton. *Habits of the Heart: Individualism and Commitment in American Life.* New York: Harper & Row, 1986.

Berry, Wendell. *The Unsettling of America: Culture and Agriculture.* San Francisco: Sierra Club Books, 1977.

Black, Earl, and Merle Black. *Politics and Society in the South.* Cambridge, Mass.: Harvard University Press, 1987.

Bloom, Allan. *The Closing of the American Mind.* New York: Simon & Schuster, 1987.

Blouet, Brian W., and Frederick C. Luebke, eds. *The Great Plains: Environment and Culture.* Lincoln: University of Nebraska Press, 1979.

Boorstin, Daniel J. *The Image.* New York: Atheneum, 1962.

_____. *The Republic of Technology: Reflections on Our Future Community.* New York: Harper & Row, 1978.

Brooks, Van Wyck. "On Creating a Usable Past." *Dial* 64 (1918): 337–41.

Brownell, Joseph W. "The Cultural Midwest." *Journal of Geography* 59 (1960): 81–85.

Buttimer, Anne, and David Seamon, eds. *The Human Experience of Space and Place.* New York: St. Martin's Press, 1980.

Campbell, Angus. *The Sense of Well-Being in America: Recent Patterns and Trends.* New York: McGraw-Hill Book Co., 1981.

Carter, William. *Middle West Country.* Boston, Mass.: Houghton Mifflin, 1975.

Cooper, Charles J., ed. *The Status of Federalism in America: A Report of the Working Group on Federalism of the Domestic Policy Council.* Washington, D.C.: Government Printing Office, 1986.

Elazer, Daniel J. "Political Culture on the Plains." *Western Historical Quarterly* 11 (1980): 261–83.

_____. *American Federalism: A View from the States.* 3d ed. New York: Harper & Row, 1984.

Gastil, Raymond D. *Cultural Regions of the United States.* Seattle: University of Washington Press, 1975.

_____. *Internal Origins of State Populations.* Seattle, Wash.: Battelle Seattle Research Center, 1975.

Geertz, Clifford. *The Interpretation of Cultures.* New York: Basic Books, 1973.

_____. *Local Knowledge: Further Essays in Interpretive Anthropology.* New York: Basic Books, 1983.

Gelfand, Lawrence E., and Robert J. Neymeyer, eds. *Changing Patterns in American Federal-State Relations during the 1950s, the 1960s, and the 1970s.* Iowa City: Center for the Study of the Recent History of the United States, University of Iowa, 1985.

Ginzburg, Eli, and George Vojta. *Beyond Human Scale: The Large Corporation at Risk.* New York: Basic Books, 1985.

Golembiewski, Robert T., and Aaron Wildavsky, eds. *The Costs of Federalism.* New Brunswick, N.J.: Transaction Books, 1984.

Gould, Peter. *The Geographer at Work*. Boston, Mass.: Routledge & Kegan Paul, 1985.

_____, and Rodney White. *Mental Maps*. Baltimore, Md.: Penguin Books, 1974.

Graubard, Stephen R., ed. "The No-Growth Society." *Daedalus* (Fall 1973): 1–245.

Hagood, Margaret Jarman. "Statistical Methods for Delineation of Regions Applied to Data on Agriculture and Population." *Social Forces* 21 (1943): 287–97.

Hart, John Fraser. "The Middle West." *Annals of the Association of American Geographers* 62 (1972): 258–82.

Heilbroner, Robert L. *An Inquiry into the Human Prospect: Updated and Reconsidered for the 1980s*. New York: W. W. Norton, 1980.

Hertzberg, Arthur. "The Triumph of the Jews." *New York Review of Books*, 21 Nov. 1985, pp. 18–22.

Hirsch, Fred. *Social Limits to Growth*. Cambridge, Mass.: Harvard University Press, 1976.

Jensen, Merrill, ed. *Regionalism in America*. Madison: University of Wisconsin Press, 1951.

Jones, Alfred Haworth. "The Search for a Usable American Past in the New Deal Era." *American Quarterly* 23 (1971): 710–24.

Kilpatrick, James Jackson. *The Sovereign States: Notes of a Citizen of Virginia*. Chicago: Henry Regnery Co., 1957.

Krutch, Joseph Wood. "The Usable Past." *Nation* 138 (1934): 191–92.

Ley, David, and Marwyn S. Samuels, eds. *Humanistic Geography: Prospects and Problems*. Chicago: Maaroufa Press, 1978.

Liu, Ben-Chieh. *The Quality of Life in the United States, 1970: Index, Rating, and Statistics*. Kansas City, Mo.: Midwest Research Institute, 1973.

Lowenthal, David, and Martyn J. Bowden, eds. *Geographies of the Mind*. New York: Oxford University Press, 1976.

Luebke, Frederick C. "Regionalism and the Great Plains: Problems of Concept and Method." *Western Historical Quarterly* 15 (1984): 19–38.

Lundborg, Louis B. *Future without Shock*. New York: W. W. Norton & Co., 1974.

Maslow, Abraham H. *Toward a Psychology of Being*. New York: D. Van Nostrand Co., 1968.

Meinig, D. W., ed. *The Interpretation of Ordinary Landscapes: Geographical Essays*. New York: Oxford University Press, 1979.

Menninger, Karl. *Whatever Became of Sin?* New York: Hawthorn Books, 1973.

Meyrowitz, Joshua. *No Sense of Place.* New York: Oxford University Press, 1985.

Mishan, E. J. *The Economic Growth Debate.* London: George Allen & Unwin Ltd., 1977.

Mol, Hans. *Meaning and Place: An Introduction to the Social Scientific Study of Religion.* New York: Pilgrim Press, 1983.

Molotch, Harvey. "The City as a Growth Machine: Toward a Political Economy of Place." *American Journal of Sociology* 82 (1976): 309–32.

Naisbitt, John. *Megatrends: Ten New Directions Transforming Our Lives.* New York: Warner Books, 1982.

Neuhaus, Richard John. *The Naked Public Square.* Grand Rapids, Mich.: Wm. B. Eerdmans, 1984.

Pawley, Martin. *The Private Future: Causes and Consequences of Community Collapse in the West.* New York: Random House, 1974.

Peirce, Neal R. *The Megastates of America: People, Politics, and Power in the Ten Great States.* New York: W. W. Norton, 1972.

Postman, Neil. *Amusing Ourselves to Death: Public Discourse in the Age of Show Business.* New York: Viking Penguin, 1985.

Reichley, A. James. *Religion in American Public Life.* Washington, D.C.: Brookings Institution, 1985.

Relph, E. *Place and Placelessness.* London: Pion Ltd., 1976.

Rubenstein, Carin. "Regional States of Mind." *Psychology Today* 16 (Feb. 1982): 22–30.

Sale, Kirkpatrick. *Human Scale.* New York: Coward, McCann & Geoghegan, 1980.

_____. *Dwellers in the Land: The Bioregional Vision.* San Francisco: Sierra Club Books, 1985.

Schumacher, E. F. *Small Is Beautiful: Economics as if People Mattered.* New York: Harper & Row, 1973.

Seabrook, Jeremy. *What Went Wrong? Why Hasn't Having More Made People Happier?* New York: Pantheon Books, 1978.

Shepard, Paul. "Place in American Culture." *North American Review* 262 (1977): 22–32.

Shortridge, James R. "The Emergence of 'Middle West' as an American Regional Label." *Annals of the Association of American Geographers* 74 (1984): 209–20.

_____. "The Vernacular Middle West." *Annals of the Association of American Geographers* 75 (1985): 48–57.

Smith, David M. *The Geography of Social Well-Being in the United States.* New York: McGraw-Hill, 1973.

Steiner, Michael C. "Regionalism in the Great Depression." *Geographical Review* 73 (1983): 430–46.

Sullivan, John L. "Political Correlates of Social, Economic, and Religious Diversity in the American States." *Journal of Politics* 35 (1973): 70–84.

Tocqueville, Alexis de. *Democracy in America*. 2 vols. New York: Alfred A. Knopf, 1956.

Toffler, Alvin. *The Third Wave*. New York: William Morrow & Co., 1980.

Trounstine, Philip J., and Terry Christensen. *Movers and Shakers: The Study of Community Power*. New York: St. Martin's Press, 1982.

Tuan, Yi-Fu. *Topophilia: A Study of Environmental Perception, Attitudes, and Values*. Englewood Cliffs, N.J.: Prentice-Hall, 1974.

_____. "Place: An Experiential Perspective." *Geographical Review* 65 (1975): 151–65.

_____. "Humanistic Geography." *Annals of the Association of American Geographers* 66 (1976): 266–76.

_____. *Space and Place: The Perspective of Experience*. Minneapolis: University of Minnesota Press, 1977.

Walmsley, D. J., and G. J. Lewis. *Human Geography: Behavioral Approaches*. New York: Longman, 1984.

Williams, William Appleman. "Radicals and Regionalism." *Democracy* 1 (1981): 87–98.

Wyner, Alan J. "Governor—Salesman." *National Civic Review* 56 (1967): 81–86.

Zelinsky, Wilbur. *The Cultural Geography of the United States*. Englewood Cliffs, N.J.: Prentice-Hall, 1973.

_____. "The Demigod's Dilemma." *Annals of the Association of American Geographers* 65 (1975): 123–43.

226

INDEX

LaVergne, TN USA
30 March 2010
177578LV00002B/47/P